with

All Good Wishes

To

Richard Rohde

For

a very Happy

christmas Season

THE NINE LIVES OF STERLING W. SILL

THE NINE LIVES OF STERLING W. SILL

An
Autobiography

INTERNATIONAL STANDARD BOOK NUMBER
0-88290-118-4

LIBRARY OF CONGRESS CATALOG CARD NUMBER
79-89354

Second Printing, July 1980

Printed and Distributed in the
United States of America
by

Horizon
Publishers &
Distributors

P.O. Box 490
50 South 500 West
Bountiful, Utah 84010

Table of Contents

Chapter One

My Nine Lives

For some time I have been expecting that someday I would write my autobiography. I do not know all of the reasons I have wanted to do this. I suppose that everyone has a kind of natural urge to think of himself as being recorded by having his history preserved on paper. There are several other reasons for a biography. I suppose that this is one way of achieving a kind of literary immortality.

Life is the greatest commodity in the universe; and to live on, even in a book, has an appeal which probably touches most people in an important way. It may be that my children or grandchildren or someone else may have enough interest in my life and work to want to know a little more about what their grandfather thought, how he felt, what he did during his lifetime, and why he did it. Someone has said that no one cares very much what we know until they know how much we care. This paper account of my life may also serve as one version of a life-text from which someone else may learn to know and to care. My greatest hope is that some of the things I have learned or done may be of benefit or encouragement to someone else. It is also possible that this wonderful possession of life may be seen and understood a little more clearly by me, its possessor, in both its favorable and unfavorable aspects as it looks back to me from the printed page.

In my role as a church worker, and in my business and other activities, I have often had interested people come to visit me with the request that I tell them what I think about some religious, business, family, or personal matter. Mostly they would like to know about my own particular views and feelings in regard to myself and my work. While I have always felt that an inspection of someone else is a very good way to get helpful ideas, and I have always been anxious to help anyone who may be interested, there were other appointments that sometimes made it impossible to spend the required time. Also, in some instances, a lack of previous thought and organization may make an impromptu recitation of ones acts or motives very weak, temporary, and unprofitable.

I have been very sympathetic with the idea, however, that I, myself, have very frequently felt a kind of hunger or longing to know the details of the accomplishments of some particular person and the secrets of his successes, as well as his failures, to help me safeguard and upgrade my own life. But I have usually been discouraged from most of these attempted inquiries because I realized the one I wished to approach was very busy and had a lot of other things on his mind so that he was not in the mood, nor had he made the necessary preparation for the particular kind of investigation of his experience that I would like to make. And even assuming my proposed teacher would give me an interview, it could not possibly be very long or complete because of the limitations of this particular kind of communication. It may also be subject to the natural human limit wherein a false modesty prevents people from giving a full thrust to their qualities of excellence. Nor would their contribution long be preserved by me because of the natural elimination process constantly taking place in the memory. This verbal kind of communication has never proven very adequate in the vast majority of cases. And so through this paper account I give myself and my experience in written form, to whoever may be interested.

Actually, the thing we know less about than almost any other thing is our own individual selves. You can ask a man questions about science, or invention, or history, or politics and he may answer you. But if you ask him to sit down and write out an analysis of himself and tell you about his mind and soul qualities, you may not get a very good answer. Or if you ask someone where he came from, or why he is here, or what the purpose or philosophy of his life is, he may stand silent and uncomprehending before you. Frequently we fail to spend much time in trying to understand why we ourselves do things or what our real ambitions are or what kind of destiny we desire or are working out for ourselves. Usually we are not even aware of why we do as we do in the very face of the fact that we believe as we believe. And when someone sits down in an attempt to write the story of his own life, he might be encouraged to get some answers based on his great experiences in this primal element of existence in which we all have our being. This education may not only be helpful to someone else but would also be put in a form that would be more easily communicated. But in addition, the more understandable form would also greatly benefit the subject who himself was doing the research.

Sometimes we hear a rather loose statement made that someone's life is like an open book. So far as I know, that is never a very accurate statement, at least our lives are seldom opened at the right place to the right people. Most of us are closed books in hardback binding with no windows. Most of us have some inner sanctuaries where our thoughts are all our own, or deep inside us we have some important private libraries that are not open to the public.

We may walk down a lighted street at night where the interior house lights are all ablaze in every room and the shades are all undrawn so that we can see into any corner of the house. But that is not true of the people who live in the houses. They keep their personal blinds more tightly drawn, and they have many inner chambers that have no windows and no doors and through which other people are never permitted to enter or even see.

But even if we were taken on a verbal excursion into the inner recesses of one's life, words are soon diffused throughout the atmosphere and most of them are soon lost from our memory. The printed page is much more permanent than any verbal statement, and written language contains a great deal more of its color and power for a much longer period. And when someone comes out of his inner sanctum and puts himself down in a book, he offers a much greater opportunity for anyone who may be interested, not only to get acquainted with him, but to learn from both his successes and his mistakes.

During the years of my own life, I have had a very substantial fascination for the biography as well as the philosophy of life of people of both sexes and all ages. I think I know a great deal more about the intimate life of Abraham Lincoln, George Washington, Benjamin Franklin, and Franklin D. Roosevelt than did many of their most intimate friends and family members. During the last twenty-five years of my church service, I have done a great deal of counseling with people about their marital affairs or their successes in their occupations or their church work. Even after an hour's discussion, I have frequently felt that I knew a great deal more about what made a person what he was than even his own wife or husband, or parents, or children, or intimate friends, as one can much more easily make himself available for inspection if there is some good reason to do so. It is frequently much easier to get an accurate picture of someone else even than he himself has, because of these troublesome blind spots where we can never quite learn to see ourselves as others see us. And for those who are anxious to learn, there is no better subject that can be studied than people.

Many people live the most productive lives in vain because the great lessons learned are so seldom transferred to others. Life is also more mysterious, and people are always more interesting than are events or ideas, and people are much more interesting as you get to know more about them or have a closer association with them.

Some time ago, I had occasion to go down the list of names listed in the American Hall of Fame. These were all outstanding people, with special accomplishments. However, most of them had very little interest for me because I was unfamiliar with their actual experiences and knew nothing about their ambitions, hopes, disappointments, weaknesses, and successes. I suppose that very few people were ever as interested in Abraham Lincoln as was Carl Sandburg, who was his biographer. One of the special delights of my life is that I have written down my own version of the biographies of over a hundred people in a literary collection I refer to as "My Hall of Fame." Though these are not necessarily the people that I admire the most, they are still very interesting to me. Even great wickedness can be fascinating and productive to study. Someone has jokingly said that "if everything goes wrong and nothing works out right, don't be discouraged. You can still serve as a horrible example to someone else."

You can also develop a special interest in someone that you have never seen. I have a sincere love for those great prophets, those stimulating poets, those wise philosophers, and those profound statesmen whom I know the most about as that gives them the greatest power to uplift my life. Joan of Arc is a kind of special heroine of mine, as is Madame Curie and my grandmother and my mother. For that matter, one may become very attached to someone who never even existed. For example, I have a great love in my heart for some of my fictional benefactors such as *Bunker Bean,* Everett Hale's Phillip Nolan, who is famous to us as *"The Man Without a Country,"* Henry Van Dyke's Artiban—*"The Other Wise Man,"* Elijah Kellog's *Regulus the Roman,* and the characters that act out the parables of Jesus. I like to think about the Unknown Soldier and the great actors brought upon the stage of life by William Shakespeare. I like to contemplate the character qualities of Leigh Hunt's *Abou Ben Adam,* or think about the work of Apelles the Athenian artist who painted the portrait of the goddess of beauty, and to relive the experiences with Matthew Arnold's great father and son team of *Sohrab and Rustum.*

If you would like to form a special attraction for some of the great captains of industry, or the great men from history, get together all of the things that are known about them and then write up your own version of their lives so that you can feel their good qualities all in one place.

Of course, no one is or should be as interesting to us as we ourselves are. When we were being fashioned in the workshop of Deity, he put into us a little gadget regulating our self-interest, which, if we exercise it enough, can make us very interesting to ourselves. And as we have a large portion of instinct centered on self-preservation, so we have another great instinctive interest centered on self-improvement, personal growth, and other mental and spiritual polishing that make us more interested in ourselves.

Robert Louis Stevenson once said that everyone should always carry with him two books, one to read from and the other to write in. Every human being ought to have some great books to read from, and one of the books that he ought to have to write in is his own autobiography. This ought not to be a book that he writes after his life has largely been finished. Actually, he ought to write his life's story in a day-by-day diary as he goes along. As a part of his diary, everyone should keep a book of remembrance, not only about his ancestors, but he should have a pictorial, mathematical, and literary record of his life thoughts and accomplishments for each year as he lives it. This not only records achievement, but it helps to produce it. Nothing succeeds like success, and there is nothing that stimulates accomplishment quite so much as accomplishment itself. And if these accomplishments, both actual and projected, are recorded on a regular basis, without allowing any exceptions in their excellence, the motivation both on the outside and the inside of life will be greatly multiplied. Then I suppose it might be a fitting thing to write a kind of overview of life. The end of life may not be far away when one comes to that place when our declining activities are set in pointing to that finish marker indicating the end of the journey.

In my own case, I have already procrastinated this biographical assignment much too long, as it has been six years since I went by that milepose on which Father Time had marked my days as three score years and ten. This is an interesting point for me, as it is already four years since I began receiving my Social Security checks which I started to pay toward forty-two years ago.

Jesus seemed to be a little partial to age seventy-two when he said to nine of the twelve disciples who organized his church upon this western continent that when they were seventy-and-two years old, they should come speedily to him in his kingdom. And it is very interesting to me that I am four years past the finishing mark that he set for them so long ago. I have already lived more than twice as many mortal years as was permitted to the Savior of the world himself. I hope and expect to live a great many years even beyond age seventy-two, and I am in no hurry to wind up my affairs in this life. In fact, I have a great many wonderful things that I would like to accomplish over a number of future years. Yet it is significant that I am getting older each year. I still have a large number of things to do, and I feel an increasing sense of urgency to get them done. I am not even quite sure about how much time might be involved in writing my autobiography. I have already published twenty-five books and have the manuscripts of twelve more written that have not been published, so I suppose that one more in either category would not make too much difference.

If I had my "druthers," I would hope that this one volume of my biography might be interesting and possibly even helpful to someone else. I am particularly interested in those people whose lives have some connection with my own. And yet in the sense that I would like to think of it, that would include everyone else upon our planet. My life, to this point, has been very interesting and very satisfying to me. I might say as many others have said and who will yet say, the world has been very good to me; God has been very good to me; my employers, my family, and my friends have all been very good to me. Life itself has been a tremendous experience to this date. And while I suppose I could have done a lot better, yet in a general way I am very happy with the results as they are. And I think the next ten years will be even more pleasant, and I hope more productive.

It might be assumed the ordinary biography would open when one is born and close when he dies. Actually, there is quite a lot more to life than that. And everyone's life is actually divided into three great sections looking backward to the beginning of his premortal existence and looking out forward beyond mortality into the everlasting stretches of eternity. Even these three sections of life are not sufficient. They all concern themselves with the length of life. But life has several other dimensions.

We usually think first of the *length* of life or how *long* we live, but then there is the *breadth* of life or how *interestingly* we live. Third, there is the *depth* of life represented by those human qualities of love, righteousness, excellence, and faith, or how *much* we live. Then number four there is a fourth dimension of life which might correspond to that more or less mysterious fourth dimension of space which is the *purpose* of life or *why* we live.

We get the total volume of something by multiplying its dimensions. That rule we might also apply to life. And so we multiply the *length* of life or *how long* we live times the *breadth* of life or how *interestingly* we live times the *depth* of life or *how much* we live times the *purpose* of life or *why* we live. And we can get a pretty good score for ourselves with this equation of how long, times how interestingly, times how much, times how come. Each of us lives a different life; each of us is a different kind of person. God makes no duplicates, and each one excels the other in some way. In fact, each of us is made up of a great group of different personality traits.

Edwin Sanford Martin once wrote some interesting lines about our human plurality under the title of "My Name is Legion." He said,

> Within my earthly temple there's a crowd;
> There's one of us that's humble, one that's proud,
> There's one that's broken hearted for his sins,
> And one that unrepentant sits and grins:
> There's one that loves his neighbor as himself,
> And one that cares for naught but fame and self.
> From such corroding cares I should be free,
> If I could once determine which is me.

But no one is just one person. All of us are a lot of people. We might be one person with our family, but another person in our work, and a completely different kind of person in our religion or in our social activities.

Robert Louis Stevenson wrote a famous book entitled *Dr. Jekyll and Mr. Hyde,* indicating the extremes of personality of Dr. Jekyll who became a desperate, ruthless, immoral criminal by night. This makes the job of each one of us a little more complicated as we must not only assume the responsibility of oneself, but we have the added problem of keeping all of our many selves going along that straight and narrow way, in the right direction, at the right speed, and at the same time.

I don't know where the idea got started that a cat has nine lives, but I know a lot of people that have at least that many and then some. As I have tried to keep score on myself, I have discovered that I live many different lives and actually live them in different worlds. My nine lives are as follows:

1. I had a very long *pre-mortal life.*
2. I had an interesting *early mortal life.*
3. One life was set aside for *my education.*

4. The world in which we live insists that every one of us should have an *occupational life* based on that great command in which the God of heaven himself said, "In the sweat of thy face shalt thou eat thy bread." (Gen. 3:19.)

5. I have had a very pleasant and inspiring *married life.*

6. Jesus came to this earth and in a most important message said that each one of us should be born again into a *religious life.*

7. One of the great wonders of our world is our ability to carry over the great ideas, the great poetry, the great music from one generation to another and from one country to another. And the total of anyone's life is reduced substantially when we fail to have a full, complete, exciting *cultural life.*

8. Because all men and women have a large measure of gregariousness in their very makeup and we are required to live and work together, every person whether he likes it or not must have a *social life,* a life of cooperation and integration in which many other people are included. It is one of the divine pronouncements that no man liveth unto himself alone, and no man dieth unto himself alone. Tennyson said, "I am a part of all that I have met," and we are all a part of each other. And what I write as my autobiography will also be a part of your biography, because we are all involved in mankind.

9. Then we have an existence that reaches out beyond the sunset in what we might think of as an *eternal, everlasting life.*

Each of our nine lives would have some subheadings. And we have some other main headings that may be large or small which reach beyond nine. We have some financial lives, some emotional lives. We have lives of adventure and excellence. Sometimes we lead military lives or degraded lives. Into each of our lives some rain must fall, and each has some of the elements of beauty, failure, and success. And each of these separate situations and conditions coming under these many headings is influenced by and made up out of the others.

And each of us might best serve the purpose of this biographical occasion by getting a little better acquainted with himself or making a summary inspection with an idea of the improvement of each one of our many lives.

Chapter Two

The Pre-Mortal Years

Nothing is more plainly written in the scriptures than the fact that the life of Christ did not begin at Bethlehem nor end on Calvary. Jesus said, "I came forth from the Father, and am come into the world: again, I leave the world, and go to the Father." (John 16:28.) In his intercessory prayer in Gethsemane he said to his Father, "I have glorified thee upon the earth: I have finished the work which thou gavest me to do. And now, O Father, glorify thou me with thine own self, with the glory which I had with thee before the world was." (John 17:4, 5.)

It is just as certain that our lives did not begin when we were born on this earth. Neither will they end when we die. There are things we sometimes do by assumption or imagination, but it is especially interesting to try and reconstruct the first chapter of one's own life.

We know a great many things about our antemortal years, just as we know a great many things about our postmortal lives. To these facts we might add a little bit by speculation or hearsay. To begin with, I know quite a little bit about myself. First, I know that I am a child of God, created in his image and formed in his likeness. The First Begotten Son of our Eternal Heavenly Parents was the being that we knew during our antemortal state as Jehovah and who came to this earth as Jesus Christ of Nazareth.

But all of the children of our Eternal Heavenly Parents were also begotten in heaven as spirit children. We know that our spirits are in the same form and likeness of our mortal bodies. Jesus was only a spirit up until the time of his birth in Bethlehem, yet prior to Bethlehem He was a personage of great power and influence. In a revelation to Moses, God the Father said of him, "Worlds without number have I created; and I also created them for mine own purpose; and by the Son I created them, which is mine Only Begotten." (Moses 1:33.) That He did not have a body of flesh and bones at that time is no indication that he was not possessed of great power, great intelligence, and great personality and character qualities. On one occasion the premortal Jehovah appeared to the Brother of Jared, some 2,200 years B.C., when the Jaredites were being prepared for their expedition to the western continent to re-people this hemisphere after the flood. On that occasion, Jehovah showed himself to the prophet. The prophet expressed surprise that the Lord had a body so nearly resembling that of his own, and Jehovah said, "This body, which ye now behold, is the body of my spirit; and man have I created after the body of my spirit; and even as I appear unto thee to be in the spirit will I appear unto my people in the flesh." (Ether 3:16.) In the Book of Genesis and in the Book of Moses it says, "For I, the Lord God, created all things, of which I have spoken, spiritually, before they were naturally upon the face of the earth. For I, the Lord God, had not caused it to rain upon the face of the earth. And I, the Lord God, had created all the children of men; and not yet a man to till the ground; for in heaven created I them; and there was not yet flesh upon the earth, neither in the water, neither in the air; But I, the Lord God spake, and there went up a mist from the earth, and watered the whole face of the ground. And I, the Lord God, formed man from the dust of the ground, and breathed into his nostrils the breath of life; and man became a living soul, the first flesh upon the earth, the first man also; nevertheless, all things were before created; but spiritually were they created and made . according to my word." (Moses 3:5-7.)

I know quite a lot about myself because I know quite a lot about the other spirit children of God, including the First Begotten. I know that I have an immortal spirit which is indestructible. It is temporarily clothed with a body of flesh and bones and is now subject to separation and bodily dissolution. However, I have an understanding of that great principle of resurrection. It is interesting to me that in this life I have never once seen my own spirit, and yet I know that I have one. I know it is a valuable and delightful possession.

Abraham and others were permitted to see a rerun of the council in heaven where we were all present as spirits. We know what took place there. We know that there was a great rebellion led by Lucifer against the program of God, and we know that those who were permitted to progress beyond the outcome of that war in heaven were the ones who were faithful to God and upheld by vote and covenant the program which he proposed. I am perfectly delighted by the fact that I feel so comfortable with every one of the principles of the gospel. There is not one single one of which I have ever felt any antagonism for, or disbelief in, or doubt about.

It is a safe conjecture that we were all among that group mentioned by Job when we were permitted to see the foundations of this earth being laid, and we were so happy at our good fortune that the morning stars sang together and all the sons of God shouted for joy. I still feel exactly that way about it. During those long ante-mortal years we learned a great many things from God our Eternal Heavenly Father. Much of this knowledge has been withheld from us while we prove ourselves in this life.

William Wordsworth called our birth "a sleep and a forgetting." But a great deal of our knowledge and glory comes with us. He says:

> The soul that rises with us, our life's star,
> Hath had elsewhere its setting, and cometh from afar,
> Not in entire forgetfulness,
> Not in utter nakedness,
> But trailing clouds of glory do we come
> From God, who is our home.

And what an exciting experience it will be when at the conclusion of our mortal lives all of this information and this exciting knowledge will be made perfect and given back to us in its fullness.

On some occasions I feel a kind of glory that comes to me out of the past, and I am very grateful that with billions of others of God's children I found myself on the right side of that important heavenly controversy instead of with those who chose to follow Lucifer.

In the conversation between the Creator and Job, some vague indications are given that we were permitted to see the foundations of this earth being laid with the knowledge that we were going to have the privilege of coming here and living upon it where we would be added upon with these beautiful, wonderful bodies of flesh and bones, without which we should never have a fullness of joy either in this life or in the next.

If all the sons of God were present for this occasion, then that included me. And I am very grateful. And while my physical possessions have never won any beauty prizes or any great athletic contests, yet I am very thankful for them. I remember on one occasion during my high school football days realizing how good it felt to be physically capable, to be able to flex my muscles and run and jump and feel that sheer joy of being a person and being alive with a healthy mortal body and great physical power and health. And I have never lost the tremendous gratitude that I have for my good fortune.

An early American philosopher, Henry Thoreau, once said that "we should thank God every day of our lives for the privilege of having been born," and then he went on to speculate on the rather unique supposition of what it might have been like if we had not been born. He pointed out some of the great thrills and blessings that we would have missed as a consequence. However, what Mr. Thoreau may not have known was that one-third of all the children of God never were born and never can be born, because they failed to pass the requirements of their first estate. And yet every spirit child of God hungers for a body. We remember the unembodied spirits who appeared to Jesus in his day, who preferred the bodies of swine rather than to have no bodies at all. And I am sure that if we could go back and stand now as we walk by faith where we once stood when we walked by sight, we would all be willing to crawl on our hands and knees through life for this tremendous privilege which we presently enjoy: To have the most broken, twisted, unsightly body would be far better than to have no body at all.

And on October 9, 1923, a patriarch laid his hands upon my head and gave my lineage into the tribe of Joseph and Ephraim, which right I had earned through my antemortal faithfulness. The greatest good fortune of my life took place during the antemortal years when I was begotten by the Eternal God of the universe who is my Heavenly Father. And how grateful I am for him and to him for the many blessings, not only for those antemortal years, but for the countless eternities which lie ahead in the postmortal years. And I hope that I do not offend him, if after I put the many known facts of my antemortal life together, I do a little conjecturing about some of the other things that may have taken place during that antemortal life.

I believe the statement of the Prophet Joseph Smith who said, "Every man who has a calling to minister to the inhabitants of this earth was ordained to that very purpose in the grand council in heaven before the earth was." I interpret that to mean that my name was presented and approved not only for the rights of an immortal body but for an important earthly ministry limited only by my own ambition and industry. The conditions of my first estate also entitled me to live in this greatest of all dispensations, in this most favored of all nations, in the midst of the greatest freedom and opportunity.

And what a glorious experience my second estate has been. As I am presently looking ahead a few years to the end of my mortality,

I like to go back in my time machine to that period in my pre-existence when I was looking forward to my birth. As we are not permitted to see clearly the conditions beyond our death, we may not have been able to see any more clearly the conditions that would lie on the other side of our birth. What an awful feeling it must have been for one to have the fear that he might be born into the home of drunkards, or criminals, or atheists who during his mortal years would lead him away from God.

Edgar A. Guest had something like this in mind when he wrote out an imaginary conversation that could have taken place between any one of us and God. He said:

I'm going to send you down to earth
Said God to me one day,
I'm giving you what men call birth,
Tonight you'll start away.
I want you there to live with men
Until I call you back again.
I trembled as I heard him speak
Yet I knew that I must go
I felt his hand upon my cheek
And wished that I might know
What on the earth would be my task
And timidly I dared to ask.
Tell me before I start away
What thou wouldst have me do.
What message thou wouldst have me say
When will my work be through?
That I may serve thee on the earth,
Tell me the purpose of my birth.
God smiled at me and softly said
Oh you shall find your task
I want you free life's path to tread
So do not stay to ask.
Remember that if your best you do
That I shall ask no more of you.

Then Mr. Guest said:
How often as my work I do
So common place and grim,
I sit and sigh and wish I knew
If I were pleasing Him.
I wonder if with every test
I've really tried to do my best.

And while I suppose that during this life we live under a kind of an opiate of forgetfulness where we don't understand as we walk by faith what we understood as we walked by sight: We don't always realize the all-important consequences of getting off that straight and narrow way, and losing our eternal life opportunities. Of those who become Sons of Perdition, God has said that it would have been better for them if they had never been born. That is, they would have been better off if they had gone with Satan and his crowd in the beginning. What an awful tragedy that would have been. How important it is in this life that we stay away from all of those snares and pitfalls that open along life's way, leading us to eternal failure and misery.

What a frightening situation it must have been to have realized then the great truth announced by Jesus that "...strait is the gate, and narrow the way, that leadeth to life, and few there be that go in thereat." (Matt. 7:14.) In this statement the Lord was speaking of the celestial kingdom. There are many people who will go to the lower kingdom, but just a few who will qualify for that heaven of heavens which God has prepared for those who keep all of his command-ments. And yet that is the place where God wants all of us to be, and to get there we must be true and faithful and *valiant in the testi-mony of Jesus.* (D&C 76:79.)

Sometime ago I heard a story of a great king who, when his only son was born, took him to the far corner of the kingdom and handed him over to a poor peasant couple with the instruction that they were to rear him as though he were their own son. And they were instructed that they should not tell this young man who he was until he was old enough to reign, and then his parents would come back and make his identity known. Now just suppose that you were that son, and now for the first time you stand in the presence of your father, and your mother, and your court, and all your people, knowing who you are. And how terrible it would be if then you show yourself before them as unclean and unworthy and undeserving. On the other hand, what a delight it will be if then, even though you didn't know that you were a king, you had behaved like a king. Even though you didn't know that you were going to handle great wealth and power, you have shown yourself as capable of handling great wealth and power. And then you feel on your shoulder your father's hand, and hear Him say, "...Well done, thou good and faithful servant: thou hast been faithful over a few things, I will make thee ruler over many things: enter thou into the joy of thy Lord." (Matt. 25:21.)

And someone has said that that is exactly our situation in life, except that we are not merely children of a great king, we are the children of the great God who created the universe. But during mortality we are as strangers traveling through life incognito. Someone once said to his friend, "Who do you think you are?" and he whispered quietly to himself and said, "I wish I knew." Someday we are going to make the wonderful discovery that we are the children of God, created in his image, and endowed with his attributes, and heirs to his glory; that we are very important people with a rich heritage and background and a brilliant future possible.

Someone has said that if you plan to make a man out of someone, it's a pretty good procedure to start with his grandmother. But God started even further back and began laying the foundation of our success and happiness as we originally lived with him in heaven. What a magnificent heredity we all have; and what a brilliant future—if we make the most of our possibilities.

I like to go back and follow my family history while I was still in the spirit world, waiting my time and turn to be born. The Church was organized in 1830. That was only 73 years before my birth. My great-grandmother was Elvira A. Cowles, who was the first treasurer of the Mormon Relief Society. In the historical record of the Church, December 1889, Vol. III, is given the following:

"Elvira A. Cowles, a daughter of Austin Cowles and a wife of Joseph Smith the Prophet, born at Unadilla, Ostego County, New York, November 28, 1813. She was afterwards married to Jonathan H. Holmes and died in Farmington, Utah, March 10, 1871." Jonathan Holmes and Elvira A. Cowles had three daughters: Marietta (my grandmother), Phoebe, and Emma Lucinda.

Emma Lucinda died before I was born. And my grandmother, Marietta, died when I was only two years old, and I have no recollection of her. But Aunt Phoebe lived until I was a grown man, over 36 years of age. Very frequently she used to tell me about my great-grandmother, Elvira, and on February 5, 1938, when I was 35 years of age, I got her a pen and paper and asked her to write some of it down. This is what she wrote, which I had copied on the typewriter and had her sign and date. She said:

"My father, Jonathan H. Holmes, with his young wife, passed the winter of 1845-6 in a temporary shelter on the plains of Iowa. In the early spring of 1846 the request was made of Brigham Young to furnish a battalion of 500 men to march to California to take part in the Mexican War. At the direction of Brigham Young, my father volunteered his services in the United States Army as a member of the Mormon Battalion. With that organization he marched from Fort Leavenworth, Kansas in April 1846, arriving in San Diego, California on January 1, 1847. This is said to be the longest march of infantry in the history of the nation.

"After father had gone, mother came on to Utah with the pioneers of 1847. Her team consisted of an ox and a cow. She drove the team the entire way across the plains. Before they reached the end of their journey, her ox died, seemingly making it impossible for her to go on. However, she put the yoke of the fallen ox on her own shoulders and continued her journey with the company."

/s/ Phoebe L. Welling,
February 5, 1938

I put this statement by her picture in my book of remembrance, and over the years I have often not only read it to myself, but in my imagination I have gone back to Fort Leavenworth and marched with my great-grandmother across the plains with the thought that my strong back may take some of the burden belonging to that fallen ox off of her frail shoulders and transfer it to my own which would have been more able to bear it.

These three sisters all married my grandfather, Job Welling. Between these three sisters and their husband they accounted for twenty-one children, one of whom was my mother.

My Uncle Milton, my mother's brother, wrote down a very interesting resume of their early family life as it was being enacted while I was still a resident of the spirit world. I do not know whether I knew at that time whether I was going to be permitted to be a part of this very outstanding family, but I am sure that I would have been delighted had I known that that would be one of my honors, and that I would carry the Welling identification tag as the second part of my name. And I have prayed many times that I would never do anything that would bring any embarrassment or shame to any other member of this family.

Uncle Milton said;

"Jonathan H. Holmes and Elvira Cowles had but three children: Marietta, Phoebe, and my mother—Emma Lucinda. That was quite enough. There was somehow compounded into the lives of these three, the finest qualities God has given to the world. I can speak with detached restraint of everyone else, but these women stand apart and above all else and all others—they were my mothers.

* * * *

"My father died of heart disease March 1886. A few hours after his body was lowered into the grave I crept miserably away alone in the dark behind an old granary and prayed to God not to let us starve—a thing which I thought would be perfectly natural and quite likely to happen.

* * * *

"Marietta became a widow at 37 years of age; Phoebe, at 35; and Emma Lucinda, at 30. When my father died our fortifications were all destroyed. Disaster beckoned and gaunt hunger stood looking in at our door. Our family had to be mobilized for war by three soft-spoken, gentle-faced mothers.

"There were born to these three sisters 21 children. Aunt Marietta had her own home; Aunt Phoebe had her home. My mother had both homes—or no home at all, as you please to state it. She was the shock troop who led this family into the world.

"If these women ever had a misunderstanding or a disagreement, I never saw it or heard of it. If a voice was ever raised in anger in the high command of this family then or during the next fifteen years, I do not know of it, neither does any other living man.

"There must have been many mid-night conferences and anxious decisions, but at dawn we were always on the march, always forward under the dauntless leadership of these pleasant-faced, quiet, heroic women.

* * * *

"My mother was sent to the State University. I have no idea whether she regarded this as a blessing or a hardship—perhaps both. To me and the family she was just a soldier going to war. She received sound, professional training and for the rest of her life was the public-man of this family.

"Meanwhile my brother, three sisters, and I lived with our Aunts. We had as much as the others had, and if a hairline decision had to be made, just to show that they were utterly and unselfishly just, I always fancied I, at least, got the best of it.

* * * *

"My mother became a tramp school teacher all over the north end of Davis County from the old Stake Academy at Farmington to the Weber County line. She traveled year after year. Sometimes she taught near our home in North Farmington; sometimes as far away as Syracuse—twenty miles northwest.

"I never knew her to murmur or complain. In every kind of weather—rain or snow—over wretched roads, always in an old rattly open buggy, frequently with a borrowed horse, this dauntless spirit came and went.

"At this time of my life I did not think of school as a warm, comfortable, well-equipped classroom. To me, school represented a phantom institution from which my mother came home late Friday nights on four rickety wheels, or to which she went before day Monday morning behind the scrawny horse.

"I see her frail body, cold and weary at the end of her journey, coming to a warm home for shelter and rest, and I feel again the bitterness of spirit which I then knew because this self-forgetting, human sacrifice was necessary.

"At this time my mother's earnings—perhaps from $30 to $45 per month—represented the chief cash income of the family. She was our banker and tax-payer. Some of the older boys were earning money at this time, but when I worked I was paid in molasses, or potatoes, or milk, or beans, or other farm produce.

"At the end of the day or week these heroic women would divide up their spoils of war and plan together the next week's campaign. One decision of that council was fundamental: Every child must go to school at whatever sacrifice and whenever possible—it might be a short term for the older boys, a month or so longer for those my age, but school was regarded as much of a necessity as food or clothing.

"Aunt Marietta as long as she lived was the head of the house. She was the oldest and by right of experience the wisest. I think no gentler spirit ever lived. She had a title as definite and distinctive as any other ruler. I do not know, but I think the title must have originated with her sisters themselves. At any rate, I regarded it as their acknowledgment of her regal state. She was Auntie; the others had to be Aunt Phoebe or Aunt Emma. Her state needed no qualifying phrase or word. Aunt Emma might be wrong—Auntie, never. She was the chief justice. There was no appeal from her decision. She was more remote to me than the others. She had kingship. She could do no wrong.

"Aunt Phoebe, the second in command, was a prodigious worker. She could move mountains, and did from day to day. I might think of the others as frail or tired—she was tireless. She was the ultimate in strength. If there was to be a forced march with short rations, Aunt Phoebe led the attack. Her energy was equal to her strength. No task was too humble and no work too hard. She was sturdy. She had a fighting heart. I am sure she always gloried in taking the hardest physical tasks and shielding, wherever possible, the other members of the high command. She was shorter and heavier than Aunt Marietta. I make no comparison of their minds.

"My mother was without doubt the frailest. She was the tallest of the three and probably the lightest. I used to fear that her thin body would wear in two. I always wanted her to grow heavier, as if I felt she needed food. Aunt Marietta had delicate refined strength; Aunt Phoebe had the sort of strength best defined as power, unlimited vitality, energy. My mother was the aesthetic type. Her strength was the strength of the spirit.

* * * *

"By then we felt able to take care of ourselves. I think our mothers at this time might have had a just pride in their work and might with satisfaction have looked forward to years of comparative peace. They had, so far as I know, never received a penny of charity, and they saw about them grown sons and daughters educated and ready to take hold of the work of the world.

* * * *

"My mother was the first to go. Without warning she awoke one morning in June 1901 and calmly announced that she was going to die. There were two or three days of bitter struggle against death, but the fighting was all done by her sisters. Good men and women pled with her and prayed for her. With a tired smile she waved them all aside. She knew that she was going out alone, as she had done so many times before, on her last journey. She said she was quite willing to live, but she let it be perfectly understood that the beckoning forms of other loved ones were inviting her through open doorways, and she wanted to be with them. She died beautifully in her forty-fifth year.

"Aunt Marietta died probably four years later, while enjoying a pleasant visit at the home of her son in Riverside. She was 56 years of age. For 19 years she led a family of 24 people from helpless infancy to strong manhood. I felt again the loss of a real mother— the most gentle and strongest spirit I have ever known.

"These two deaths happened an average of 35 years ago. Still Aunt Phoebe, 5 years older than the one and 2 years younger than the other, lives on and on. Today, January 25, 1938, she is still in good health and justifies all I have said of her toughness. She is the last of the Mohicans, the end of a good house, the living witness of what I have here written. Today, almost 87, with serene untroubled fortitude, she sits alone on the throne of this kingdom. It is just 52 years since her husband died. She is looking with unhurried gaze in his direction, and when she goes to him, she will report that save only one she has kept every child she brought into the world safe from death or harm. She will make the same report to her sisters, and when she turns for a moment to greet her own father and mother, I expect they will say that their march across one continent was only a skirmish compared with her campaign of 52 lonely but triumphant years.

—Milton H. Welling—"

Aunt Phoebe was 52 years old when I was born, and she was 87 years of age when I was 35. But she has always been one of my great heroes. And I look forward with great anticipation to meeting her sister, my grandmother, Marietta. Of her, Uncle Milton said, "No gentler spirit ever lived. She was the chief justice of our family. She had kingship. She could do no wrong."

I feel very envious of children who have had the chance of living and having a friendly association with fine grandparents. I never knew my Grandfather or Grandmother Welling. I never knew my Grandfather Sill, and my Grandmother Sill died when I was a very young child. I do have a distinct image of her, however, as she used to come to Church in her horse and buggy. I never remember of a family dinner, or of hearing her speak, or hearing anything about her.

My information from the Welling side of my family is very meager, but it is even more meager from the Sill side of my family. I wish that my grandparents and my parents had all taken the time to write down something about themselves and their lives that I could treasure as I do those few lines that I have. That is, I don't know very much more about my grandparents in this life than I did about them in the pre-existence. But I am very grateful to them because of the fine characters that I know they all possessed, and of the part they took in bringing about the greatest blessing that has ever occurred to me in this life, and that is that I was born and made eligible to enjoy the fantastic blessings of this life.

Chapter Three

The Early Years

I was born March 31, 1903, about a half a block west of the Farmers Union Store on Gentile Street in Layton, Utah. The old Oregon Short Line section of the Union Pacific ran down the main street of Layton at one time, and then a little later it was moved a little bit west and ran just west of our home, butting through the corner of our family's property.

My father had twenty acres of land about a mile and a half north of Layton, on a little street that ran north from the main road up the street which now serves as the south entrance to Hill Field. Soon after my birth we moved out on this farm where we stayed until I was in the seventh grade.

In those days there were a number of small homes on this street which housed the families that lived on their farms. This street, for some reason that I could never understand, was called Easy Street. Going from south to north up the street on both sides of the road, as I remember them at a later date, first was the home of Morris Whitesides; next M. P. Whitesides; directly across the street was Joseph A. Sill; then north John H. Gibson; next John Watson; next O'Keith Adams; next Royal Robbins; across the street on the east, Isaac Adams; up the street on the west, Charles W. Robbins; on the corner of what is now Hill Field and Antelope Road was the Joseph King residence, and later Dee Harris built a house across east on the other corner; then going up the street Jesse Harris; next D. D. Harris. Across the street on the east was Henry Thornley; just above the canal was Daniel B. Harris, father of Ezra Harris who succeeded his parents as occupants of this home; next up the street was David B. Weaver; and on the top of the hill and the last resident up the street was Christopher Weaver, the father of Parley Weaver who was succeeded in the home by his son. Thus a total of sixteen families lived on Easy Street.

I guess it would not be possible for me to have been granted any privileges in my antemortal existence, like taking a sail up this street to get a sense of the locale in which I was going to spend the early years of my life. If I had have been, I'm sure I would have been a little bit disappointed with the fact that the Sill residence was the smallest, the cheapest and the most unsightly and uncomfortable one on the street. And I could have picked out some other disadvantages. We were not very good farmers, and I am sure it would have been the concensus of opinion that we had the greatest number of weeds per square foot, the poorest crops, made the least money, and had one of the largest families to support.

This house on Easy Street was made up of two rooms: a little bedroom for my parents, which was probably eight by ten; and the long room which served as the living quarters for the family was probably ten by fifteen. Then there was a little lean-to on the end in which my brother, Russell, and I slept. It was about six by eight feet.

In 1913 we homesteaded some land in Delta, Utah and lived there for sixty days during which we built another house which was about eight by ten feet in dimension. And the nicest house we ever owned is the house still standing in Layton which, as I remember, cost $1,100 to build, on which we had a $700 mortgage.

I used to be invited occasionally to have Sunday dinner with one of the boy friends with whom I played, but because of the serious limitations of our facilities and budget, I only remember one occasion when I ever had anyone to my house to dinner. That experiment turned out rather badly. However, the most serious part of this burden fell on my mother as she tried to provide for her family. Of course, we had some farm produce which we ourselves raised. We grew our own meat. We usually had quite a lot of fruit, and my mother used to care for a limited number of chickens and used the eggs to trade at the store. But all in all, we seemed to get along without any serious problems. We had no rebellions or bad habits that I was aware of. As I look back on it now, I can't think of anything that I would like to have changed about it, except even in those earlier years I could have contributed more than I did.

I have recently listened to records of the early lives of Franklin and Eleanor Roosevelt, who were born into families of great wealth and high society. They were brought up with the greatest care in the finest environment. Both of them made a great success of their lives, and yet I think I would not care to exchange even my early years with them.

My wife and I have also recently listened to the early life stories of Abraham Lincoln and Mary Todd Lincoln. Mary Todd was brought up in a fine home with the greatest culture and a love for fine things. Abe was brought up in a backwoods cabin on the dirt floor where nothing much mattered. And I suppose that each of these situations have some advantages and some disadvantages.

I remember the institution of the Saturday night bath where my mother used to improvise a little bathroom around the kitchen stove in the south end of our living room. She would put some chairs across the room and put some quilts over the backs of the chairs and then put some warm water in a No. 3 galvanized tub in which one child after another would take his bath without bothering to change the water in the tub. Then mother would lay out our clean clothing ready for Sunday. Back in those days, the hot water supply was heated in a water reservoir on the side of the stove or in some buckets or pans which were placed on the top of the stove. The water to be heated was brought in from the well outside.

There was usually somebody in the community who owned a threshing machine, which was made up of a large steam engine turning a powerful flywheel, and then a belt from the engine ran the threshing machine. And they would go around the community and thresh people's crops for them, and take a share of the wheat as their toll. Then we would take part of our wheat down to the mill and have it turned into the flour we needed. We would have rolled oats or rolled barley to help the horses out during the hard working season. The threshing time was always a very special occasion, and for a number of years I would work on one of these threshing crews and every place we went they had a great feed of tomatoes, corn on the cob, and all sorts of good things for the threshers to eat.

One of the miserable jobs that I never did like very much was to be the straw stacker and stand under that blower that would blow the straw and chaff up onto the stack. It seemed that most of it went down my neck or got into my lungs. But I liked the food, and I could even tolerate the barley beards down my back and in my eyes.

On some occasions when we had company come in the evening, we would fill our milkpan with apples and place some plates and knives around among the guests and we would peel and eat the apples.

I am very grateful that my parents were good members of the Church. In my early years, my mother was President of the ward Primary, and while I don't remember very much of the detail, yet I could not help but be the beneficiary of her teaching and also her great spirit and noble heart.

I have frequently gone back in my memory and tried to identify the first things that I can remember. One of the great wonders of that day was the telephone line that was put up Easy Street. I must have been very young, but I can remember them putting up the poles. We had a telephone installed in our house. It was a big box fastened on the wall, and I remember that we had a party line with many people all hooked into the same wire so that we could listen in on each other's conversations if we wanted to. The telephone company tried to signal the person they wanted by a particular kind of ring. That is, one ring would be for one customer, two rings would be for someone else, a long ring and two short rings would indicate someone else, so that if everyone would answer only when he was summoned, some measure of privacy would be maintained, although this could not be depended upon.

Usually people would lift up the receiver to see if anyone was already using the line and when someone tried to signal the operator by winding the crank on the side, the operator would reply, "The line is busy." I remember my older sister, Mable, holding me up to talk to someone on the telephone as I was just learning to talk. In fact, one of the first phrases that I ever learned was to give my own version of the operator's statement, "The line is busy."

When someone stayed on the line too long and someone else was waiting for what he thought was an urgent call, there used to be some arguments over the wire about whether what the other person was talking about was important enough to tie up the telephone line.

One of the most distinctive of my early recollections was the occasion when Margurite and Genevieve were born. At that time, I was a little over five years of age. The birth took place at home in the small bedroom of my parents. I was asked to take my younger brother, Russell, then three years old, out to play in one of our usual playgrounds while the event took place. I have many early memories of those early days on Easy Street. One of these was:

Our Home

My parents slept in their little bedroom, which was a separate construction but pushed up against the other main room and connected by a door. The very small children frequently slept in the room with our parents. My brother and I slept in a little six by eight lean-to on the back of the house. The rest of the family slept in the main room which served as living room, dining room, kitchen, and bathroom, or they were parceled out in some out of doors sleeping arrangement.

The house had no plaster, but my father had obtained some filter cloths from the sugar factory through which the syrup was strained and nailed these up on the studding, then they were cal-cimined to improve their appearance. When the wind blew, the air would get behind them and flap them back and forth or they would bulge to show the pressure of the wind. Naturally such a house was very difficult to keep warm during the winter. We had only one stove in the house and that was the coal cook stove in the extreme south end of the long room. When bedtime came, the fire was allowed to die out so that the temperature was pretty much the same on the inside of the house as it was on the outside.

It was my job to make the fire in the morning. My father would call to me from his room when it was time, and because of the extreme cold and because there was no time to dress, I became very expert in making a fire in the shortest possible time. I would be prepared with kindling, paper and coal the night before. Then I would dump the grate, take off the stove lids, put in the paper, then the kindling, then the coal, then light the match to the paper, put the lids back on and see if I could get back in bed with my brother before I froze to death. Sometimes it was about an even race.

Back in those days, I had four pieces of clothing, a blue denim shirt that pulled on over my head, a pair of overalls, a pair of shoes and a straw hat. I used to get the straw hat for five cents at Arthur Ellis's store, then I would thread a shoelace around where a hatband ordinarily would have gone and I could make the hat any size by drawing in the shoelace. I have a picture of myself in the middle of the winter with the snow on the ground, still wearing my five cent straw hat. I do not remember wearing underwear or stockings except on Sunday.

My older brother was in a little better condition than I was so far as clothing was concerned. He had two hats, a felt work hat and a Sunday hat. I wore my five-cent straw hat during the week to work in, and he let me borrow his felt work hat to go to Sunday School.

At that time, we lived about a mile and a half from the Church house. I have always been a regular church-goer, even though at that time I was the only member of our family that I remember who attended. I used to walk the mile-and-a-half to church and I used to go about an hour early so that I would get there before the other people started to arrive, as the other members went by families in surries or buggies or some other kind of horse-drawn vehicles, and I felt self-conscious having to walk. So, I would always try to be at the church before any of them came along. And even though the other members of my family at that period did not attend, yet I think that since I was old enough to attend at all, there has never been a month when I was not active. And it seems that I have always had a great desire to go as I never remember that the suggestion ever came from other members of my family or from teachers or workers in the ward. I did have some Sunday clothes and I remember no embarrassment for my Sunday dress.

However, my work and school garb was a little meager. As given above, I had four pieces of work clothing for the day time; and when I went to bed, I took off my shoes and my straw hat and my overalls, and slept in my blue denim shirt, which served as a rather abbreviated night gown.

It used to be my job also to do the chores, which included feeding the pigs, milking the cow, keeping the stable clean, and feeding the other animals, which used to be a problem as we very frequently had little to feed them. During the summer, I used to herd the cow out on the street. She would eat the grass along the ditchbank and at the sides of the road. And one of the great trials of my life was that sometimes I had to herd her on Sunday. Otherwise, she would not get anything to eat, and she furnished a large part of our food supply.

One of the vivid memories of my life was the irrigation reservoir that my father built. During the week we used to play on the reservoir. I got a couple of railroad ties and made a raft on which I could sail. Or frequently we went swimming in the reservoir. I remember one great event when the reservoir sprung a leak in the bank along the line of the pipe running out of the exit. It soon became a little trickle and then a larger stream and then before we were aware, it had gone so far that we were unable to stop it and the water washed away a part of the dike serving as the reservoir bank. Several men from around the neighborhood were shoveling in dirt, throwing in rocks, sandbags, and in other ways trying to stop the water flow which was tearing the gulley through the bank. But it got out of control and did a great deal of damage by washing away the crops that were below it. This seems to have made an extraordinary imprint on my mind; and on many occasions since that time, I have had a dream in the night of our farm being washed away. This always has a very terrifying, depressing effect upon me.

As I got a little older, my father permitted me to have a little bit of land of my own to cultivate. I planted raspberries and blackberries and dewberries, and all kinds of garden stuff to supplement our food supply. I also had a watermelon patch, cucumbers, onions, carrots, radishes, and a lot of other things. I used to get a seed catalog every year and I loved to look at these beautiful pictures and realize what you could produce by putting a few seeds in the ground. I suppose these seed catalogs served me instead of the comic books and murder stories of the present day. I remember for two or three years I used to send for some raw peanuts and had myself a few hills of peanuts. But I love the soil and I love to see things grow.

Later on, after I was out of high school, I took over the running of my father's farm, which had been considerably run down because the renter had not taken time to keep the soil properly fertilized. We had a man who raised cattle close by, and I made a deal with him one winter that I would clean up all of his yards if he would loan me his manure spreader, and I hauled all of his manure out and spread it on my land. I took great delight in the crops that resulted.

In 1921, and for a number of years before that, the land had been rented. Prices were very high following the end of World War I. I took over the land in 1922. I borrowed money to buy some horses and a minimum of necessary equipment. But that year there was a great falling off in the farm prices and I did not make enough money to pay for my equipment. However, the next year I had the soil in better shape, the crop was greater, and I was able to clear up my bills and have enough over to help pay my way on a mission.

I remember some tragedies in those early days. When I was very young, our cow died. I very well remember that long night. The veterinarian came and stayed for a long time after dark working with our cow. I was holding the lantern and most of the other members of the family were standing around far into the night hoping and praying that our cow, which seemed to us like one of the members of the family, would not die. But our hopes were in vain, and the next morning someone came to salvage what they could and skinned the cow to sell the hide. I can still remember how badly I felt that such a desperate economy was necessary. Then the cow was loaded on a slip and dragged down into the sand hills at the west of our property, which was to serve as her final resting place.

I also remember the death of my dog, Tip. I do not remember the cause of his death, however. He used to sleep in the little shed that I had improvised as a place to keep my kindling dry, and I remember the night that he died. I spent most of the night holding him in my arms, praying that he would get well. But Tip also died, and left a very large, open place in my heart.

For some of those early years I attended school in the little one-room school house out in what we used to think of as the sand hills, a little east of where the new freeway crosses what is now Antelope Drive or Syracuse Road. One teacher used to take care of the entire eight grades. To get to school required a round trip walk of probably a mile and three quarters, except when we would go through the sand knolls, we would cut down the distance a little bit.

As I began to grow up a little, I was aware of our comparative poverty. We didn't have any money to buy hay for the cow. My mother was extremely limited in what she could do for her family by way of both food, clothing, and housing. Because I was a pretty good worker and my services were needed, I used to stay out of school a great deal to help with the planting and harvesting of our crops so that I had a very spotty attendance record at best. I didn't think of myself as handicapped at all, however, because I was always able to make up the work so that I could be promoted. And in one year I had a special promotion, being promoted from the seventh to the eighth grade in the middle of the year with a group of other students.

I think I was a pretty good worker and learned to do most of the things necessary to run the farm. Later on the school out in the sand hills was closed up and we used to walk to Layton to school. We finally moved to Layton, which was much closer to the school house, when my father became the postmaster. And though he had a severe amount of debt, things brightened up a little financially. My farm labor had qualified me to get what I thought was a very good farm labor job during my three years in high school. The money that I thus earned made it possible for me to have a full outfit of underwear, sox, and even a hat of my own, and also prepared me to take over the farm on my own after graduation.

I have always thought that I learned more on the farm to serve my success throughout the balance of my life than I did in any other place. It was in my farming operations that I learned how to work consistently and continuously near the very top of my possibility. This I was able to do on my own power, motivated by my own enthusiasm, without any prompting or even any suggestion from someone else.

I have seen so many people who have fallen down in those things that they attempt to do because they have been unable to keep their work out of the area of becoming drudgery, where they had to force themselves to do it more or less against their will. I would like to make it an official part of my life's report that of all of the jobs I have ever done, including those early years on the farm, my undertakings as a student, my later farm work, my missionary activities, my school teaching, my work as a salesman and a sales manager, as well as all of the work that I have done in the Church, I have nver had a job I didn't like. Some of them I didn't like to begin wtih, but to use another paraphrase—if you can't get a dinner to suit your taste, then get a taste to suit your dinner.

If I were asked to name the most outstanding and profitable characteristic of my life, it would be my ability to keep going. For some thirty-five years with the New York Life, I have been entitled to a month's vacation each year, and the company has urged and almost threatened me to get me to take it. I would, of course, make just as much money. They thought I would make a lot more money, but it is a matter of official record that I have taken only one week's vacation during that period. The reason being that I could just not think of anything that I would enjoy doing as much as working at my job. And when I finally retired, the official report showed that I was 35 months behind on my vacation.

It has been the same with my church work and everything else that I have done. Throughout my lifetime I have worked Saturdays and most of the holidays except the very major ones. Over the years I have been cautioned by doctors and other people to diversify my activities more and take it a little easier. I remember Roy D. Thatcher, Chairman of the Board of Regents when I became a member of the University of Utah governing board, said to me one day, "Of course, you can't keep it up." But it has never been any effort to keep it up. Nor have I ever had any problems trying to force myself to do my work. I have merely done the thing that I wanted to do and seemed the easier for me to do at the time, all of which has been greatly enjoyed.

And I am very grateful for the opportunity to be continuously employed as many hours per day as I want to be. I now have a large number of good friends who are over sixty-five who have given up their employment or had it taken away from them. And some of them will live for another twenty or thirty years without the pressure or excitement of a daily occupational demand being made upon them. This would be one of the most unpleasant of life's conditions to me. I am very grateful that so far as my prospects presently indicate, I will never have that forced upon me while I maintain good physical and mental health.

And this great lesson of life was learned by me in my earliest youth when I was completely unsuspecting that any significant thing was taking place in my life. Not only is the moment of birth an unconscious moment, but many of the great events in our lives take place while we are not aware of their significance or actually what is happening.

Chapter Four

Out On The Farm

Over the years I have often thought of some of the important things that happened when I lived out on the farm, both in my childhood days and later when I took over its work and management. I now find myself fully convinced that these were some of the very most important experiences of my life. I feel a little bit sorry for my children, grandchildren, and others who do not have a substantial agricultural experience under the conditions of those early days. In fact, it seems to me that one of the problems of our day is that we are getting too far away from the soil.

Since the beginning of time, most of the people have lived on the land and have devoted themselves to supplying their own needs by wresting them from the soil. During the early history of our country, most people were farmers. There are many people who feel that there is a closer relationship existing between our physical, mental, and spiritual welfare and the soil out of which we ourselves were taken. It is interesting that Adam, who in his antemortal existence was Michael, the archangel, was a farmer; and most of the people since his time have devoted their interests to agriculture, horticulture, livestock and the other occupations that are concerned with the land. And yet life was quite different in those days to the life that we now know in our homes of luxury and convenience. And I thought I would like to draw a picture of the farm life that I knew many years ago.

I was impressed in my earliest years, as I have been ever since, about the wonders of God's great creation of top soil wherein He placed all of the elements to furnish an everlasting food supply for billions of people. What miracles and wonders can come from twenty acres of farm land.

In settling on his farm, my father marked off an area of two to three acres as a kind of homesite. The house was set back quite a little way from the road and we had some cherry trees and did some other gardening in the area between the house and the street. The house was lighted at night by coal oil lamps which could be carried from room to room as needed. One of the interesting things was that most of our utilities, plumbing, and supplies were outside the house itself. Back of the house my father had built an irrigation reservoir where our turn of water could be impounded when someone was sick, or needed the daylight to do the irrigation, or wanted to save the water to be used later in the week. And I would like to give, as well as I can, a picture of the conditions around our home on Easy Street.

Immediately south of the house, my father dug a well to furnish our cullinary water supply. The well had a wooden casing. A frame over the top of the well supported a pulley, through which a rope hung with a bucket on each end. I remember the dirt that came out of the well had a lot of clay in it with which as children we used to model things. At the west of the house we had a refrigerator. This was a wooden frame covered with burlap. On the top of the refrigerator was a large galvanized pan filled with water which was about six inches deep and large enough to cover the refrigerator, probably two feet wide and four feet long. One end of the burlap was immersed in the water and the other hung down the sides of the framework. This acted as a natural siphon to keep the entire burlap wet. The evaporation produced the coolness to keep the milk, cream, fruit, and other things inside the refrigerator cool.

A path ran from the south door of our house west past the refrigerator. Next on the left was a brooder house which was built to house an incubator to hatch our chickens. Later this idea was given up and then the brooder house was cleaned up and used as an auxiliary detached bedroom. Continuing west along the path, the next institution was the coal house which held several tons of coal, enough to furnish the heat for the home during the winter. The next building on the right was the tool shed. At one time my father had been something of a carpenter and he had a good set of carpentry tools, plus shovels, etc.

Going on west you next came to the chicken coop where my mother had a few chickens. This was near the south east corner of the irrigation reservoir.

Going down the path a little further was a kind of "Chick Sales" outside lavatory which had a simultaneous seating capacity of three. Under this a deep hole was dug and as necessary this institution was moved to cover a new digging in some new location. Then turning north around the west bank of the reservoir, there was a large pig pen made out of logs and separated into various pens. Continuing north were the corrals and the stable where the animals were kept. In front of this was an area which contained the haystack and the year's supply of straw used for bedding down the animals. The harnesses for the horses were hung in the back of the stable.

Then turning east along the north side of the reservoir was the main roadway connecting the farm with the street on the east. There was also a large irrigation ditch that ran down the north side of our property to irrigate that part of the land which was not under the reservoir. Going east, we had another building called the granary where we kept the wheat which we took to the mill to have flour made. Also we had wheat to feed the chickens. There were other grains like rolled oats, etc., that we had to feed the horses and some special grain processed for the pigs.

Next to the granary was a large building called the buggy shed, which was a large shed intended to keep the buggy, when we had one, out of the wet. We could also put other pieces of farm machinery in the buggy shed. Between the buggy shed and the granary I built a woodshed where I could store a great quantity of wood suitable for kindling the fire in the morning, as this was my particular responsibility. And there must be an ample supply of dry kindling in wet and snowy weather, otherwise there would be no fire in the house.

Then, proceeding back south toward the house, we had on the west between the path and the reservoir a cellar dug in the earth, with dirt walls and floor over which we had built a roof of timbers covered with brush with an overburden of dirt. In this cellar we kept our winter supply of apples and any vegetables which might be available like onions, carrots, parsnips, etc. We also had some shelves where the years supply of bottled fruit might be kept. We usually kept our potato supply in a potato pit dug in the ground and lined with straw. Straw was also placed over the potatoes, and then a large covering of dirt sufficient to keep the frost out of the potatoes in the winter time was added.

Occasionally when I was very small, we would hitch up the horse in between the shaves of the buggy and drive to Farmington where my mother's family lived. My mother, with Ralph and Mabel, would sit in the buggy seat and my brother, Russell, and I would sit down in the bottom of the buggy. And it seemed that each of the two lines used to drive the horse would always fit conveniently under my ears on the side of my head and my ears used to take quite a beating when my mother would flap the horse with the reins. We would come home with various kinds of fruits under the seat and in the back of the buggy. I do not know how long it would take for a round trip to North Farmington. I imagine it might be about three or four hours. But even the harnessing and unharnessing of the horse was quite an operation as one had to go to the pasture or barn to get the horse, which usually had to be curried and brushed to make it presentable, then harnessed and hooked up to the buggy. This was quite a different operation than merely stepping on the automobile starter in our day.

My father had planted about ten acres of apples and four or five acres of peaches. We also had some cherry trees. One of these was an early variety and it seems to me I used to stand under this tree all spring waiting for the first red color to touch these green cherries. Then I would climb up the tree and get the cherries. This hunger apparently stamped itself rather deeply into my brain, as throughout my life I have occasionally had dreams of being out in the most beautiful cherry orchard with the trees all laden down with large black, fully-ripe cherries, none of which I have ever tasted because just as I get ready to eat them I always wake up. This has seemed like a dreadful waste to me to create these wonderful imaginary cherries which my dream did not last long enough for me to enjoy.

Later on the apples and peach trees were mostly pulled out because of the difficulty in marketing the fruit. I remember one year that we sold our peach and apple crop on consignment. The fruit was shipped to one of the big cities in the east. But either the consignment went unsold or we were in the hands of fraudulent dealers as we received no money at all in payment. In one case we were asked to pay the freight.

Jesus said that if a tree did not produce, it should be cut down. He said, "Why cumbereth it the ground." And I suppose my father felt that would also apply even though the tree could produce but the fruit could not be profitably sold. Back in those days, most people seemed to grow their own fruit and most communities like our own were more or less self-supporting. There were many advantages in living on the farm in that if there was sufficient industry and a little capital to work with, one might grow his own food.

One of the most beautiful sights that I have ever seen in my lifetime was our ten acres of apple trees all in full bloom. William Martin described this situation when he said:

Have you seen an apple orchard in the spring
          In the spring?
An English apple orchard in the spring?
     When the spreading trees are hoary
     With their wealth of promised glory,
     And the mavis sings its story
          In the spring.

Have you plucked the apple blossoms in the spring?
          In the spring?
And caught their subtle odours in the spring?
     Pink buds pouting at the light,
     Crumpled petals baby white,
     Just to touch them a delight—
          In the spring.

Have you walked beneath the blossoms in the spring?
          In the spring?
Beneath the apple blossoms in the spring
     When the pink cascades are falling,
     And the silver brooklets brawling,
     And the cuckoo bird soft calling,
          In the spring.

If you have not, then you know not, in the spring,
          In the spring,
Half the colour, beauty, wonder of the spring,
     No sweet sight can remember
     Half so precious, half so tender,
     As the apple blossoms render
          In the spring.

   I was just a little boy then, but I used to like to lie on my back on the ground and listen to the birds and the bees and enjoy the great beauty of the wonder of God's creation. And all of the raw materials for a good fruit crop and every other crop to last the occupants of the earth for thousands of years had been provided for and put into the soil on that early morning of creation so long ago. It is a small wonder that after the intelligence that God put into his work of creation, he looked out upon the earth and called it very good. With far less understanding but with great appreciation, I have done a similar thing millions of times when I have thought of this earth and its great productive powers as very good.

Later we built a combination fence around several acres of apple trees and planted some red clover in between the trees to provide a pasture for the pigs from which we got a great deal of our year's meat supply. Pigs can turn wormy apples and clover into pork chops, spare ribs, and bacon. We got our bread from the grain we grew and our butter and cream from the alfalfa field. And even the smoke that went curling up from the chimney each day had a certain air of glamour and romance about which the most extreme environmentalist of that day had not the slightest objections.

Some of the farmers on our street used to have a kind of fore-runner of the station wagon which was called a white top or surrey. At least it was a two seated vehicle with a top to keep out any rain or snow, and canvases could be let down to give protection from the sides. These more luxurious conveniences were usually drawn by two horses instead of one.

I am sure that I would not like to make a permanent trip back into the past and live on the farm, but in my imagination I like to go back and make the rounds of doing the chores, milking the cows, etc., etc., with this young boy that I used to be. I like to feed the pigs, swim in the reservoir and do the other things that were so very important and interesting to me in those long ago days out on the farm.

Chapter Five

My Educational Life

The dictionary says that education is the process of nourishing a child or young animal. It is a manner of training youth for their ultimate station in life. The dictionary also refers to education as the impartation or acquisition of knowledge, attitudes, skills, habits or the disciplines of character development.

We speak of a grade school education, or a college education. Some people have a liberal education and some have a specialized education. There have been a lot of people in the past who have had little or no formal education—their only instruction and discipline has been received in the school of their own experience, sometimes called the university of hard knocks. Herbert Spencer said, "To prepare us for complete living is the function which education is supposed to discharge." And complete living involves training in the physical, the psychological, the sociological, the artistic, and the spiritual.

There are many other facts and laws involved in our educations. One of the synonyms of education is "good breeding." The dictionary says breeding is training in the amenities and courtesies of life. We should begin studying these definitions of education during the first part of our lives, not waiting until our future is largely behind us. From my point of view, my own formal education left much to be desired, yet as I look back on my experience, I receive a great thrill of joy.

Of course, most all of life is in one way or another education. Some education points out those areas that should be developed while some shows the quicksands that should be avoided. We study medicine to learn how to keep ourselves well physically. We study psychiatry, psychology, and the other studies of the mind to learn how to keep ourselves well mentally. Agriculture is how we feed ourselves. Sociology is how we live together agreeably. Law is how we keep our lives orderly. Then we have this great science of religion to learn how to keep ourselves well spiritually.

We have a great deal of educational philosophy under the heading of "thou shalt not." Much of our finest education has to do with those pitfalls that should be avoided. One of the striking things about education, as is the case with most other things, is that we don't know very much about it. For example, we have never yet discovered any process or any educational instructions which can guarantee to everybody alike the most desirable and profitable kind of education. Even effective home training does not produce the same result in all family members. Elbert Hubbard used to conjecture about the reasons why it so frequently happened that from the same family nest could come one or two eagles and a dozen ordinary barnyard fowls. Actually no one seems very definite in his convictions about how to guarantee, even to ourselves, the highest kind of accomplishment. Some people do well in their formal studies and some do not. And someone has posed this question, "Where is the teacher who could have taught Shakespeare?" The same person gave it as his opinion that if, instead of having his ears boxed leaving him deaf in one ear, and then being kicked out of school at age fourteen because he couldn't learn, Thomas A. Edison had taken electrical engineering courses at college, he may have turned out to be a hypocritical professor instead of the electrical wizard who repeated that great command to our entire world, "Let there be light!" But this box on the ears and kicking out of school procedure has not worked very well as a general thing. Some people graduate from the university of hard knocks as captains of industry, while others come forth as hopeless derelicts.

In spite of many disadvantages and shortcomings, my own education has been like the other parts of my life—a thrilling, exciting experience. If one should add up the total of my years spent in formal schooling, I would probably be a freshman or sophomore in high school, as work on the farm in my early years, plus earning the funds to attend school later on, caused me to spend a part of each school year since the fourth grade in physical labor instead of study. This had some disadvantages, but I think this deprivation greatly increased my hunger for learning and added something on the positive side of my education. I was awarded a high school diploma from Davis High School in 1921 and have credit for three quarters of unmatriculated college study, one at the USAC in Logan and two at the University of Utah. Even in my 70's,

I have a great hunger for study. There are still a great many things that I would like to know about and skills I would like to develop.

In my recent years, I have done a large amount of independent reading. In my twenty-five looseleaf note books (8½" x 11" size, with approximately 300 pages in each one) I have a rather complete set of notes on over a thousand of the world's greatest books, from which I have received a great deal by way of attitudes and skills, as well as receiving some pleasant training in the "amenities and courtesies" of life. And I am very grateful for this combination of practical experience and formal schooling. Even my formal education is far more than Benjamin Franklin, Thomas A. Edison, Abraham Lincoln, or Jesus of Nazareth ever had. In addition, I am grateful for those men who, through their books, have tried to help me solve some of the problems for which education at its best was intended. I hope to have a great many more years to continue my studies, to help me prepare for graduation into that interesting area beyond the boundaries of this life where we will be enrolled in a process of eternal progression.

In 1925, while a missionary in Alabama, I visited the famous Tuskeegee Institute. They were practicing a theory of education which has always made good sense to me. That is, they would attend class for three days each week, and then they would actually go out on the job and do the work for an additional three days that had been motivated in their studies. After reading the books and getting ideas about agriculture from the teacher for three days, they would actually go out and do the work involved for three days so that they not only had the knowledge in their brains, but they also had the complimentary skills, attitudes and habits in their muscles. They would study carpentry, and then take their hammers and saws and do the things that they had studied. I was impressed that that was a pretty good idea, and I had begun this same work routine when I was in about the fourth grade. I don't remember that I ever went to school a full year after that time, as it was necessary to stay out in the fall to help get in the crops. One of our big crops was the apple harvest, and while some people may not think my work with the apples and study in other fields was very well correlated, yet there is a theory that no ability or character or improvement is ever lost, and sometimes our greatest successes swing on the most insignificant events.

At a very early age I learned something about taking the responsibility of the farm work, and I was motivated to work as hard as possible so that I could get back to school as soon as I could. I was also impressed by natural necessity that every job ought to be done effectively. There are some young people, particularly the children of well-to-do parents, to whom education becomes a little boring, and they sometimes sluff school to get a little release. This was something that never bothered me. Neither boredom with my studies, nor any kind of lack of interest in my work, has ever been even a small part of my experience. I never sluffed school one day in my life. On the contrary, being forced to stay out whetted my appetite to get back into school as soon and for as long as I could. There are some people who can loaf along and still keep up with the crowd in the classroom. By this procedure, some people form the habits of loafing or ineffective work. I had many advantages because I had to work harder than most of the others in order to make up the back work, and consequently I was benefited both ways, toward greater physical industry and toward more diligent mental study.

However, this prolonged absenteeism involved a problem in my freshman year of high school, as when I reported six weeks late, the algebra teacher refused to let me take algebra. I had the idea I could make up the work I had missed, but she thought it would be too difficult for me to make up the back work, and her own teaching load prevented her from spending the personal time with me that would be involved in this particular study. Therefore, I missed algebra and geometry in high school. And while I received my high school diploma, yet this lack of required credit made it impossible for me to matriculate in college.

Later, when I became the Chairman of the Board of Regents of the University of Utah, and had something to do with trying to help students toward their graduation, I was given a little feeling of envy toward all graduates as I had been unable not only to get *out* of the University, but I had even been unable to get *into* the University.

At least in part, life has made some of these shortcomings up to me. After the conclusion of my eleven years as a member of the Board of Regents, I was given an honorary Doctor of Laws degree. At least I can wear my doctor's hood on the outside, even though I may not have the required mental furnishings on the inside. I have never ceased to be grateful, however, for this labor part of my Tuskeegee-like education. A part of this balance came from my athletic experience, particularly from the football training received in my last high school year, as I have always felt that I learned a great many things about sportsmanship and courage that I had never found in the classroom books. I think it is a great accomplishment to be able to be knocked down, knocked out, and generally bruised and mussed up in rather vigorous play, and then be able to put your arm around the one who almost cracked your skull and feel kindly toward him.

My senior year in high school was one of the high points of my education and my life. My coach was Wilford Romney. I was very exact in following training rules and I felt the great thrill that comes when one feels that he has abundant, glowing, good health. Each night at home I used to like to run a mile or two just for the fun of it. It was a great thrill to jump over fences and flex my muscles and feel the joy of being abundantly alive physically. But also because of my starting early, I was elected President of the senior class, and I had a lot of other great privileges. I was given a part in the school play. I had some wonderful friends both on the faculty and among the students.

A part of my education went beyond the few things I learned in formal course work, much of which I have forgotten; I also learned to feel great confidence in other human beings, both my instructors and my classmates. There was a little luncheon stand just off the campus that we used to call The Beanery, where we sometimes went to have lunch. Mrs. Wilcox, the proprietress, became one of my heroines.

For many of my recent years, high school students have seemed to me like children who need to be supervised and checked up on to keep them from getting into all kinds of serious problems and falling down before the most trivial temptation, but back in my own high school days they seemed like adults, having a great character and the ability to handle their own affairs successfully.

My senior year at Davis High School was a delightful experience, but good things come to an end. Because I had arranged to rent my father's farm for the next summer, I left school on the first of March in order to buy some horses, the necessary equipment, and get my spring work under way at the earliest moment. To give up my class presidency and this pleasant association with my teachers and other friends was not easy, yet it seemed to me to involve no difficult problems because it was the thing to do. At the time, I planned to make farming my life's work. I loved to make things grow and to participate in this miracle of creation. God Himself planted a garden eastward in Eden in which He made grow many wonderful things. Many of us would be better off if we kept a closer interest in the soil. On the other hand, I hated to give up my education. But lack of funds, both with my father's family and for myself, seemed to make that necessary. The responsibility of being on my own farm was another great educational experience. I did go to the Agricultural College at Logan during one winter quarter when there was not much doing on the farm. During those winter months I studied Agronomy, animal husbandry, and related subjects. years. When financial considerations made it necessary for me to give up teaching, I went into selling, which was also an important educational experience. At first I did not like selling, but I was successful right from the start because I worked at my selling the way I had worked on the farm, long and continuously. But I hated the prospect of being a salesman.

Then I made a very important discovery—that it is not a wise procedure to hate such important things as your own life's work, and so I began to emphasize in my mind the advantages of my job rather than the disadvantages. I looked at the pleasant parts of selling through the big end of my psychological telescope which made them bigger, and I looked at the unpleasant parts of selling through the little end of my telescope, so that they seemed to shrivel up and disappear. When I went into sales management, I repeated this process of accentuating the positive and mastering those parts that might otherwise cause me negative feelings. In my sales management work I maintained the same hours and vigor that I practiced on the farm and in my sales work.

There is one sure way for someone to learn to love what he is doing, and that is to do it well. On one occasion I heard President Clark refer to Alexander Hamilton as a genius, and Alexander Hamilton tells how he became a genius. He said, "Men give me some credit for genius but all of the genius I have, lies in this; when I have a subject in mind, I study it profoundly. Day and night it is before me. I explore it in all its bearings. My mind becomes pervaded with it. The result is in the fruits of study and labor." And I am convinced that if anyone wants to be a genius in any field, he may easily become one by following the formula of Mr. Hamilton. I have discovered that whether I am doing physical labor, public relations work, or sitting hour after hour, month after month at the writing desk, the success formula continues to be the same—study and labor. And for good measure, I might add a third factor—that one should always have fun in the process.

I have seen so many people who are always trying to pull themselves out of some prolonged depression. They almost can't wait until quitting time, and the high point of the year for some people is vacation time. Most people tell themselves that they ought to have a hobby or something that they enjoy doing to furnish them relief from the drudgery of their occupations, which they hate. Ralph Waldo Emerson had a much better philosophy when he combined these two success elements and said, "May the work that you do be the play that you love."

It was once suggested to Abraham Lincoln that his eyes looked tired, and that he ought to rest. Mr. Lincoln replied, "It's my heart that is tired and in order to rest my heart, I must go on at an accelerated pace." If your son is a little bored with his school work and you tell him to go fishing for a couple of weeks and forget the school, you will find that when he comes back and discovers himself that much further behind, he will probably be more tired and more bored than he was before the vacation. The best way to rest is to work twice as hard, because no one ever gets tired or bored while he is winning.

This same principle makes some people say, "It is so difficult to live my religion." And to rest up they feel they need to get away from their righteousness for a binge into some kind of monkey business to make them feel rested and at home.

An important part of my education began on Janaury 4, 1924, when I left for a mission to the Southern States and was assigned to labor in the Alabama Conference. On May 8, 1925, I was appointed conference president and served in that assignment until my release in April 1926. At that period the Southern States Mission led all of the missions of the Church in number of baptisms. The baptismal report for the year 1926 is as follows:

Southern States Mission	1,170
Central States Mission	589
California Mission	583
German-Austria Mission	575
Hawaiian Mission	455
Swiss-German Mission	389
North Western States Mission	350
Western States Mission	338
Northern States Mission	272
Eastern States Mission	258
British Mission	246
New Zealand Mission	222
North Central States Mission	160
Mexican Mission	134
Netherlands Mission	133
Samoan Mission	111
Australian Mission	78
Canadian Mission	77
Swedish Mission	62
Danish Mission	60
Norwegian Mission	57
Tongan Mission	47
French Mission	44
South African Mission	28
Tahitian Mission	10
Armenian Mission	7
South American Mission	5

And the Alabama Conference led by nearly double any other conference in the Southern States Mission and had more than half the total number of baptisms of any other entire mission. They are as follows:

Alabama	253
South Carolina	159
Florida	150
North Carolina	114
Mississippi	89
Virginia	81
Georgia	76
Eastern Kentucky	73
Eastern Tennessee	51
Middle Tennessee	50
Kentucky	46
South Georgia	27

During the last eleven months, while supervising the other missionaries, it was my job to travel with the newest arrival and try to teach him how to do missionary work. When there was an uneven number of missionaries, I very frequently travelled alone as I went from one set of missionaries to another in giving them what supervision and motivation was possible. In those days there were no assistants to the mission president, and no zone leaders, and no one else to do training work except the mission president and the conference president.

I liked all of my missionary companions, though I did enjoy some far more than others. I discovered that there are some who, in the mission field, like in school and on the farm, were not equipped with very much ambition or industry and it was a little difficult for them to work very consistently or effectively. Then I had some other missionary companions who were delightful. They were filled with the spirit of the gospel, they were filled with the spirit of industry. They were filled with the Spirit of the Lord. They wanted to get the job done. With them I felt as I did back in my football days and in my farm work when I wanted to run, jump over fences, etc. And for twenty-seven months I had another great experience.

The Alabama Conference consisted of the State of Alabama and the thirteen counties of Florida running along the Gulf of Mexico west of the Appalachicola River. Because we had only about twenty-five missionaries, we did not have enough to work the entire area simultaneously, so we divided our territory at Montgomery and would work the northern half in the summer time to get away from the excessive heat and humidity of the Gulf area, and then we would work the southern half in the winter when it was more pleasant in the south.

Of course, we were all on foot. We would hold about four conferences a year and would usually change companions about every three months. We would then be assigned to a particular territory and would receive the names and addresses of all the Church members, investigators and friends living in that territory. Then we would work our way around to see them and do missionary work as we went. Our mail was all sent to the mission headquarters at Atlanta. Then each week we would send in the report of our work done and let the mission office know where we were going to be on our mail day which was Friday. We could also order any supplies or materials, Books of Mormon, etc. We would also requisition money from our account in the mission office. We knew the members that were able and willing to put the missionaries up at their homes, and so we would indicate to the mission office that our mailing address would be in care of some member or friend or the post office General Delivery where we were going to be that Friday. We would write to the person where our mail was to come and have them, if possible, set up some meetings for us when we arrived. We would get there in time to do our laundry, have our clothes pressed, etc. Then we would go around the community calling on the people and letting them know that we were going to have a meeting in the school house or in somebody's home at a certain time and invite them to be present. We would also discuss with them the principles of the gospel, trying, of course, to get as many new qualified members of the Church as we could.

We would usually stay in that place over Sunday and set our mailing address for the next Friday at some place sufficiently distant where we could have time to do the tracting, hold whatever meetings were possible, and yet arrive on schedule. Sometimes we would be invited to ride with someone, which we usually accepted. We would talk with him about the gospel, then take up our work where he let us out of the car. It might seem to some people to be a little strange and cause a substantial inconvenience for one to give up his family and friends, his educational opportunities, his employment, his social advantages, to preach to strange people doctrines which most of them did not want to hear and also pay his own expenses and expect to enjoy the total experience, especially when some people were very antagonistic and unpleasant. And yet many returned missionaries declare after such an experience that this was one of the happiest periods of their life. This was certainly so in my case. I do not remember having a single unpleasant experience with members or companions or non-members during my entire mission.

Very frequently one may live in a community all of his life and not get very well acquainted with even those people who live next door. But during this 27-month missionary experience, I became more completely acquainted with hundreds of people than I had ever done before or since. We lived in their homes, slept in their beds, ate at their tables, knelt with them in family prayer. We enjoyed a friendly relationship with a lot of people, on a more intimate basis than is ever known by many people during their lifetime.

Most of these people were very humble, and yet one feels the bonds of love that can connect former strangers and hold them together. The work done by even the most humble and, in some ways unprepared, missionaries can have great consequences.

On several occasions I was in Pensacola during my missionary period when Pensacola was just a little fishing village. A few years ago, I went back there to attend their quarterly stake conference. A woman came up after the meeting and presented to me her grandmother's baptismal certificate, which indicated that I had baptized her on May 5, 1925. The lady told me that 120 of her grandmother's posterity were now members of the Church, and ten of these had filled missions or were presently on a mission.

This is an example of the little mustard seed that sometimes grows into a great tree. It was a thrill to be able to go back there, after a lapse of fifty years, and still find many of those faithful souls that I had known and loved a half a century earlier still faithful to their trust as human beings and as children of the Lord.

In those earlier days we usually had a little one-room chapel which may not have cost $75 to build. Now many of these have been replaced with great houses of worship, sometimes approaching a million dollars in cost.

I was released in early 1926 and arrived in Salt Lake City during the April general conference. Someone told me that my mother was in attendance at the conference meeting in the Tabernacle and they knew where she was sitting. I went into the Tabernacle and sat down beside her. After she had recovered from her shock, we enjoyed the balance of the meeting together.

One of the other great experiences that would come under the heading of my education was the experience of teaching the seventh grade at the Layton school for two years. While I did not qualify for a state teachers' certificate, the superintendent of Davis County School, Mr. Hubert C. Burton, who was a very good friend of mine, had a vacancy that he told me I could fill. He told me that if I would go to the University of Utah for the two summer quarters and take a specified number of classes he would give me this assignment. This was a great experience.

E. G. King, who is one of the great teachers I have known, was my principal and I learned a great deal from him. But I suppose that teaching itself is the greatest learning process. Almost every other experience in my life might properly come under this heading of my educational life. I started out by teaching spelling, arithmetic, history, etc., to young people, then I changed into the life insurance business where I have tried to teach thrift and the advantages of providing for one's family to prospective purchasers of life insurance. Then I changed again to teaching industry, selling, planning, and character training to prospective life insurance salesmen. And finally, I have tried to teach religion and enthusiasm for the word of the Lord to other human beings.

In all of these personal experiences, as in most other experiences, the teacher learns more than the student.

Chapter Six

My Minor Occupations

$\mathcal{I}$ do not remember those first occasions when I began to take upon my immature and inexperienced shoulders some part of the responsibility for my share of the work as the opportunity was presented to my father's family. I remember a rather prolonged period of herding the cows, feeding the calf, doing other chores like keeping the woodshed full of kindling wood to start the morning fire, and keeping the coal bucket full of coal from the coal house to keep the fire going after it was started. For a long period, it was my job to make the fire in the family stove in the morning. We also had a swill barrel and some grain in the granary together with wormy apples, beet tops, and other things which I fed the pigs.

Monday was washday, and I remember we had a washing machine that required a lot of turning. Our washing machine had a handle and a foot pedal which you worked at the same time. I used to serve as the motor that powered the machine. Then I would turn the wringer that squeezed the water out of the washed clothes for my mother.

At a very early age I learned to milk the cows, clean out the stables, water and feed the horses. When a new calf would arrive at our farm premises, it would be my job to be a kind of nursemaid to see that it was given the right amount and quality of attention. As these calves were weaned from their mother so that the milk supply could again go back to the family, I used to stake the calf out in some grassy area where it could eat the grass and leave the milk for us. But the calf had to have a drink of water occasionally, so at regular intervals I would untie his long tether rope and take the calf out to the water ditch in the street where he could drink his fill. Usually the calf was a little more playful and had a little more energy than I. Frequently I didn't lead the calf, the calf led me. He knew where we were going and I held onto the rope as he ran toward the place of our rendezvous at the water ditch. Eventually the calf became too big and too strong for me to handle. On one occasion he was feeling a little too much of his strength and his desire for exercise. He ran up through the field a little beyond my speed with me hanging on to the end of the rope. But he was going so fast that I couldn't look up to see where we were going and the calf jumped through a wire fence and pulled me at great speed into the barbed wire, which cut a big gash into my right cheek. The calf won his freedom temporarily and the deep gash and the flowing bloodstream caused me to seek the aid of my family.

Someone hitched up the horse to our old family buggy and with a homemade bandage on my wound, my mother held me on her lap as we went to see the doctor. I remember very distinctly the security that I felt and the comforting feeling that I had in having her arms around me during my trouble. And even though I felt great pain, I am sure it was much less because of her sympathy and the confidence that I felt that everything would come out all right and that nothing could go very wrong while she was on the job.

We arrived at the doctor's and the doctor disinfected the wound, then put some kind of adhesive plaster over it to close the gash. In time my cheek grew back together, but it left a scar on the right side of my face.

My little bovine friend has long since grown up and gone the way of all calves. I hold him no ill will for our accident. My bloody experience with him was just a part of the program for boys and calves by which they attempt to fulfill the purpose of their existence.

I had another very much more agonizing experience while I was still very young. My mother had a long sick spell, and I wondered what would ever become of us if she were to die.

Later, I assumed more major roles like pulling weeds, picking tomatoes and even running the business end of a pitchfork or shovel. This eventually turned into pitching sugar beets and heaving one-hundred pound grain bags onto the wagon. Farm work in that day was never thought of as very easy, yet it always seemed to me very pleasant. As I grew older, the increasing weight of the job was offset by the extra satisfaction that I had in doing it. I have never felt any irritation or dislike even at the heaviest farm work.

As I now think back on those very early years, I think of a lot of things I could have done that I did not always do. That is, I could have cultivated a better vegetable garden, which would have added to the family food supply. I could have kept more of the weeds out of the strawberries and tomatoes, and I am sure the chickens would have appreciated it if I had kept the chicken coops a little cleaner.

Back in those days we used to have some weeds which were called pigweeds. We called them "greens," and my mother used to cook them as a kind of substitute for spinach, which seemed to me then to be very acceptable. I have always had a very robust appetite which seems to date from the moment of my birth and has grown steadily ever since. This also may have been a carry over from the pre-existence, and I will be very disappointed if we don't have a lot of good things to eat in the postmoral period of our lives. In my early days, encouraged by our poverty, we also had another dish which consisted of hot water with some salt and pepper and butter in it. We called it poor man's soup.

I remember how important I felt when I got a job picking tomatoes for Bishop Harris at four cents a bushel. Later, his son, Jess, gave me a job thinning sugar beets. I seemed to have a lot of trouble in always leaving only one beet in a place and Mr. Harris would always follow down my row to remind me of my errors. Yet I, from even that early age, had a great experience and friendship with Jess Harris and the members of his family. For a number of years during the pea and canning season, I worked at the Woods Cross Cannery at Layton. And during the sugar campaign in the fall for a number of years, I worked at the Layton Sugar Factory with a twelve hour shift that ran from seven till seven.

The most menial job at the sugar factory was the one that I first had of getting down on my knees with a bucket of soda and a bucket of water, a scrubbing brush, and scouring the grease and the syrup off the concrete floor. I remember with awe how I looked at some of the other jobs that required a lot more know-how than I had, and it seemed to me at that time that it would be impossible for me ever to acquire the skill and intellectual power that would enable me to do some job other than scrubbing grease off the concrete floor.

However, eventually I was assigned to higher jobs. At one time I worked on the battery, filling up the large tank-like cells with the beet cossettes, where the juice was extracted out of the shredded beet. I also learned to run the carbonators. For a couple of years I worked in the beet sheds getting the beets into the flumes. I worked in the sugar room, trucking six one hundred-pound sacks of sugar per load to the sugar stackers. And my last job for the Layton Sugar Company was to work in the storeroom, checking out the supplies that were to be charged to the various job operations.

I remember that occasionally, especially on the night shift, three or four of us used to gang up and buy a pie from Rachael

Whitesides, who ran the boarding house next door to the sugar factory. She made the most marvelous, great big banana cream pies for twenty-five cents! They used to put a lot of vigor and power into us when we ate one in the middle of the night.

In these early years, I made two or three adventures into crime. One of the most exciting of these was an occasion when at about age eight with half a dozen companions of my own age we broke the eighth commandment which says, "Thou shalt not steal." We had gone swimming in a reservoir up in East Kaysville. When we got out of the water about 3:30 in the afternoon, we felt some need for refreshment and we thought our guardian angel was working in our behalf when we saw that someone had provided a watermelon patch up on the side of the hill just a little way from the reservoir. Without taking time to notice that the owner was standing up at the head of the field watching us, we crawled through the barbed wire fence and began thumping the melons to see which ones we would take. The owner ran down through the field and caught us and took down our names. Then he reported us to T. McClure Peters, then Justice of the Peace in Kaysville.

Judge Peters sent some kind of summons to each of our parents that they should bring their offending sons before his court for judgment. I was about frightened to death as I had no idea whether I would be electrocuted, hanged, or guillotined. I remember that my mother and father and I waited in the judge's outer office and I have never had any more terrible moments. I decided at that time that if I got through this alive I was never going to steal any more watermelons or anything else. I don't remember what, if anything, the judge did. I suppose he tried to help me understand that stealing was not a profitable enterprise to be carried on. But that was not necessary, as I had already arrived at that conclusion on my own power. I have thought since that time that this was probably one of the very profitable experiences of my life because the pendulum of my possible criminal inclinations swung to the extreme other side. Not only did I decide not to steal watermelons, but I also resolved to obey the law, so far as I knew it, in every other thing. And I think I have been fairly successful. You could put all of the tea, coffee, beer, Coca Cola and other kinds of drugs together with all of the tobacco that I have ever used in my lifetime in one teacup and would still have room to spare.

However, a couple of my friends and I, on three or four occasions as we were walking through the sandhills to school, would stop in a little favorite hideaway and manufacture our own brand of tobacco from some of the cedar bark that we would strip off the fence posts. And we would roll this up in a piece of Deseret News and puff the smoke. While it seemed that we were breaking one of the Ten Commandments or the Word of Wisdom or something, I am not sure that a cedar bark and Deseret News combination would qualify as a serious infraction of either of these two great commandments, "Thou shalt not steal" or "thou shalt not use tobacco."

Carl Sandberg said of Abraham Lincoln that Mr. Lincoln used enough tobacco to find out that he did not want to smoke, and he drank enough liquor to discover that he did not want to be a drunkard. I think I got the message on both these points from infractions of these laws that were about as minimal as possible.

I also did my gambling on a minimum basis. One time when I was working in the pea vinery, an older boy came along who owned a pair of dice and was going to teach some of us how to earn money by throwing the dice. I remember that I very proudly had in my pocket two nickels. When it came my turn for the gambling lesson, he asked me how much I wanted to play for and I told him I had two nickels and he asked me to put one of my nickels down on the pavement and he put a nickel down beside it. Then I threw the dice and he picked up my nickel. Then I put my other nickel down and lost that also on the first throw. Inasmuch as my valuable financial treasure was now depleted, I was out of the game and he went on to demonstrate his teaching ability to someone else. But I have always remembered how much I hurt at losing my money.

A number of years later, I took my wife and two young sons along on one of my business trips to Las Vegas. We went into one of the early day casinos in Las Vegas and I was explaining to my young sons the disadvantages of gambling, how these machines were set so that the players got back only a very small part of what they put in. And sometimes it worked about like my crap game experience, where you lost everything. I thought an actual demonstration would be worth a couple of quarters and so I asked them to watch while I performed. I put in the first quarter and then pulled the lever, and I was the most surprised person in the casino when I got the jackpot. On at least that one occasion the infernal machine spewed out money all over the place.

In view of the demonstration, my sons had a little trouble in understanding my moralizing. However, I knew what I had said was true and I did not allow myself to be drawn into a certain loss by a one time win. Nor have I offered any demonstrations to anyone since.

In my very early business career, I used to travel a great deal by automobile. I was doing a great amount of automobile traveling in my early days as a General Authority of the Church. On a few occasions over this period I have allowed myself to get a little bit impatient and, consciously or unconsciously, exceeded the speed limits. One time I was going out through Davis County and an officer stopped me in Farmington. I said to him, "Officer, I am sorry I was going a little fast. What are you going to do with me?" And he said, "I am going to send you over to Judge Hellewell." I said, "Why are you going to send me to him?" He replied, "He is the Justice of the Peace in Farmington." He said, "Is there any reason why you shouldn't go to him?" And I said, "Why don't you send me to the Justice of the Peace out to Layton?" He said, "Why should I send you to Layton?" And I said, "Because my father is the Justice of the Peace there and if I am going to spend any money, I would like to keep as much of it as possible in the family." He thought this request was a little peculiar, but he good heartedly went along with the idea and said okay, and he wrote me a ticket to go to my father who fined me $5 for speeding. He kept three dollars and the state got two.

On another occasion I went to Gooding, Idaho to a stake conference. We dedicated a meeting house and didn't get through with our business and settings apart, etc., until about 9:30 p.m. I had to drive from Gooding, Idaho to Salt Lake City after that time. I got on to the broad highway between Clearfield and Layton, a big wide road with which I was thoroughly familiar. It was about 3:30 in the morning and I thought this would be a good time to gain a few minutes. The streets were almost completely vacated and I had a new car, so I pressed down a little bit on the accelerator. All of a sudden, from nowhere, I saw a traffic officer's red flashing light in my mirror. I pulled over to the side of the road and got out of my car and went around to the back of my automobile just as the officer was getting out of his car.

He said to me, "You seemed to be in a little bit of a hurry." I said, "Officer, I am in a hurry." He said, "Where are you going?" And I said, "I am going home." He said, "Where do you live?" And I said, "Salt Lake." He said, "Where have you been?" I said, "I have been up to Gooding, Idaho." He said, "What have you been doing in Gooding, Idaho?" I said, "I have been attending a stake conference." He said, "Do you know what the 12th Article of Faith is?" And I said, "Yes, sir, 'We believe in being subject to kings, presidents, rulers, and traffic officers.'" And he said, "That is very good, you may go on home." But this seems to me to prove that everybody ought to memorize the Articles of Faith.

I had another interesting experience with the law. I had just hired Gordon Hawkins as a new agent for the New York Life. He was very anxious to learn, and asked if he could go along on some of my Church appointments. One time I had an assignment in Midvale. When we were riding home, we were visiting and having an interesting time when we were stopped by a traffic officer. I couldn't imagine what was wrong, as I knew I hadn't been exceeding the speed limit. The officer came up to the window and I said to him, "What's the trouble, officer?" And he said, "Don't you know?" And I said, "I am sorry, but I don't. I know I haven't been speeding." And he said, "I know you haven't been speeding." I said, "Then what have I done?" And he told me some technical minor violation which I had made with which I was not even familiar. I said to him, "Officer, I suppose you ought to charge me double, one for my violation of the law and one for my ignorance, because I didn't even know that there was a violation." He seemed to think that was a reasonable attitude, and he cautioned me to watch it in the future and he let me go without a ticket.

Young Gordon was very much impressed with what he thought was the great power of this psychology of admitting guilt and offering to pay the fine double. A few weeks later he had a very similar violation. As a budding young salesman he was hopeful of making a good impression and so he said, "Officer, you ought to charge me double." And the office said, "That is exactly what I intend to do." And that is exactly how it worked out with the result Gordon lost some of his faith in the power of psychology.

At one time, I had a paper route. I delivered the *Deseret News* on horseback. I never did get affluent enough to afford any kind of saddle, and so I used to ride bareback on a horse that had a rather knife-like backbone. The extent of my route was several miles and I used to ride with one bagful of *Deseret News* papers over one shoulder and another bagful over the other shoulder. The up-and-down gallop of the horse had a tendency to saw me up the middle as I made my daily trip to deliver my papers. Though that was a little rough, after sixty years I feel no permanent disabilities as a consequence.

My main occupational interest, however, seemed to always be in the soil. I loved the idea of using fertilizer, irrigation water, cultivation, seeds, etc., aided by the sunshine, the atmosphere, and the rainfall to bring wonderful crops and all kinds of good things to eat out of the naked soil. I feel that there aren't very many more pleasant or profitable occupations than to live out on the soil that one owns and loves, to manage and help it to produce its many miracles so necessary to the continued life and happiness of all men and women upon the earth.

Later on, I cannot remember exactly when or for how long, I worked at the Farmer's Union Store, where I sold groceries, dry goods, hardware, confections, harnesses, and lumber. I also had a period working at the Layton-Kaysville Milling Company. As I look back upon them now, each one of these employments and each set of people I worked for had something very substantial to teach me. I take considerable pleasure from them even yet, as I think I was a good worker. In all of the time, I do not remember one occasion where I was ever criticized, or any word of anger was ever said to me, or where I think I could not have worked again, had I desired so to do. Nor do I remember any occasion when I felt the least resentment or any criticism for any of my employers. Nor did I even once feel that any of them were unfair or made any improper demands upon me. I think at some time each one of them indicated to me that I should not work as hard or as many hours as I did. But I am very grateful that I was not obsessed with the spirit of rebellion and the desire to tear down the establishment that seems to come as standard equipment in many young people in this latter-day. I did not realize at that time what I think I now know, that my character and entire future was being molded with so little thought being given to it by me. And I am very grateful that I seemed to take to work more or less as a duck takes to the water.

We are usually being educated the most when we are the least aware of what is happening. I remember that Charles Kingsley once said that we should thank God every morning when we get up that we have something to do that day that must be done whether we like it or not. Being forced to work and forced to do our best builds into us virtues, temperance, industry and a hundred different virtues that the idle never know. As I commemorate my advancing birthdays, while I am very grateful for the experiences of those major employments of my life, I am also very grateful for the minor employments by which the major ones were preceded, as they also make up an indispensable and very important part of my life. It is fundamental that before one can run he must first learn to crawl and then learn to walk.

Up to a certain date in my life, I always intended to be a farmer. However, during my period as a missionary, I had some other ideas. When I came home from my mission, it was necessary for me to get a job as quickly as I could to replenish my badly-depleted financial resources. I got home in the early spring, just as they were starting to clean out the Davis and Weber County Canal. My old friend and former employer, Dee Harris, offered me a job with several others to get down into the bottom of the canal with a shovel and clean out the dirt and gravel that had accumulated in the canal during the last season. I soon discovered that my hands were not as tough as they had been when I left home twenty-seven months before and it was not very long before they were pretty sore. Mr. Harris felt a little sorry about the pain in my hands and so he promoted me to the job of timekeeper. But this was not a very good permanent prospect to look forward to, so I sought employment at several other places, sometimes with discouraging results.

I was now twenty-three years old and had a high school graduation diploma which would not permit me to matriculate at the university. I had one quarter of college training in agriculture at the USAC in Logan. It seemed to me that my chances for an education had pretty largely passed me by. My friends who had gone on to college had already graduated the year before and now were all accepting good jobs.

It seemed to me that there was no possibility that I might ever become a doctor or a lawyer or some other thing that required a college degree. And I had no particularly strong urge to do so. The thought occurred to me that I might be a mail carrier. I had a good strong back and pretty good legs. I read in the paper about a civil service examination that was going to be given soon, and so I got information about it and spent quite a little time preparing to take the examination. And I thought I would be able to pass it rather easily. I was disappointed, however, when I received my examination report to discover that I did not get a grade high enough to justify even putting me on the list.

Occasionally I have passed some mail carriers on the street and tried to appraise them for their intelligence or to understand what it was that they had that I didn't. Some time ago, I passed two mail carriers both of different racial extraction, and while I mentally saluted them for their accomplishment, I had a case of envy that they passed the test and I did not.

For many years I had carried a $1,000 life insurance policy in the Metropolitan Life Insurance Company. One day when the agent came to collect my premium, I asked him if he thought that his company would hire me to be a debit agent and collect the industrial premiums of some of their policy holders. He very obligingly escorted me over to Ogden and introduced me to his manager, with whom I had an interview to become a life insurance debit man. After the interview he asked me to come back a few days later and bring my father and a financial statement from both my father and myself. He also indicated that if I was given the job, I would need to put up a $500 cash bond to guarantee my honesty to always turn in my collections to the company.

Before the next interview I went to see my banker, Lawrence E. Ellison, and told him of the circumstance and asked him if he would loan me the $500 bond. He indicated that he would, but after two more interviews this insurance man indicated to me that because of my inaptitude he thought it would not be advisable for me to go into the life insurance business. I think he felt that my inferiority complexes or personality disadvantages would prevent my success. Anyway, whatever it was, he refused to give me the job. One of the interesting things about it was that I agreed with him—I also felt that I was not qualified to be a salesman.

However, a couple of weeks later Wilford Brimley, general agent for a small Chicago company, came into the bank and told Mr. Ellison that he was looking for someone in Layton to represent his company as a salesman, and asked Mr. Ellison for some suggestions. Mr. Ellison told him that I had tried to get a job representing the Metropolitan and had been declined. Wilford came to see me and while I was very apathetic about it for several reasons (first I didn't think I could do it, second, I wasn't very enthusiastic about his company, of whom I had never heard before), he persuaded me to sign a contract, and I worked at it spasmodically for a few months but never did do very much.

One of the other jobs that I tried to obtain was a job teaching seminary. I had always felt comfortable with the doctrines of the Church and my membership in it. I thought I could probably do well at it, though I had the problem of lacking in education. Anyway, I sent in an application which was promptly declined. Many years later after I had become a General Authority of the Church, I was introduced on two or three occasions to speak at public meetings by apostle Adam S. Bennion, former Church Commissioner of Education, and on each occasion he said, "Sterling is a product of our seminary system." What he remembered was that I applied for a job to teach seminary, but what he did not remember was that he declined the application.

While these "turned down" experiences were a little bit painful at the time, I now count them as valuable steps in my education. And while I did not like being a life insurance agent, I stayed with that company long enough to see in it some possibilities. Because I was thinking about getting married, I thought that I myself ought to buy some more life insurance. But when I began to check into it a little bit, I decided that I did not want to buy any life insurance in my own company. Then it occurred to me that if I did not want to buy life insurance in my own company, then I certainly ought not to sell it in that company to someone else. And so I decided on my own power to go into the life insurance business. But I thought that before I did, I ought to rectify what I had done in the past.

And so I went back to my banker friend and told him that I would like to borrow some money, so that I could go to all of my policy holders, which weren't very many, and give them their money back. I didn't want to start out in the insurance business and take some money from some people and then jump the ship and abandon them. So the banker loaned me the money and I took what little savings I had and went around to every one of my policy holders and gave them their money back in full. I explained to them that I was going to quit this company, and I didn't want them to think that I was going to leave them holding the sack for something that I myself could not now recommend. Each of them remonstrated and said that was not my fault, but I knew I would feel a lot better about it if I made full restitution before making my next start.

After this job of reimbursement was completed I spent a couple of weeks in investigating insurance companies and finally I walked into the office of the New York Life on June 7, 1927, and asked them if they would give me a job selling life insurance. And because I had definitely made up my mind, I thought it would be in their interest to do so, even though the Metropolitan and myself had felt otherwise. But there was a little difference in the job inasmuch as the Metropolitan had to wait until a debit was opened and they were obligated to pay a salary for the collection. And they could not afford to take one man when they could get someone that was better. The New York Life was only going to pay me a commission, and if I didn't perform as I should, I would solve my own problem. On June 7, 1927 I had another of those unconscious moments when something tremendous happened in my life where I was not aware of its importance when it was happening. But in one way, June 7, 1927 is a very significant day. It was a kind of graduation day, and while my education for my life's work was just beginning and it would last over my entire lifetime, yet it is also the day that my life's work began; and so I take this day as the point for the finishing of my education and the beginning of my life's work— my occupational life.

Chapter Seven

My Occupational Life

When God closed up the Garden of Eden so that the real work of the world could get under way, he took Adam and Eve out and introduced them to the great opportunity of providing for themselves. Then he gave that great, all-important command in which he said, "In the sweat of thy face shalt thou eat (thy) bread...... (Gen. 3:19.) But like a lot of other great commands, this one has also been misunderstood and abused. To begin with, this command to labor is not a command of punishment, it is a command of opportunity.

Work is not merely how we get our bread, it is how we build our characters, develop our personalities, learn initiative, cause our bodies to grow, and do almost every other worthwhile thing in the world, including saving our souls. Most all of the satisfactions in life also come from useful labor satisfactorily performed.

The gospel of Jesus Christ itself is largely a gospel of work. We not only earn our bread in the sweat of our faces, but we also work out the degree of our eternal exaltation in fear and trembling before God by that same process. To me, labor is a kind of sub-religion. The Lord gave an interesting recommendation of our part of the work of the world when he gave an important revelation in which he said, "Wherefore, verily I say unto you that all things unto me are spiritual, and not at any time have I given unto you a law which was temporal; neither any man, not the children of men; neither Adam, your father, whom I created." (D&C 29:34.) The Church is a divine institution. Governments were also instituted by God for the benefit of man, and God himself also ordained and established our occupations.

Sometime ago, I read an article which made reference to a catalog listing over 17,000 different occupations. Every human being has a vast array of at least this many fields from which to choose what he will do with his occupational life. I have thought, "What an exciting idea it is that we may help to carry on the work of the world and the work of the Lord by having our choice of those 17,000 interests which may most appeal to us." Elbert Hubbard once made a helpful comment about our occupational lives by saying: "Business is the process of ministering to human needs." Therefore, business is essentially a divine calling; that is, the doctor, the teacher, the plumber, and the farmer, are ministering to human needs and therefore, each is entitled to say that he is engaged in a divine occupation. The quality of our work will be greatly increased if we think of it in that way and do it in that spirit.

I have had a little smattering of two or three occupations that have all been intensely exciting to me. I'm reminded of Robert Frost's poem describing the man who came to a fork in the road—though he had to choose which road he would follow, he felt a little sorry in his heart that he could not travel both. To some extent, that is the way I have felt because of the many exciting choices that have been available to me.

For example, I have done some farming. A man may own a little section of God's great earth and then perform with it the most fantastic miracles. With the aid of the sun, the rain, and the atmosphere, one may bring out of the soil all tastes, colors, and varieties of the most delicious fruits, the most wholesome herbs and vegetables, the most energizing grains, and every variety of meats.

Someone once announced that he had made a great invention—he had discovered how to manufacture butter out of grass. He said, "All I need now is a cow and a churn." But even cows and churns and horses and houses may be brought out of the soil. In addition, out of raw land one may get strawberry jam, or chocolate milk shakes, or T-bone steaks, or blueberry pie. Jesus told of a sower who went forth to sow, and while some of his seed fell among the thorns and some on rocky ground, and the harvest was very sparse, yet it was still an exciting fact that a farmer could create the food to provide physical, mental, and spiritual power for human beings.

In our day one man may produce 5,000 tons of wheat in a single year, thus multiplying by many thousands of times the most effective effort of the sower mentioned by Jesus. Out of 16 inches of topsoil, over a period of a few years, one may grow enough potatoes to stack up a pile twenty feet high and still have every one of his sixteen inches of topsoil left undiminished.

When I was born, I weighed only eight pounds. I couldn't speak, or walk, or understand. And yet because of what has come out of the soil and gone into me, I have developed a mind and body that will do fantastic things and go with me throughout eternity. God himself is the greatest agriculturist. He is the greatest horticulturalist. He established the livestock industry and all of the other righteous occupations.

For two years I taught school and had a class of seventh grade boys and girls. This educational road is one that I would also have liked to have followed permanently. For twenty-seven months I was a missionary, teaching as best I could the principles of the gospel. What a thrilling thing it is to be an authorized minister of religion, teaching the principles of life and salvation to other human beings! And what a wonderful occupational roadway this is to travel. In many of these occupational fields, the Lord is our guide and example. He was the Master Teacher, the Great Physician, the Light of the World, our finest example of industry, courage and faith. If a man chooses, he may spend his entire lifetime teaching great truths. Or he may be a doctor and spend his lifetime in curing diseases and relieving people of pain, or he even can go much further than that and find ways of preventing disease.

In 1886, over 120,000 people in the United States died of smallpox. But we haven't had a death from smallpox in the entire country for many years. I had two sisters who died of that terrible malady called diptheria. This has all been eliminated by the research and study of people engaged in that godly occupation known as medicine. Many of the dread diseases that have caused the plagues and broken up families in the past are now largely non-existent. Franklin D. Roosevelt's life was almost ruined by polio. This disease has also been largely eliminated from the dreadful classification it used to occupy.

But there are thousands of other exciting employments. One may be a great musician, a great artist. One may be a religious leader, or an inventor, or an architect, or a scientist. I know of a zoology teacher who loves to study cockroaches. His eyes light up at the mention or sight of some particular specimen.

Someone has said that success in marriage does not come primarily from finding the right person, it is mostly in being the right person. Occupational success is achieved, not only through finding something that fits our tastes, more frequently it is accomplished through developing our tastes to fit our occupation. What a great delight it is for some people to spend their lives as gardeners, bringing all kinds of beautiful flowers, grass and out of the soil. And as there are no ordinary people, so there are no ordinary occupations. There is no such thing as common labor if it is done with an uncommon attitude and uncommon excellence.

But of all of the great occupations from which one may choose, I was fortunate enough to choose one of the best when I decided to be a salesman. Millions of people have found great enjoyment in life by going fishing as a kind of recreation. And many think there are few things more thrilling than getting a fish on the hook that one is able to land by his skill and understanding. But Jesus said to some fishermen, "Follow me and I will make you fishers of men." (Matt. 4:19.) So far as I know, there isn't anything more exciting than to get a *man* on the spiritual hook and bring him into the right place by your mental skill and persuasion.

A doctor usually puts his patient to sleep before he begins a serious operation. A lawyer takes his client into court and by the superior power of judges and policemen, forces him to do as he should. A fisherman takes an unfair advantage of the fish he expects to capture by taking the most attractive bait and disguising in it a vicious steel hook. But a good salesman lays out the hook in front of the prospect without any attempt at disguise or concealment. Instead of putting the patient to sleep while he cuts into him, a good salesman wakes the prospect up and then by reason, logic, persuasion, and an explanation of advantages, leads the prospect voluntarily to the place where the salesman wants him to go.

I am reminded of a story that came out of the first World War. A Frenchman, an Englishman, and an American were making an excursion out into "no man's land." All of a sudden, they came upon some Germans sleeping in a large shell hole. The Frenchman said, "Let's shoot them where they lie." The Englishman said, "No, let's disarm them and take them prisoner." The American said, "Let's wake them up and have a right good fight." The job of a good salesman is to wake people up and give them greater objectives to fight for and put higher power in their motivations.

There are missionaries, salesmen, debaters, and other leaders who have the spice of competition and challenge stirring in their hearts. They thrill at the chance to teach, persuade, convert, and convince other people to a cause in which they are highly interested and to which they are fully converted.

The concept that all great men are salesmen is an idea which is very interesting to me. They are sometimes called by other names, such as governors or generals or presidents, but their success depends on their ability to get their ideas over to other people so as to produce action.

No one wants a lawyer who merely knows the law. He wants a lawyer who knows how to win cases, and persuades people to live orderly lives. No one is very interested in a bishop who merely knows the difference between sprinkling and immersion. What everyone is interested in is the bishop who can get people to come to church, pay their tithing, and who can build success and happiness into the lives of all of those who come under his direction. It is the job of the missionary, not only to enlighten, but to convert and get all of the people under his influence marching happily down that straight and narrow way that leads to eternal life.

The greatest task of the President of the United States is to be a salesman. It is his responsibility to persuade other nations to cooperate in programs of righteousness, and to make loyal, deserving citizens out of those people over whom he presides. It was the business of Jesus to get people to follow that straight and narrow path leading to eternal life which he had already marked out for them.

But I became a life insurance salesman. This would not be a very exciting idea to most people. It certainly would not be listed at the top of the social register for occupations. Sometimes it happens that life is cut off before we have finished rearing our families, paying our bills, and doing the job for which we were sent here. For a small monthly payment, one may provide the great future benefits of sending his children to school, providing his widow with an income, paying off the mortgage on the home, and doing the other things that he would have done if he had been permitted more time in which to do it.

Life insurance is one means of buying time. It can be paid for on a convenient monthly basis, and it may be purchased at cost. That is, there are no stock holders in the New York Life. After expenses and the claims have been paid, all the rest of the money, including the interest earned on funds held by the company, is paid to the policy owners in the form of dividends. Even on these there are no taxes to be paid.

If a life insurance salesman needed an advocate to promote his cause, one of the best is the Bible. The Bible says, "Pure religion and undefiled before God and the Father is this, to visit the fatherless and widows in their affliction, and to keep himself unspotted from the world." (James 1:29.)

When the breadwinner dies, everyone in an abstract way wants to help, but if the life insurance man has properly done his job, there will be money to pay off the mortgage, and pay the grocery bills, and send the children to school, etc. The apostle Paul made a famous insurance speech to Timothy when he said, "But if any provide not for his own, and specially for those of his own house, he hath denied the faith, and is worse than an infidel." (I Timothy 5:8.) And that makes very good sense to me. Everyone in good health has the ability to earn money. Now he may spend that money for liquor, or tobacco, or other things, but the most important need is for one to take care of his own family. He might be able to pray the longest and sing the loudest, but if he doesn't provide for his own family, he has left out something that is very important. In a great many places we have gotten away from the old-fashioned virtues of thrift. Life insurance, in addition to the protection, provides thrift on a kind of semi-compulsory basis.

Somebody has pointed to Joseph who went into Egypt as having served as the president of the first life insurance undertaking. He interpreted the dream of the Pharoah, foretelling that there would be seven years of plenty throughout all the lands of Egypt when crops would be produced in abundance, but these would be followed by seven years of famine. And then Joseph was appointed to build granaries and store up the corn during the good years so that there would be food in Egypt when the poor years arrived. Since then money has taken the place of corn as the medium of exchange. We now save our money during the good years to provide for our families during the periods of scarcity that usually follow.

As I understand it, there are many purposes to be served by one's employment.

1. It is the means by which he supports his family, and helps to provide for them the necessities of life.

2. It is one of the best ways ever devised of developing one's self.

3. It is a means of developing excellence in one's self because of the rewards and motivations of one's skills. That is, the better we perform our labors, the more compensation we receive. And a high powered motivation is frequently very helpful in making the most of ourselves.

Our work is also the source from which many of our enthusiasms and satisfactions come.

Life insurance is not only one of the biggest businesses of the world, it enables one to perform a useful service. Yet one of the biggest advantages that I have enjoyed in the business is the association and training that I have received from the great men that I have met along the way, who have given me encouragement and inspiration.

One of the most outstanding of these men was Fred A. Wickett, vice president of the company. I had had some difficulty in making up my mind about what I wanted to do in my life. Many of the popular professions were beyond my reach because of my lack of education. Lack of capital also ruled out other possibilities. To me there was something of the providential in my finding enough courage to walk into the office of the New York Life Insurance Company on June 7, 1927 and asking them for a job to sell life insurance on a commission, as I had one of the most advanced sets of inferiority complexes that I thought there was in the world.

Mr. Wickett was in Salt Lake very soon after my appointment and suggested that we have a sales contest to motivate business and also to celebrate the thirtieth anniversary with the company of agent John D. Spencer, a son-in-law of Brigham Young. Mr. Wickett agreed to buy a policy on his own life from the agent who could sell the largest amount of business over a pre-determined allotment that would be given him. The allotment was designed as a kind of handicap to put everybody on a basis as nearly equal as possible.

To begin with, it never occurred to me that I, a brand new agent without sales experience, could ever win this sales contest; but when the report came out at the end of the first week, I had made about as good a record as anyone. I got a faint hope that at least there was a chance, so I went to work with all diligence. I did not know very much about the business or about selling, but I did know quite a lot from past experience about industry. I worked very hard and very long. At the end of the month I was delighted to find that I not only had the largest excess over my very small allotment given because of my newness and inexperience, but I also had the largest actual total volume. I therefore had the privilege of writing the vice president a life insurance policy. I not only received a substantial commission, but it was a good beginning to a wonderful relationship with Mr. Wickett, which lasted until his death over forty years later.

In August 1932, I was invited to be a speaker at the National Association of Life Underwriters in San Francisco. Mr. Wickett, who was Inspector of Agencies in charge of the West Coast, including the State of Utah, knew of this invitation. He invited me to come and spend the night of August 17, 1932 at his home in Palo Alto, which I did. After some discussion, he told me that he would like to have me become the agency organizer of the Intermountain Branch Office to begin October 1, 1932, with the idea that I would become the Agency Director or Manager on January 1, 1933 when the present Agency Director, Mr. L. H. Stohr, was to be retired. I was very greatly honored and very enthused about the possibilities, though in many ways it did not offer the challenge, rewards, or freedom that personal selling did. But in any event, that night of August 17, 1932, the foundations were laid for some of the really great experiences of my life.

At a later date, I received a letter from Golden K. Driggs who in 1932 had worked in Mr. Wickett's office in San Francisco. I met him that day in August, 1932 and we became fast friends from the very beginning. Later, he wrote me a letter in which he mentioned this occasion as follows, "Just before the national convention in San Francisco, Mr. Wickett called me into his office and told me of a great young man, also a Mormon, who was a New York Life agent in Utah who was making all kinds of sales records as an agent in a very small town. Mr. Wickett told me that this young man was twenty-nine years of age, was scheduled to speak before the National Association of Life Underwriters. He told me he wanted me to get acquainted with you and then he confided to me that he hoped to sell you on the idea of going into agency work when Mr. Stohr retired.

"Since that day, Mr. Wickett has told me many times that he considers you one of the greatest young men with whom he has to do. In 1936 when he transferred me to Boise to work under your direction, he made this prediction that Sterling Sill will some day be a principle in the Mormon Church. He was then just leaving for New York to become the vice-president of the company and he also told me that the officers of the company thought that you would also some day be an officer in the Church. Mr. Wickett inquired of me as to some aspects of your dedication to the Church and whether or not I thought that you would consider going to New York to accept a high executive position in the New York Life. He indicated to me that you had indicated some reluctance at the thought of leaving Utah, although he felt that your great ideas and forceful leadership should extend over the country and not be confined to the Intermountain West. You have never told me, but I have an idea that you have been approached along this line several times. Many of our top agency and field men have wondered why you were not drafted for executive service and stationed at company headquarters. They didn't know, but I did, that you were destined to become a General Authority of the Church and your world-wide influence through your talks over radio and television and your popular books have done much more for many people than if you had become the president of the greatest company on earth, the New York Life.

"I wanted you to know how our wonderful friend, Mr. Wickett, as well as myself have thought about you."

After Mr. Wickett retired, he moved from New York back to his home in Palo Alto.

Some time later I received another letter from Golden Driggs who had visited with both Regional Vice-President Vern Van Leuven and retired Vice-President Fred A. Wickett. He reported that Vern Van Leuven had said that Mr. Wickett had said to him, "Vern, if I were you, I would join the Mormon Church. There is nothing else like it in the world. Mormons put Christ's teaching into practice in their daily lives and they have the finest program for young people with which I am familiar." Mr. Wickett has said to me not once but many times that if he were a little younger, he would join the Mormon Church.

Outside of my own family, Mr. Wickett was one of the two or three men that I would name as my greatest benefactors. He himself had a considerable amount of interest in Utah because at one time he had been the New York Life manager here for a short period. He was a man of great wisdom, great character, and great ability in handling people. He had an interesting philosophy which he always practiced. It was to the effect that everyone had an obligation to everyone that he met or did business with to give him something on every occasion of contact. It may be a word of encouragement, or some constructive business suggestion, or an inspiring idea. But everyone should leave his contacts better than he found them.

This is a restatement of the verse which says that "He has achieved success who has lived well, laughed often and loved much; who has gained the respect of intelligent men and the love of little children; who has not lacked appreciation of earth's beauty or failed to express it, whether by an improved poppy, a perfect poem, or a rescued soul whose life has been an inspiration and his memory a benediction."

This was the philosophy of George Washington Carver, the great Negro scientist, who spent much of his life in educational work among the southern negroes. Dr. Carver lived in the day of the southern sharecropper when it was a common practice to move out on the soil and drain out of it as much of the fertility as possible and then move on and repeat the process in some other location. There are some people who remember George Washington Carver because of his educational effort among the southern negroes. Other people remember George Washington Carver because he made some three hundred commercial products out of the common peanut. But I remember George Washington Carver because he said that every human being had an obligation to leave the soil richer than when he found it. That is, he ought to leave the wood-pile of life a little higher when he left than when he came. And this was the philosophy of Fred A. Wickett. This is also a part of great salesmanship.

Between the time I began with the company and the time when I went into agency work, I had attended several club conventions where Mr. Wickett was in charge. I felt the great strength of his leadership. I was very interested in the Church. He was not a member of the church to which I belonged, and yet I felt as close to him as I have ever done to almost any other human being outside of my own family. I had absolute trust in him, which continued until the time of his death in October 1970, and beyond that event to the present day.

After I went into agency work, as long as he was an officer on the West Coast, he used to come and see me about three or four times a year, and would spend a couple of days. He spent some time with some of his business friends, particularly James A. Hogle, while in Salt Lake; and he spent some time with the agents. He always had a sales meeting while he was in town, and he talked to the salesmen about the company, and about success procedures and sales techniques, all of which was very interesting to everyone. But most of the time he spent trying to build a little of his success into me.

Any good ideas that he had he would go over with me. He would also ask me for my ideas, and I used to spend a lot of time telling him what I thought about things. As I expressed my own ideas, I always seemed to get better ones. But after each contact with him, I felt lifted up, the sun seemed to shine a little brighter. It frequently seemed to me, while he was with me, that I stood about ten feet tall and could accomplish about any objective that I set my heart on.

I was aware that there were some managers under his direction who did not like him very well, and who did not like to see him come to their offices. They felt he was critical and demanding and a little harsh; but I never once had this kind of a feeling. He was always my best friend, and while he was in town, time went by in a great hurry. I could always depend on it that when he was counseling me, he was telling me exactly what he thought. There was no insincerity or sham about him. There was no subterfuge. Though he was very free with his criticisms, I always rejoiced in them. While I did not always agree with everything that he said, yet I was never offended and I felt free to argue a point if I wanted to do so. I also felt that my feeling toward him was fully returned, at least so far as an older man can return this affection and confidence to a much younger employee.

From the very beginning of my agency work, I had a good record and he used to quote me frequently as he visited the other offices. I have no accurate record, but it seems to me that I had a part on every club program or divisional agency manager's meeting that he ever conducted where I was present. I never once had the feeling of being uncomfortable in his presence, or that he was unfriendly, or that I had to be continually on guard against making a mistake. This is a feeling that I have not felt to the same degree in the presence of other people who were my superiors, either in the company or out of it.

In my business, in the Church, and in other places, I have sometimes become acquainted with individuals who found it difficult and unnatural to be friendly and helpful. I know a number of these at the present time. They profess love and friendship for everybody, but either they are insincere or they lack the ability to get that over into their actual relations. But that was never true with Mr. Wickett, and it made my work a great delight as well as a great deal more profitable to everyone.

To me, almost every day in my company's service has been a kind of vacation, as I have very greatly enjoyed my work and have felt that I was doing something constructive and helpful to other people. When I began with the company, the work week was five days, plus a half a day on Saturday. Then some place along the line they dropped the Saturday work and had it five days. But as of today, I have never dropped Saturday as a work day. I suppose that I am still clinging to the old Mosaic Law that says, "Six days shalt thou labor."

But then in 1936, when I became a bishop, the seventh day was also added as a day for rather intensive activity. In 1954, when I became a General Authority of the Church, the seventh day became a primary day, at least for spiritual and a great amount of physical and mental exercise.

And throughout my life, from my days on the farm, I have started very early and worked very late and usually took a briefcase full of work home to be done after dinner.

For a great number of years, the people at the home office tried to get Mr. Wickett to come to New York and help all agency men as he had already helped those under his direction while on the West Coast, many of whom had been transplanted into key positions in other parts of the country. Finally, in 1937, he moved to

New York where he remained until shortly before his retirement on November 1, 1944. One of the days that stands out in my memory was the day that I received a letter from him indicating that he was being officially retired and would no longer be active with the company. And while this was something that I fully understood and expected, yet when I received the letter I was in my office by myself and I broke down and cried. Because I was by myself, I didn't try to restrain my tears and it felt very good to me to relieve myself in my tears. I have wept very few times in my life and never as I did on that occasion. I could not help but have a great surge of emotion go through my heart to think that officially, he would no longer be a part of the company. In his retirement, however, my opinion of him never lessened.

On several occasions since his retirement, I have visited him in his home. I attended Palo Alto Stake Conference on August 25-26, 1962 and I invited him to attend the meetings, which he did. He invited me and I accepted the privilege of staying with him Sunday night in his home. Monday morning he took me with him up to San Francisco, and he and I and Vern Van Leuven had a pleasant lunch together at the exclusive Bohemian Club of which he was very fond. But from my point of view, my business experience was very pleasant and very successful.

My last period as an agent was the first nine months of 1932. For that year, I ranked eleventh in number of applications sold among the entire agency force of 11,243 agents in the United States and Canada.

My official agency life amounted to thirty-five years. The office rose from a rank of 101 in 1932 to number one during my pre-retirement years. Of the men recruited and trained during that period, we had exported from the state sixty-two who became managers or assistant managers in other places, or men who were transferred to fill group or other important company positions. Two of my NYLIC posterity have become vice-presidents. During that thirty-five year period, our office or I personally held first place twenty-five times in the entire company from the business received by the men which we had recruited and trained.

It has been my privilege to start in the business some very excellent life insurance salesmen, three of whom have led the entire company in sales in a particular year.

In 1947 the company established a program of keeping track of the agency man who had the largest production from the men that he had appointed personally during his career. This was called the Lifetime Recruiting Review. On February 14, 1949, Vice President

Dudley Dowell wrote me a letter in which he said, "Dear Sterling: I am sure you will be interested to know that a recent survey disclosed that the agents who had been appointed and trained by you personally, sold a larger volume of life insurance in 1947 and in 1948 than any other similar group in the Company. Hearty congratulations! Sincerely yours, Dudley Dowell, Vice President."

In the twenty-one years that this program has been in existence, I had this honor every year except six.

It has been the custom for the last number of years for the Company to give a dinner for retiring agency men. I suggested to the Company that I would appreciate it if they would omit this in my case. My old office had been divided into seven general offices: four in Utah, two in Nevada, and one in Wyoming, each of which was well represented and had been effectively operating for several years. I myself had been spending my full working time for the Church, and my NYLIC service had been primarily an honorary one. Elimination of my retirement dinner would save a substantial amount of money for the Company, and I had already been honored by the Company far beyond my deserves. I felt to just let the matter pass would be the best way of handling it. However, I was overruled by the President of the Company, and so on September 13, 1968, at the end of my regular and honorary service, some 500 people including agents and their wives, townspeople that had been especially invited, some Church people, members of my family, a great number of New York Life men from around the United States that I had personally appointed or had something to do with their training, plus a delegation from the home office led by Dudley Dowell, President of the Company, and another delegation from our regional headquarters in Seattle led by Charlie Cash, Regional Vice-President, met in the Lafayette Ballroom and on the mezzanine floor of the Hotel Utah. We had a splendid program which was recorded on tape and on paper.

Chapter Eight

My New York Life Retirement Dinner

In April 1954, I was called by President David O. McKay to serve as an Assistant to the Quorum of the Twelve. In the early days of this particular program, many of those called to assist the Twelve were called primarily for the purpose of helping with stake conferences over weekends, but were asked to continue on in their occupations during the work week. Among other things, President McKay said to me that I was to keep my business, but that I should not let it interfere with any of my Church assignments.

I informed President Dudley Dowell of the New York Life of this call, and told him I did not know exactly how much of my time I would have left to devote to company business, and if he felt I should resign my New York Life assignment either now or later, I would be willing to do that. He was very pleased at the honor that had come to me. He said, "I think our company owes a great deal to America and if you can make a contribution through your Church, we would be delighted to have you do it in behalf of the company." He said he did not want me to resign, but to continue on with the company on whatever basis would be most convenient for me. He said, "We can see how it works out over this next year and make any necessary future adjustments as they seem desirable." He said, "If the time ever comes when you can't carry both of them, we will get someone to help you with your insurance work."

Accordingly I continued in both assignments until 1958, when my office became the largest office in actual production in the entire company. I could see that eventually some adjustment was going to have to be made, and this seemed to be a good time to do it. I therefore reminded President Dowell of his statement and suggested that January 1, 1959 would be a good time to turn over the actual management of the General Office to someone else. However, I was asked to continue in an honorary capacity as Inspector of Agencies. He asked me who I would like to have to take my place, and I selected Gerald L. Ericksen, whom I had started in the insurance business who was very capable and of whom I am very fond and proud. At that time, he was managing the New York Life office in Southern California. So he became the manager of the Utah Office on January 1, 1959, and I assumed my honorary capacity in the NYLIC with my full-time Church work.

My retirement dinner proved to be one of the highlights of my career which was already filled with highlights. The attendance included the president of the company, other home office officials, and many other people whom I loved and with whom I had worked very closely over many years.

My wife and I were presented with a large color television set contributed by the agents. She was also presented with a bouquet of forty-two beautiful red roses as a token of the forty-two years that had elapsed since I joined the company. This was responded to by a speech from her. I was also given three large loose-leaf notebooks which I highly prize as they contain many photographs taken at the dinner itself as well as some 253 letters from personal friends around the country expressing their friendship and appreciation.

Naturally, much of what was said at this meeting had to do with me directly and personally, and in spite of my desire to maintain some measure of modesty and accuracy, I was pleased with the program. I shook hands with the guests as they arrived, and later on someone at the dinner said that this was the first funeral he had ever attended where the corpse met him at the door and shook his hand. The entire program cannot be given here, but some excerpts from what was said are as follows:

Master of Ceremonies Gerald L. Ericksen extended a warm greeting to all of those present. He announced the great volume of business that had been done as a buildup for this occasion. A considerable number of General Authorities of the Church were present. My brothers and sisters were all recognized. The general managers that I had had something to do with recruiting and training who had come from other areas where they now served were also acknowledged. Some of these were Joel Richards, manager of the Salt Lake Office; Gordon Hawkins, Hollywood Office; David Dance, Seattle

Office; Gerald Hyde, Everett, Washington Office; Loy Maycock, Denver Office; Bryce Flamm, Ogden Office; Gerald Ericksen, Utah Office; and Dick Barnes, formerly manager of the Denver Office and presently insurance commissioner of the state of Colorado.

The agents representing the four offices in the state of Utah in the sixty days preceding this dinner exceeded all records ever before made by writing $17,466,000 of business in this two-month period.

The first speaker on the formal program was Charlie Cash, Regional Vice-President of the company with headquarters in Seattle, Washington. Vice-President Cash made, in part, the following comments:

"Thank you very much, Jerry, distinguished guests, and fellow NYLIC's. It is a real pleasure and honor tonight to be a part of this program, because rarely in a man's lifetime does he have the opportunity to help honor a truly great and dedicated man. Before saying a few words as the regional officer of our great region, I would like to be personal for just a minute if I may. I joined the New York Life almost twenty years ago in a small town in central Arkansas. This was actually five years before I had the opportunity to meet Sterling Sill. Sterling, I am sure that I would not be here this evening if it had not been for your generosity with my then General Manager, Jack Gaultney, in passing on your Regional Bulletins. Because as a detached new agent in a small town, certainly without the courage and the kindling of my enthusiasm that I received from these sales bulletins every week, I would not have made it. Because of the influence that your bulletins have had on me and my career with New York Life, I have distributed them to agents from coast to coast in all the agencies that I have managed.

"Three years ago when Frank Satter announced that he would like to be relieved of his responsibility as Regional Vice-President, President Dowell asked me to come out here and take over as leader of the region. And frankly I was delighted with the opportunity, but I must admit that I was highly concerned to try to fill the void left in this region by Frank's retirement from its management, and to live up to the tremendous records that have been made in this region seemed like an impossibility. And I might add that while they were kind enough not to mention it, I know that President Dowell and Senior Vice-President Norton shared my same fear. However, just two weeks after I arrived on the scene, we had our first North Pacific Region Star Club Meeting which Frank had so nicely arranged and then turned it over to me. During this Star Club Meeting I had the opportunity to meet with Sterling Sill and visit with him, and at this meeting, believe me, I was much relieved. Here was a man that had led our company as the records indicated, as Jerry just mentioned. He had been the outstanding recruiting and developing agency man year after year after year in the entire company; he had won every award that the company could give an agency man; he had developed more people in management of our company than anyone else in company history and had counseled with more young agency men in this business than anyone else in the company; and yet, this man not only was willing to accept me as a young regional officer, but reassured me that any time I needed his assistance or guidance he was always available.

"Now, Sterling, for all of these things that you have been and that you are today, I am grateful. But even more important than all of these, I want you and Doris to know that Mary Jane and I are most grateful for the love that you and Doris have expressed to us since we came here three years ago.

"Now I could recite many specific contributions that Sterling has made to our Region and our people in the great Northwest— contributions that he has made in the last three years. But I would like to have a man that is much better qualified than I to speak on this subject, Frank Satter, another one of NYLIC's all time great leaders, a man who for thirty years has been associated with Sterling Sill in more different capacities than any other human being, is the best qualified man to talk about Sterling's contributions to our region. So at this time it is a real pleasure for me to present retired Regional Vice-President and current member of the Million Dollar Round Table, Frank Satter."

Frank Satter:

"Thanks, Charlie. Sterling and Doris, I am glad that someone decided that they could not put this show on without me. First of all this is a tremendous privilege, and I appreciate very much being with all of you wonderful folks in Utah once again. It is awfully nice to walk around and shake hands with old friends.

"I am very grateful for the example of courage, the attitudes, and the optimism of our honored guest and the way he has handled the difficulties and the challenges of our marvelous business.

"In the interior of our consciousness, each of us has a private Hall of Fame. It is reserved exclusively for the real leaders who have influenced the direction of our lives. And relatively few men of the many men who have exercised authority over us from childhood to adult life meet our test for admission to this sacred precinct.

"Tonight we give voice and acclaim to such a hero in your world and in mine. Sterling, time nor talent will not permit any numeration of each gift, each benefit, each inspiration, each beneficial experience that we have received from you. But I want to thank you now, as I have thanked you for a good many years in my prayers, for confidence; because when you made me manager, you gave me that thirty-second training course. It was enough, it was enough. Because I had a certain amount of doubt in my mind, and you said, 'You don't have to be Vern Van Leuven, and you don't have to be Jim Brickett.' Well, that was some relief. And then you said, which has stayed with me, 'Frank, the work of the world is being done by imperfect men in an imperfect way.' So that gave me room to operate. And then you created for me a reputation with other people that as yet I haven't earned. It was tremendous, Sterling, but it's been a lot of fun trying to equal it, and I appreciate it, that challenge.

"And then above and beyond all the gifts that Sterling encouraged was spiritual ambition—the Pearl of Great Price—that we all seek.

"What did he do for us in the region? It is unnecessary to enumerate all these things: the ideas, the example, the inspiration, the records, the accomplishments, the determination, the up and down (and it was more up than down). All of this direction was reflected in millions, just as you are hearing these records quoted here tonight by these men of accomplishment that you honor at your head table. But all too often in setting these records and these millions we forget their real meaning. These are not record millions, and they are not bulletin millions. They are not home office figures; they are not insurance department figures. But these are New York Life Dollars. Now these are dollars that we created and you created. The dollars have served, are now serving, and the dollars that will serve the necessities of the needy, the widowed, the orphans, and the aged. And so, Sterling, we thank you and call you blessed, and we shall continue forever in this spirit of love for blessed is that man that seeth his brother's need and supplieth it, seeking his own in another's good.''

Reed Brinton:

Reed Brinton, life member of the Million Dollar Round Table, past President of the President's Council, and recently member of the Board of Regents of the University of Utah, and presently vice-chairman of the Advisory Board of Director's of the New York Life Club, said in part:

"Sterling has established some records that will last for generations.... In the past twenty years he has had three men work under him who have become the national sales leaders for the entire company. And if there is any one overriding virtue that Sterling has developed, it is probably this matter of self-discipline. Once he decided upon a project, he poured in all of his energy into it. And he demanded more of himself than he did of others.

"Some twenty years ago Sterling was given a list of the one hundred best books ever written. He read each one. As a result, new ideas began to well up in his mind, new concepts developed, his point of view broadened. He began to see the problems of life in new perspective. Soon he was relating ideas to current problems. He wrote weekly sales bulletins to his agents. The request for his bulletins expanded until he had a huge mailing list. And just as he had expanded the muscles of his own mind, he was now expanding the minds of others. Many years ago he began writing books instead of bulletins. He has written one each year since then. As he read more, he wrote more, he spoke more, and he accomplished more. He related the philosophies, incidents, and stories that he read into the human life situations in which he was involved. Reading, thinking, writing had made him stronger, and he wanted others to realize that they too could improve their own abilities. He wrote and talked about the value of time, the importance of attitude, the need for skill, the rewards of thoughts, and the ecstatic joy of accomplishment. He asked people to learn more, to do more, and to be more. He asked them to believe in themselves. 'Too often,' he said, 'people suffer from too small an estimate of their own ability. They spend their strength on the small tasks without putting their real power to trial. Not to believe in God is a tragedy, but not to believe in one's self is a disaster.'

"When I saw Mrs. Dowell, the wife of our President, in New York a few months ago, she said, 'Tell Sterling I'm using his books to teach my Bible classes.' I heard a man give a talk in California a few weeks ago, and he said, 'Tell Sterling that half the ideas I use are received from his books.' And a young man said, 'I have never appreciated the real need for religion in my life until I talked with Sterling Sill.'

"What does history say of a man overwhelmed by anxiety or over-burdened by sorrow who has found new hope from having read Sterling Sill? I have personally seen Sterling give of his time, his energy, and his money to people in trouble. Some he knew very well and others scarcely at all. In one case, he nearly gave his life. And at this point, I would like to call on a young man whose life Sterling saved by almost giving his own. I would like to ask that young man, George Redding, and his father, Austin Redding, from Denver, Colorado, to come to the microphone."

Austin Redding:

"Thank you very much, Reed. I am sure that all of you can understand how deeply touched the Redding family is on this occasion. Those before me on the program have enumerated Sterling Sill's many accomplishments very well, but thirty years ago as a young New York Life man in Great Falls, Montana, he also helped me too. But he has done something far more than that. Sterling is a man of strong, outstanding physical courage. I am sure that all of you are aware of the fact that he was awarded the Carnegie Hero Medal for heroism not quite ten years ago. Only the good Lord can give life. A mother brings a child into the world, but when someone saves that life and hands it back to you, then words are completely inadequate. And Sterling and Doris, Eleanor and I owe you a life-long debt, one that can never be repaid, as the Bible says, 'Greater love hath no man than this, that a man will lay down his life for his friend.' And Sterling, you offered and almost gave your life in exchange for that of our son, George. God bless you."

A. Ray Olpin:

"Sterling had been appointed to the Board of Regents of the University five years before I came here as president. He was educated in the public schools but is a self-made man. He is one of the best read men I have ever met. He loves to read the classics and is a great note-taker. These notes he has so well-organized that a moment's notice he can recall points to illustrate thoughts which he is presenting. He has a tremendous memory and a well organized mind.

"Mr. Sill was chairman of the board during the very critical university period between 1947 and 1951. He was always very congenial. He was very thoughtful. He met difficult situations courageously and boldly. But when deliberations became rather serious and difficult, his sense of humor always came to the rescue, and a little levity was introduced into the discussion which always helped a great deal.

"Working together during this period we greatly expanded the campus area by acquiring about three-hundred acres from Fort Douglas adjacent to the campus. And with money from various sources, we built a number of very important buildings. But there is one building on the university campus that is different from any other. The University needed a management house for the girls majoring in homebuilding. Because the University did not have the funds, Mr. Sill undertook to raise the money by soliciting contributions from private citizens. And the largest contribution came from Mr. Sill himself. And for two and one-half years he went throughout the community preaching the benefits of education and collecting the money that made this important building possible.

"Sterling is a real salesman. He has been a dedicated, dynamic person working for the benefit of the University when it was so seriously in need of financial and other help. Sterling, I am not going to go into the many things you did in an academic way. But this building is a great tribute and a monument to you and your efforts, and many have profited by the instruction and attitudes in home building that they have received because of your work. And so we all thank you for the many things that you have done for the University."

Gordon Hawkins:

"I think it was William James who said, 'The greatest use of life is to spend it for something that outlasts it.' Sterling Sill has done this as he has touched for good the lives of every person here. He has not only spoken to us, but he has spoken through us. And I don't know of any man in my life that has impressed me quite like he has. I regard him as my greatest benefactor next to my own father. And I am thankful that Sterling Sill passed my way. I'm thankful that he made me become a man. I'm thankful that he kicked my pants and corrected me. I kept telling him, 'Why do you keep criticizing me so much?' He said, 'Hawkins, it takes a lot of pounding to make good steel.' And I said, 'But I'm beginning to feel like an anvil.'

"At Guadalcanal there is a beautiful monument erected on the spot where an entire marine regiment was wiped out during World War II. Not one survived. This monument has an inscription which says, "When you go home, tell them of us and say, 'For their tomorrows, we gave our todays.' " Sterling gave his todays that many of us may have some brighter tomorrows."

President N. Eldon Tanner

"I remember very well when Sterling Sill came to visit my stake when I was a stake president, and how he impressed me with the need of organization and of spending my time profitably and effectively in administering the affairs of the people in that stake. He has traveled throughout the Church from stake to stake through all kind of weather by all kinds of transportation. He has instructed and encouraged and inspired the leaders of those stakes in their work to higher accomplishment, and he is widely quoted by the people throughout the Church. His influence consisted of much more than merely that which he said. I remember one time someone quoted him. We were sitting together in a stake conference, and he said to me, 'I didn't say any such thing.' But that was the message he got across to that individual. And the influence he has had in people's lives is much greater than the things that he has said.

"I remember his being called up to speak at General Conference, the time was short and he said, 'I can give a fifteen minute talk or a one minute talk.' President McKay took him at his word and said to do it in one minute. He did very well; he left a message and kept within the minute. President McKay's comment was, 'I like a man who keeps his word.'

"Sterling, I'd like to say to these people that you are properly named, and may the Lord bless you as you continue in His service."

Dudley Dowell:

In introducing President Dudley Dowell, Mr. Ericksen pointed out that in his opinion President Dowell had done more for the New York Life than any other man in its history. Mr. Dowell said in part:

"Sterling Sill was outstandingly successful as a salesman. According to our records in the home office, he made a minimum of ten sales per month for every month that he served as an agent. Then after a short tour as assistant manager, he found himself in charge of what I remember with a great deal of nostalgia as the old Intermountain Branch Office headquartered here in Salt Lake City. This began the second phase of one of the greatest agency building careers in the history of the New York Life Insurance Company. He was a great competitor, he was never content with being less than first place among New York Life recruiters. And I know because in those early 1930's I was competing against him as an ambitious New York Life Manager up in Butte, Montana and later in Seattle. I knew what a rugged contestant Sterling could be and still is.

Sterling started in agency work more than thirty-three years ago, and in all of that time, there have been very few years when he didn't lead all the New York Life recruiters, both in number of new agents appointed and in the volume that they produced during their training years. In more recent years, as the company has placed more and more emphasis on career building and persistency of agents, Sterling has produced more new men who in their second and third year had led in their classes. Needless to say, Sterling leads everyone in the results that we run of each man's lifetime career in recruiting efforts. Many of his recruits that you have heard introduced tonight have in recent years been giving the 'old master' himself a real run for the annual honors of bringing men through in our business.

"Last June, Mr. By Woodbury, Vice-President of the Zions First National Bank here in Salt Lake City, wrote me with great feeling. I can't read or answer all of my mail, but I enjoyed this one letter. He had just come, it seems, from a luncheon at which his bank had honored the membership of the Million Dollar Round Table of Utah. But let Mr. Woodbury's own words tell us the story.

"Among other things he said, 'Our concluding speaker was Sterling Sill, to whom we gave a plaque for being the greatest recruiter and motivator of men in the life insurance industry in the state of Utah. We should have said, of the entire United States, because I don't know of any person in this country who has a record of recruiting and motivating men equal to that which Sterling enjoys. As a tribute to Sterling, we asked all of the members of the Million Dollar Round Table in the room who had been recruited by him into the life insurance business regardless of company affiliation to stand. Eleven of those twenty-nine men who are currently members of this Million Dollar Round Table in Utah stood up as having been recruited by Sterling Sill. In other words, he had recruited over a third of all of the leaders in the life insurance industry in our state.'

"Mr. Woodbury continued, 'I guess each generation produces a few outstanding men, and in my generation, I want you to know, Mr. Dowell, that the most outstanding man in my acquaintance in the insurance industry has been Sterling Sill. The records he has set will go unmatched and unequaled for many years. And his sphere of influence grows wider and wider with each passing year.' And so, I think it remains for someone outside of our business to capture in words more eloquent than mine, certainly, the tremendous stature of Sterling Sill and what he has achieved as a builder of men within his own chosen profession. And this, to me, is a startling fact that Sterling has accomplished all of this and in the process has apparently used only one-half of his effective and creative hours each working day. His other full-time job, as all of you know, is in his Church; and if we could find some meaningful method of keeping his Church score, we would find a record equally astounding.

"I know his capacity of constructive influence over his fellowmen in spiritual affairs would perhaps even exceed those of his masterful agency building in the New York Life. Where has he found time to deliver the thousands of sermons in person and on the radio, to write a dozen books and to continually travel hundreds of thousands of miles, mostly on weekends? He has challenged and motivated all of those and all of us within the sound of his voice or those who have been fortunate enough to read his printed pages. What a heaven-sent gift is the sheer mental and physical energy given to one individual to accomplish so much for so many in such wholesome endeavors. Rarely does one man find so much time and harness it so successfully to the benefit of his fellowmen.

"There is another heart-warming link between New York Life and Sterling Sill's church that seems especially worth mentioning tonight, particularly to our guests because, perhaps, most of you even with the New York Life may not know of it, though I'm sure Sterling does, and I always like to tell about it. It concerns another great New York Life man, Colonel Haws, one of the great pioneers of our company who helped open up the west for the New York Life, and Heber J. Grant who, of course, was president of the Church from 1918 to 1945 and a former general agent of the New York Life. Colonel Haws was one of John Brown's men who at Harper's Ferry helped to organize an Illinois regiment during the Civil War. He became general agent for New York Life in Kansas after the war. Subsequently he was put in charge of all of the company's operations west of the Mississippi with headquarters in San Francisco.

"Eventually he came to Utah, arriving on the Overland Stage about the time the golden spike was driven at Promotory Point. Colonel Haws went to visit one of his agents who was boarding at the home of Heber J. Grant's mother when President Grant was a child, as Mr. Grant was to report later to the author of an earlier history of our company. And I am very much interested in business history because we are going through this now, and I happened to read this old anecdote.

"Colonel Haws, when he visited this home, was so taken by Mrs. Grant and her cooking that he insisted that he was going to board in her house. The Colonel would not take no for an answer in spite of Mrs. Grant's protests. Colonel Haws finally pressed a hundred dollars in ten dollar bills into her hand and insisted that she go out and buy a bed and bedding, because he soon recognized that that was the problem. He asked her to put the new bed into young Heber's room, because that was where he was going to sleep. And President Grant later became an agent and a general agent of the New York Life.

"Subsequently the Colonel brought his bride to the Grant homestead. And from those early days until the day of his death, Heber J. Grant wrote, 'of all the men I have known not of my religious faith, Colonel Haws was the most loyal and most truly steadfast friend I ever had.' And that friendship continued on with the senior officers of our company. And on my first visit to the home office of New York Life as a young manager in Montana, I had the privilege of visiting President Thomas A. Buckner's office, and the only picture I saw in Mr. Buckner's office was one of Heber J. Grant.

"The loyalty, truthfulness, and steadfastness of purpose which characterized Heber J. Grant also apply in full force to Sterling Sill. Sterling has demonstrated by work and deed that his own dedication to his Church and his profession is only achieved by hard work, organized intelligent efforts that come from an inner belief that tolerates no doubt. He has a special singleness of purpose that few men ever even contemplate, let alone achieve.

"Michelangelo, surely one of the greatest artists of all time, put it best perhaps when he observed, 'If people knew how hard I work to get my mastery, it wouldn't seem so wonderful after all.' Like Michelangelo, Sterling, too, has been largely self-taught and self-motivated. He planned from the very beginning to succeed, and he was willing to make whatever personal sacrifices were necessary to achieve his goal. And so, Sterling, on this occasion, I came out here in behalf of the officers and directors of the company to extend to you all of our sincerest congratulations on your rich career with New York Life, and to extend thanks for your tremendous contributions including the reputation and growth of the company in this area for which you are so largely responsible. All of us are in your debt. May I wish Doris and your good self great health and happiness for many long years to come.

"Wasn't it Goethe who said, 'The man who is born with a talent which he is meant to use finds his greatest happiness in using it.' God bless and prosper you, Sterling."

At the end of the program in asking me to make a response, Mr. Ericksen said: "Sterling, I know that you would like to reply to this demonstration of friendship and good will. However, before you do, I would like to make a statement. As I think of you, I am reminded of some of the quotations that you have used many times in my presence, and which I feel characterize you. There is a statement by Disraeli which says, 'Genius is the power to make continuous effort.' Elbert Hubbard said, 'The secret of success is constancy of purpose.' Leonardo da Vinci said, 'Thou, oh God, doth sell us all good things at the price of labor.' And Calvin Coolidge said, 'Nothing in the world can take the place of persistence. Talent will not, nothing is more common than unsuccessful men with talent. Genius will not, unrewarded genius is almost a proverb. Education will not, the world is full of educated derelicts. Persistence and determination alone are omnipotent.'

"And now as I present you to this group, may I say that most of us here tonight feel that at least in a business sense we are your children. Some are your grandchildren and you even have some great-great-grandchildren that are here who have been trained in your success tradition. That tradition we hope to carry on beyond your years. We will keep trying for that continuous effort and provide the price of excellence in what we do.

"Sterling, we would like to hear from you now."

Sterling W. Sill:

"President J. Reuben Clark, Jr., once said that there are two times in a person's life when he should not try to make a long speech. One was when he was accepting an office and the other was when he was relinquishing it. I have never had such a great urge as now to make a long speech, and I have never felt such inadequacy even to make a short one as now. But at this point in time where our paths may begin to grow a little further apart, I would like all of you to know that there are very few experiences in my life for which I am as grateful as the circumstances and events that are responsible for me being with this great company and for the great men and the great experiences that I have encountered along this extended pathway of forty-two years. The New York Life, its ideals, and all of you will forever remain in my heart. I might compare myself to one of Napoleon's soldiers who was having a chest operation for the removal of some shrapnel. He said to the surgeon, 'If you will cut a little deeper, you will find the emperor.'

"During this long and interesting span of years, I have had two primary tools to work with. One is the rate book and the other is the Bible. Both of these speak about many of the same things. The Bible says, 'He that provideth not for his own and especially those of his own house hath denied the faith and is worse than an infidel.' That is also what the rate book says. The Bible says that pure religion is to visit the widows and the fatherless in their affliction. And that is the beginning and the end of our business. The Bible tells of

Joseph going into Egypt and storing up corn in the seven good years so that the people would not perish during the seven poor years that followed. Since that time, money has replaced corn as the medium of exchange and life insurance provides the money for that rainy day which usually comes about seven days a week during our poor years.

"The training course says that we should build these great success qualities of industry, faith, courage, and ability into ourselves and that is also the most important message of the Bible. And because no one liveth unto himself alone, we usually take over these productive traits as we find them ready-made in each other. Alfred Lord Tennyson once said, 'I am a part of all that I have met.' And Sterling Sill has something important in him that belongs to each one of you.

"I am very grateful both to the men in the home office and in the field who have contributed so much to my life. I am very grateful *to you,* Dudley, for your great service to the company and I am very grateful *for you* because of the important contribution that you have made to my personal success and pleasure over many years. I am very grateful to God for many things. One of them is that in my opinion my connection with this company was providential, and I count it a great privilege to have been a part of NYLIC for forty-two of its hundred and nine years. And as I think of its great growth and successful service during these last four decades, I say to myself, 'All of this I have seen, a part of it I was.' And now as I close my NYLIC career and surrender my stewardship, I would like to say in the words of Dicken's Tiny Tim, 'God bless us, everyone.' God bless America, God bless NYLIC, and God bless all of you who through NYLIC's instrumentality, attempt to serve the best financial and spiritual interests of the people.

"And I would like to pronounce my own benediction upon our great business and upon all of you in the words of the ancients, who said:

> May the Lord bless thee and keep thee
> May the Lord make his face to shine upon thee
>   and be gracious unto thee
> May the Lord lift up his countenance upon thee
>   and give thee peace."

Presented to Sterling Sill at this retirement dinner was a large plaque laminated on a wooden base which was as follows:

**NEW
YORK
LIFE**

PRESENTED TO
OUR GOOD FRIEND

Sterling W. Sill, C.L.U.

• FREELY YE HAVE RECEIVED, FREELY GIVE •

FEW MEN IN NEW YORK LIFE'S LONG HISTORY HAVE GIVEN SO MUCH OF THEMSELVES TO THEIR CHURCH, THEIR COMMUNITY AND OUR COMPANY. A MAN OF TALENT, YOU HAVE USED THAT TALENT FOR EVERYONE AROUND YOU. A STRONG MAN, YOU GIVE STRENGTH TO OUR ENTIRE COMPANY.

BY WORD, PEN AND EXAMPLE, YOU HAVE INSPIRED NOT ONLY THE MEN WHO WERE FORTUNATE ENOUGH TO HAVE YOU AS A GUIDE AND FRIEND, YOU INSPIRED US ALL.

THE BIBLE SAYS, "BE STRONG AND QUIT YOURSELF LIKE MEN." THAT, STERLING, IS THE STORY OF YOUR LIFE AS A COMMUNITY AND NYLIC LEADER. IF THE COMPANY IN YOUR BEAUTIFUL UTAH HAS GROWN AND FLOURISHED, IT IS BECAUSE OF YOU MORE THAN ANYONE ELSE. AND ALL YOUR FRIENDS, ALL OVER THE NEW YORK LIFE, THANK YOU.

• SEPTEMBER, 1968 •

Dudley Dowell	_R. C. Paynter, Jr._
President	Chairman of the Board
(signed)	(signed)

Chapter Nine

My Family

It is readily acknowledged by most thoughtful people that the most important institution in this life or the next is the family. That is that intimate little group of people made up of father and mother and children. The present members look backward to their ancestors and forward to their posterity with a vital interest in those members both present and non present. The family is the source from which we get most of our education, our training, our help, our success, our love, and our happiness. The base of our family operation is the home. That is that especially hallowed spot, consecrated and made sacred as a sactuary for our family use.

After the creation God looked out upon the earth and pronounced all of it very good. But the entire earth is a very large place inhabited by billions of people, and as the poet has pointed out:

> God gave all men all earth to love,
> But since our hearts are small,
> Ordained that just one place should prove
> Beloved over all.

We also need a smaller and more intimate group of special people to serve our greatest needs.

Many years ago John Howard Payne wrote his poetic masterpiece entitled "Home Sweet Home" wherein he said:

> Mid pleasures and palaces where'er we may roam,
> Be it ever so humble, there's no place like home.

We sing another song in which we say:

> There is beauty all around
> When there's love at home
> There is joy in every sound,
> When there's love at home.
>
> Peace and plenty here abide,
> Smiling sweet on every side,
> Time doth softly, sweetly glide,
> When there's love at home.

In my own individual case, above all other things, I am grateful for my family and my home. My primary objective in this life, and it will be in the next, will be to be worthy of them, and to contribute a maximum of success and happiness to each one of those involved. If this biography was not supposed to apply particularly to me, I might best use all of the available space in writing biographies and expressing my gratitude and love for the individual members of my family.

Standing at the head of my family, I am very grateful to acknowledge God, my Eternal Heavenly Father, and express my great appreciation to Him and for Him who created me in his own image and endowed me and all of his other children, including those of my own household, with a full set of his attributes and potentialities. I am grateful for his loving and Fatherly commands directing me to develop those endowed potentialities to that far height that someday I may become even as he is. I am also grateful for my Eternal Heavenly Mother and I know that she has made, and will make, a full contribution to the success and happiness of her children.

The First Begotten Son of God in the spirit is not only our Elder Brother, he shares with our Eternal Father in creating for us the great benefits of our lives. He came here to this earth as our Saviour and Redeemer and worked out an infinite atonement in our behalf. He organized His Church upon the earth, in which He has placed those eternal principles and ordinances so necessary for our eternal welfare and happiness. He has put the Church in both His and our names. He has called this joint enterprise The Church of Jesus Christ (for Himself) and Latter-day Saints (for us).

Two of those Latter-day Saints he has given me as parents. Another very special one he ordained to be my wife. Three of them are my children. He has given me two wonderful daughters-in-law and one wonderful son-in-law. In none of these instances, even if I could, would I make any changes. And I have already acknowledged my great love and appreciation for those other men and women who were my ancestors. I am very interested in the fact that my great-grandmother was Elvira A. Cowles and was sealed for eternity to Joseph Smith, the Prophet. After the death of the Prophet, she was married to Jonathan H. Holmes. She died in Farmington, Utah on March 10, 1871.

God has ordained as a part of our destiny the literal, bodily resurrection and has sealed in His holy temple this family relationship. He has provided for a system of eternal progression and eternal exaltation. He had also ordained the great principles of the eternity of friendship and the happy relationships that may exist forever between His children.

We are not only inspired by God, but He has ordained that we may inspire, uplift, and serve each other to our heart's content. God has provided us with a gregarious characteristic where we can do our best work and be the happiest when we are living and playing and working together, with a free and full interchange of love and helpfulness. He has provided that all of this will be a part of our eternal lives and our eternal happiness.

Standing next to God in my list of benefactors are my parents. Someone has said that God could not be everywhere and so he made mothers. Lincoln referred to his mother as an "angel" and I am completely happy in the idea that Nancy Hanks Lincoln had no more of those angelic qualities than did Marietta Welling Sill. In addition to her being an angel, she is also a great heroine. Her love and devotion was a powerful instrument for good in the lives of her ten children. While, like Nancy Hanks Lincoln, she did not have much to work with in the way of material things, I will always be most grateful for her magnificent services to her children. I join with my sister Genevieve when she said, "My fondest memories were when I went home and found my mother there." A house full of the most famous people could not have made up for her absence.

With my mother, my father stands as the co-partner as my greatest benefactor. He was not very successful financially, and the ambitions that came into his mind caused him to change jobs a number of times. Then, because of some unsuccessful surgery, he was an invalid for the last eighteen years of his life. This caused many problems, not only for himself but for those who were dependent upon him. But the blood that, through the hereditary process, he passed on to his children was not tainted by alcohol or nicotine nor was his spirit corrupted by vice, dishonesty, crime, profanity, or any kind of ungodliness. My father had a very good mind and was thought of by many as the most highly educated man of his day in the small community where he lived.

I salute my mother and my father with my whole heart as they stand together next to God as my greatest benefactors. Someone has put my feeling about my parents in words when he said:

> You may have riches and wealth untold,
> With baskets of jewels and caskets of gold.
> But richer than I you will never be,
> For I had a mother who read to me.

With the endowment that I received from my Heavenly Father and Mother, as well as my father and mother upon the earth, I certainly should be able to make it the rest of the way on my own. This would be guaranteed to me if I would always follow their directions.

I appreciate my nine brothers and sisters and wish I had the ability and the space to write a creditable biography of each of them. My oldest brother, Ralph, was born July 17, 1895, and died April 20, 1952. My sister Mabel was born March 23, 1898, and died September 24, 1968. I never saw my sister Mary, named after my mother Marietta, but each year I get a little closer to what I expect will be a wonderful reunion with her. She was born on February 9, 1901, and died August 6, 1902. I came next on March 31, 1903. Russell was born August 24, 1905, and died September 24, 1963. My twin sisters, Marguerite and Genevieve were born November 16, 1908. Laura was born on Feburary 15, 1912, and died on January 2, 1919. I have written elsewhere about her. We were great pals and I thought of her as a kind of kindred spirit. Alta was born on February 17, 1915, and Claude, who finished the ten, arrived in this world on October 29, 1918.

I am very proud of my brothers and sisters. Each one has some ability and some quality of greatness that excels every other one. I am very grateful to them for the brothers-in-law and sisters-in-law, as well as the wonderful nieces and nephews that they have added to our family.

The greatest accomplishment of my life, next to being born, came about on September 4, 1929 when, in the Salt Lake Temple, I was married to Doris Mary Thornley. Her mother was not very pleased when she discovered that there was some conversation going on between her daughter and me about marriage. The

Thornley family had been one of far greater wealth, culture, and many other virtues, and I could completely understand and appreciate her point of view. I think I agreed with her appraisal of my chances in life more than I did of her daughter's appraisal of my chances in life. I think I was frightened more than she was at the thought of taking upon my unsteady shoulders the responsibility for the welfare and happiness of this wonderful person who had agreed to be my wife. Now, after nearly fifty years of marriage, my perspective has become a little clearer.

I would like to include in the record an expression of my appreciation and love for her. She has fulfilled my every hope and then some, and there has never been a minute in that long period when I wished I had married someone else. She has made our home a pleasant haven of love and peace and joy. The house in which we have lived has always been beautiful in its arrangement and immaculate in its cleanliness. Like her wonderful mother, my wife has always been a good cook and the greatest hardship I have ever suffered has been during my unsuccessful struggle to avoid eating too much of some over fifty thousand wonderful meals that she has prepared, give or take a few for Fast Days, etc.

With her violin, the piano, and her heart strings, she has filled our home with music. I don't know how she could have improved herself as a wife or as a mother. I have never seen anyone who, in my opinion, outranked her as a grandmother, or as a hostess, or as a friend, and she excels in her great character qualities. I have never known of the slightest suggestion on her part of anything unfair or unworthy.

When President Kimball suggested that in his opinion everyone ought to write his biography, I told her about it. She told me that she had already started on her own, so I will not try to muddy the water by trying to do it for her here. My purpose here is only to express my great appreciation for her and for the great indebtedness that I feel for her love, her great spirituality, her faith in God, her great love of people, and her dominant desire to help others.

I am very grateful to her for the many lessons in grammar and culture that she has given me. On one of the papers which was sent to my company on the occasion of a recommended promotion, my boss had given as one of his strongest arguments in my behalf that I was well married. That statement should be written on most of my other accomplishments. And outside of being well born, I know of no higher rating.

I have said many times that in my humble opinion women are just better human beings than men are. They are prettier, they live longer, they are more spiritual, they are more righteous, and they make better wives and better mothers. They are more effective in loving and teaching other family members, they are more worthy examples, and they make better companions. This is certainly true in my case. I am very grateful to God that he has permitted me this marriage relationship.

As we have grown older and watched the marriage association of our friends interrupted by death, we have indulged somewhat in the conjecture about which of us will be the first to finish this mortal probation, and I just can't imagine what I would do without her. I was given an awful shock recently when I arrived home from work. I found my wife lying on the dining room floor with our daughter leaning over her. I had some awful thoughts for a few seconds until Carolyn explained that her mother had wrenched her back and she was giving her an adjustment. While I hope the real event is a long way away yet, I occasionally think of the words of the poet which beautifully, though inadequately, express my feelings on this subject. He said:

> Should you go first and I remain
>   To walk the road alone,
> I'll live in memory's garden, dear,
>   With happy days we've known.
> In Spring I'll watch for roses red,
>   When fades the lilac blue,
> In early Fall when brown leaves call
>   I'll catch a glimpse of you.
>
> Should you go first and I remain
>   For battles to be fought,
> Each thing you've touched along the way
>   Will be a hallowed spot.
> I'll hear your voice, I'll see your smile,
>   Though blindly I may grope,
> The memory of your helping hand
>   Will buoy me up with hope.
>
> Should you go first and I remain
>   To finish with the scroll,
> No length'ning shadows shall creep in
>   To make this life seem droll.
> We've known so much of happiness,
>   We've had our cup of joy,

And memory is one gift of God
   That death cannot destroy.

Should you go first and I remain,
   One thing I'd have you do:
Walk slowly down that long, lone path,
   For soon I'll follow you.
I'll want to know each step you take
   That I may walk the same,
For some day down that lonely road
   You'll hear me call—your name.

To this point we have had a great life together. Each year for some fifty years, when she could get away, she has gone with me to some beautiful convention hotel to attend insurance, club, and agency meetings. We have visited many distant parts of the world when on missionary tours, attending Area General Conferences, stake conferences, etc. We have enjoyed many interesting gatherings with many wonderful people.

I think every year of our marriage since our children began to arrive, every one of our children and grandchildren have been given a birthday party by their mother and grandmother, including a birthday cake and candles, good food, presents, and love, all arranged by her for those concerned, and the end is not yet.

Our Family Home Evenings, family reunions, family picnics, and other numerous occasions when we entertain our friends, all revolve around her, and I expect that that pleasant association and program will be continued even after we have crossed the boundaries of this life.

I appreciate the sentiments of Elizabeth Barrett Browning, who wrote a sonnet expressing her immortalized love for her husband. She said:

"How do I love thee? Let me count the ways."

Then, after enumerating the many avenues that her devotion to her husband had taken, she said:

"I love thee with the hopes, smiles, breaths,
   and tears of all my life,
And if God wills I shall but love thee
   better after death."

I am sure that that same condition will prevail in my own case. After the problems of this life have been cleared away, I shall love all of my family better after death, from God at the top to my last descendant. And I hope that somewhere along the way I will have an opportunity to make up to all of them for my shortcomings in this life.

I am particularly grateful for our three children—Michael, David, and Carolyn. I am very proud of each one of them. Ralph Waldo Emerson once said, "I have never met a man who was not my superior in some particular." Each of my children are my superiors in many ways. May God bless them with every righteousness and success.

I quote in part from a magazine article written about Michael while on his mission in England.

"We are very proud to publish this very unusual story: an inspiring one about a famous body building athlete, John Michael Sill, from the Western United States, who is now stationed in Mansfield, Notts. England, filling a two year religious mission for his church.

"The Latter-day Saints religious faith, to which Mike belongs, has one of the most stringent codes of any in the world. Its members abstain from liquor in any form, tobacco, and any unhealthy foods or drinks. It is fitting, therefore, that such a healthy, virile representative of modern manhood would be sent forth to present his church's religious doctrines to the world as a missionary. In any case, here is a proof again that the age-old ideal of a sound mind in a sound body is today as important as ever.

"For the past year he has been embarked upon a two year religious mission on behalf of his church, The Church of Jesus Christ of Latter-day Saints, sometimes known as Mormons. This mission is undertaken at his own expense and is an act of devotion and loyalty during which time all his other own personal interests and activities must be laid aside.

"Mike Sill was born and reared in Salt Lake City, He received his early education there and later attended the University of Utah for two years. Here he majored in sculpture and his work in this field was highly praised as being extremely skillful and original. Interest in body building began at the early age of fourteen. Having suffered from rickets as a small child he was thin and in an attempt to build himself up he trained with the world famous George F. Jowett course. Two years later, at the age of 16, he was awarded the Jowett World Championship trophy as its most accomplished pupil.

"About this time he met the incomparable Steve Reeves who encouraged him and helped him with his training. They became great friends and Mike gives much credit to Steve Reeves for his own accomplishments.

"Within the next five years of his rigorous training it 'paid off' as follows: He won the titles of

> Mr. Utah Jr. 1955
> Mr. Utah Sr. 1956
> Mr. Rocky Mt. 1957
> Mr. Western America (2nd) 1957

"He has posed for the world famous paintings that Arnold Freiberg did for Cecil B. DeMille's film, The Ten Commandments." (Written by Domenique for *Man's World and Reg. Park Journal,* March 1959)

In a letter to me dated December 27, 1958, Michael's mission president, T. Bowring Woodbury, said of him:

"While I am writing to you, I want to tell you what a wonderful son you have in Mike. I have never seen such enthusiasm and such unbridled fervor, as your son has for the work. I note that last week he and his companion each put in 85 hours of proselyting time. This is a true figure and it does not include travel time, study time, or anything that isn't actual missionary work. This is a record for the mission. We have never had anyone go over 80 hours before. I think as a steady diet this would be too high a figure and we have encouraged your son and his fine companion Elder Asay to level off at a little lower altitude.

"I'm sure with this kind of activity and with their humility and faith that they will show wonderful results."

David graduated from the University of Utah in June 1963 and received a master's degree from Stanford University in December 1964 in Far East History. He has elected to follow in my occupation with my company and I hope to cut a second crop of occupational joys through him.

I appreciate my children for their righteousness and their frequent expressions of love to their mother and me. I have selected Carolyn to represent the others by her expression. When she was just learning to write, she wrote me a seven word letter which I have preserved, in which she said, "I love you because you love me. Carolyn" To this date she is the leader of our family in the number of grandchildren she has presented to her parents. She has also excelled somewhat as a poetess and a few years ago on Father's day, she wrote me a poem in which she said:

To my father on his day, June 20th, 1971
By your daughter, Mary Carolyn Sill Fitzgerald

On Father's Day
This lovely June of 1971
I'm going to be so happy and
There will be a lot of fun.

We're going to have a visit from
Grandpa and Grandma Sill
And when they come to Draper
It gives us such a thrill.

There is a man who stands so tall
Whose hair looks like a cloud
He is my daddy, Sterling, of
Him I am so proud.

He sets a fine example
With almost perfect presence
Who shows us all the way, indeed
His quest for excellence.

Within my heart I have a hope
Which always shines so bright
That God, our Heavenly Father,
Will let you keep your sight.

You are a special father
And husband I am sure
And as a grandpa to the kids
You really, really score.

It isn't often, dear, sweet Dad
I tell you how I feel
But with all my heart I love you
And I am sure I always will.

Our two sons and our son-in-law have all filled honorable
missions. All of our children have been married in the temple
and I am very proud of and grateful for our two daughters-in-law
and our one son-in-law.

I am also grateful to my grandchildren and I would like to recommend to them that they listen to their parents, that they obey God, that they love their country. I hope that in time to come they may on occasion remember their grandparents who, like their parents, will love them sincerely and always be praying for their success and happiness, whether in this life or the next. It was largely for them and others of their generation that this book was being written. I would now like to recommend to them an acceptance of the philosophy of May Riley Smith, who said:

Sometime, when all life's lessons have been learned,
    And the sun and stars forevermore have set
And the things which our weak judgments here have spurned,
    The things o'er which we grieved with lashes wet,
Will flash before us out of life's dark night.
    As stars shine most in deeper tints of blue;
And we shall see how all God's plans are right,
    And how what seemed reproof was love most true.

And we shall see how, while we frown and sigh,
    God's plans go on as best for you and me;
How, when we called, He heeded not our cry
    Because His wisdom to the end could see.
And e'en as prudent parents disallow
    Too much of sweet to craving babyhood,
So God, perhaps is keeping from us now
    Life's sweetest things, because it seemeth good.

And you shall shortly know that lengthened breath
    Is not the sweetest gift God sends his friend.
And that, sometimes, the sable pall of death
    Conceals the fairest bloom His love can send.
If we could push ajar the gates of life,
    And stand within and all God's workings see,
We could interpret all this doubt and strife,
    And for each mystery could find a key.

But not today. Then be content, dear heart;
    God's plans, like lilies pure and white, unfold.
We must not tear the close-shut leaves apart—
    Time will reveal the calyxes of gold.
And if, through patient toil, we reach the land
    Where tired feet, with sandals loosed, may rest,

When we shall clearly see and understand
I think that we will say, "God knew the best."

In this biography I have tried to express my own philosophy of life in my own words, reinforced by the words of others, and I hope that in what is written here those who come after me may see a picture of their own lives lived at their best.

I have tried to recommend to all the great value of right-eousness, industry, excellence, and all of those other traits of human possibility by which we attempt to make the best and the most of our individual lives, enabling us to reach our divine destiny.

I am sure of this, that the one business of life is to succeed. Certainly God did not endow us with these magnificent mental, spiritual, emotional, and physical resources and permit us to live under such favorable conditions on his beautiful earth, and then expect us to waste our lives in any degree of failure.

We might well keep in our minds that important statement made by a prophet of the Lord, that no other kind of success can compensate for failure in the home. When we do well, all other members of God's family are lifted up.

Chapter Ten

The Men In My Life

After a careful study of ten thousand personnel records by a large research organization, it was decided that eighty-five percent of all success comes about because of the use of our personality traits. In this survey involving over one hundred commercial companies, basic character and the ability to cooperate with and influence other people was listed among the most important attributes of those who made good. I make reference to *other* people in *my* biography because if you eliminated from me that which properly belongs to someone else, there would not be very much of me left.

The human element in success has always been far more important than any mere technical competence. Personality can create wealth, but wealth cannot create personality. Therefore, personality is greater than wealth, and no matter how you look at it, personality is one of the most amazing qualities in the universe.

We think of the immortality of the soul as being our greatest concept. But what would even the immortality of the soul amount to without the immortality of the personality? This great personality endowment which comes down to us from creation makes God man's only fellow in the universe. Probably the last thing that any individual would want to give up, either here or hereafter, would be those individual traits that make him a distinctive person. And as a part of my biography, I would like to include an acknowledgment to just a few of those great men who have influenced my life, with the result that many of their ready-made personality traits have been compounded into me.

I might also include some of the many women who are also among my greatest benefactors: my mother, my wife, my daughter, my granddaughters, my sisters, my friends, and particularly those great women who have served over many years as my secretaries, without whose help, especially in my non-reading years, I would have been largely helpless. I am especially grateful to Linda Bishop who has done much of the reading, writing, and indexing of this manuscript.

At just about the time that my degenerating eyesight had made me completely unable to read, Afton Affleck organized a group of volunteer women to come into the church office building to do volunteer work in the various departments where needed. Then, for the next several years, some of these noble souls led by my wonderful friend Sister Affleck spent a day or a half a day a week or a month serving as my eyes and doing other secretarial duties which enabled me to triple or quadruple the amount of work that I have been able to do. I have been most grateful for this whole-hearted volunteer service, and I have received dozens of letters from them expressing their appreciation for the chance to serve and reflecting my whole soul's gratitude for their incomparable service, friendship, and motivation.

Sister Ila Adams might represent these fine women when she said:

"Dear Elder Sill,

As I write to you on your birthday, I have difficulty in expressing in words my deep appreciation for the privilege of working with you. When I was young I often heard my father speak of your great advice and successful business and spiritual ideas. At that time I didn't dream that I would ever meet you personally. I only wish I had the physical strength, mental ability and whatever else might be necessary for permanent employment in your office.

"I am deeply sorry for your present great trial and someday we will all know the reason for it. Someday when 'we shall know even as also we are known' we will all realize the great good you have done and are doing for others in many ways. If it were not for the problems with your eyesight, many of us would never have had the opportunity of associating with your wonderful spirit and being taught by you. Thank you for the most edifying experience of my life.

"As I may be of continuing assistance to you I will hope you will call on me.

"May you have many more happy birthdays is my wish, with love, Ila."

How pleasant are such constructive associations that we may have with each other and how much we borrow from these influences that ripen our lives.

We are impressed with the great scriptural statement which says that no one lives unto himself alone. We remember John Donne's philosophy that:

> No man is an island entire by himself.
> Each is a piece of the continent
> A part of the main.
> If any part of the continent is washed away by
> the sea,
> Then every man is the loser by just that much,
> As we are all involved in mankind.
> But each of *us* is also heavily and intimately
> involved in mankind,
> When the frontiers of our faith and knowledge are
> increased,
> When everyone is made better as a consequence,
> When the tide of righteousness comes in,
> Then all of the ships in the harbor are lifted up.

Everyone's good enriches us because we are all involved in everything around us.

Jabez S. Adams:

I have been very pleased with the men with whom I have associated in my occupational activities. As a young boy, I worked around in various kinds of labor; thinning sugar beets, working on the thresher, and doing various other kinds of farm day labor. From the time I was very young, I used to work at the Layton Sugar Company at various jobs which may appear to some people as menial.

I had a friendship with Jabez S. Adams, who was the plant's general foreman. This friendship has lasted the many years beyond his death. He was much older than I, but he took a very friendly interest in me which made me realize how pleasant it can be when an older person gets down on the level of those who come far below him, not only in occupation, but in knowledge and in about every other consideration. I spent a great many hours with him at a time in my life when my character was assuming its permanent mold.

Charles Sill:

During the summers while I was in high school, I worked on the farm. Between my freshman and sophomore years, I worked for my uncle, Charlie Sill. Much of his land was devoted to raising hay and grain. I used to haul hay for him out of the Black Hills a few miles north of his home and occasionally had the distressing experience of having a big load of hay tip over. But he also had sugar beets and some other crops. I had a great regard for my uncle Charlie.

Daniel Dee Harris:

Between my sophomore and junior year, I worked for Daniel Dee Harris, who was the superintendent of the Davis and Weber County Canal, which took most of his time. And so I ran the farm for him. He had eighty acres of wheat in the middle of the area now known as Hill Field. Half of the land he cropped the year I worked for him, and the other half he summer-fallowed to conserve the moisture so that he could get a better crop every other year. His farm was too far away from home for me to come home every night, so I used to take a big load of hay to last the horses for the week and also take my other equipment, such as seed grain during the planting period, and spend the week out on the top of what we called the Sand Ridge, now Hill Field. I used to take enough food with me on Monday morning to last until Wednesday night. Then Mr. Harris would come out Wednesday night and bring me enough food to last through Saturday noon. Saturday night I would come home for Sunday and start out again new the next Monday morning.

Mr. Harris was a very jovial, friendly person, and I don't know that I ever enjoyed seeing anything quite so much as I did seeing his little Ford Runabout appear on the horizon Wednesday afternoons and to spend some time with him upon his arrival. He had a very hearty laugh and it sent little chills of happiness all through my system. He always used to leave me feeling that the world was a wonderful place to live in. I had great joy in working for him, and I even had a fine association with his horses, because they were my only friends and cooperators during the week.

In hiring me he asked me if I would be willing to work until the first of November, by which time the beets would all be harvested, and then I could go to school. This was agreeable to me as I needed the extra money and I was confident that I could make up the work as I had done in other years and I wanted to play football for at least one year.

I had always liked Mr. Harris very much before I went to work for him, but forever after this experience of being his employee he has been one of my very special heroes. And just thinking about him is to me the equivalent of reading half a dozen books. Later on when I applied for employment with the New York Life Insurance Company, I gave Dee Harris' name as a reference and on the questionnaire form that he returned he said, "I congratulate the New York Life Insurance Company, if you are successful in obtaining the services of Sterling Sill." And I count it as a tremendous part of my education to have known Daniel Dee Harris.

A few days before he died, he left a request that I be asked to speak at his funeral. It was a great disappointment to me that on that particular date I had to be out of town on a Church assignment and was unable to fulfill the desire that both he and I felt. I myself am getting a little older and if perchance I might some day get where he is, I will have as one of the first things listed on my agenda to look him up and talk with him about his wheat crop out on Hill Field. I was grateful for the ninety dollars a month that he paid me as wages, but I am a lot more grateful for that training in the amenities and courtesies of life that I received from him.

Morris H. Ellison:

I worked for Morris H. Ellison between my junior and senior year, with the understanding that I could be released when school started. Mr. Ellison consulted with Dee Harris before he hired me and Mr. Harris gave me a very glowing recommendation. Because I put in very long hours, he cautioned Mr. Ellison that I might kill his horses. But this was also a very great experience, and I had a wonderful relationship with Mr. Ellison.

Charles A. Callis:

Another of the great heroes of my life was my mission president, Charles A. Callis. I left Salt Lake on January 4, 1924, and arrived four days later in Atlanta, Georgia, the mission headquarters of the Southern States Mission. We were directed to go to the Terminal Hotel near the railroad station in Atlanta, where we would stay while we were being assigned to our various conferences where we would work. I occupied a hotel room with another elder. Because the entire group was generally together, we went to the mission home together, and I did not notice that my room companion did not show up at the meeting. After the meeting was over at the mission home, we went back to the hotel. I went back to my room and was startled upon opening the door to see President Callis sitting there waiting in the room. He had not overlooked the fact that my companion did not show up.

We waited there together for an hour or so and finally the delinquent elder put in his appearance. President Callis was very unhappy about this delinquency at the very beginning of this elder's mission. I do not now remember what this elder was doing, or where he was, but only that he was not where he should have been. And from the conversation that went on between President Callis and this elder, I decided that I would not like to have any similar delinquencies to discuss with the mission president during my term in the mission field. But for me, this meeting with Charles A. Callis was the beginning of one of my greatest experiences with one of my life's greatest men.

Some time ago, I read an article in *Reader's Digest* telling how someone placed a block of silver up against a block of gold and left them there for two years. When they were finally taken apart, it was found that the molecular action in each of these solids had thrown little flecks of itself across the boundaries to be embedded in the other. That is, they found little flecks of gold in the silver and little flecks of silver in the gold. That type of principle operates at its best, and possibly at its worst, in human beings also. We are constantly throwing out little bits of ourselves in the forms of inspiration, knowledge, attitudes, fears, and prejudices, which become embedded in those within our range. A great deal of what is now known as Sterling Sill actually had its beginning as Charles A. Callis. I have received much from him by this process of cross fertilization of ideals, standards, and ideas.

He was a great preacher of the Gospel. He had been an attorney, and he had a great confidence in his power as a judge of human beings. He was a great salesman. In those days the meeting houses throughout Alabama were mostly little flimsy shacks built up on stilts where you could usually see through the floorboards to the ground. President Callis had a deep sense of the dramatic. He would build up to a crescendo, then come down on his heels with great force. This not only sent a shiver through his listeners, but the building itself would quiver and shake. The message would also frequently get to the chickens or the pigs that would wander underneath the church house, and they would sometimes run for their lives as if the final judgment was taking place inside the church.

The first time he came to Alabama to a conference during my term, I had a little visit with him. He went back to Atlanta and told one of the missionaries who was a friend of mine some very complimentary things about me. This very pleasant relationship continued and increased throughout the balance of his life, both in and out of the mission field.

I looked forward to his coming to conference, and to the weekly letters that we would get commenting on our reports sent to the mission office. Later, when I became the conference president, it was my very great good fortune to spend a lot of time with President Callis when he visited my jurisdiction. He would usually walk me out through those beautiful southern woods and preach to me about missionary work. He also loved to preach the gospel to me as a kind of one-man audience. And this he also did with great power and effectiveness, which always used to send a shiver running up and down my backbone.

President Callis was to me a kind of modern-day apostle Paul. He was born in Ireland and worked in the coal mines for many years. He was converted by a missionary who was not a very good missionary. When this missionary left Ireland to come home, some members gave him a little going away dinner at which this missionary apologized for his lack of missionary effectiveness. He said in substance, "I have not been a very good missionary and my accomplishments have been almost nil during all of my time here. I have baptized only one person and that was a dirty little miner Irish kid."

Later on, when President Callis was a member of the Council of the Twelve, he went out to attend a conference in the stake where this man lived. Following the pattern he set in the mission field, this man had long since become completely inactive in the Church. But President Callis wanted to see him again, and so he went to his place of residence and knocked on his door and the former missionary opened it. President Callis said to him, "Your name is so and so?" And the man said, "That's right." President Callis said to him, "You were in Ireland on a mission at such and such a time?" The man said, "That's right." President Callis said, "You weren't a very good missionary." And the man answered, "That's right." President Callis said, "You didn't do much good while you were there." And the man said, "That is right." President Callis said, "About the only thing you did worth mentioning was to baptize one dirty little miner Irish Kid." The man said, "That's right." Then President Callis introduced himself by saying, "I am that dirty little miner Irish Kid. I am Charles A. Callis, a member of the Quorum of the Twelve."

President Callis was called to the Southern States Mission and was assigned to the Florida Conference in May of 1906 and served until the spring of 1908. He was made the mission president August 20, 1908. He was released from his mission February 1934, so his mission lasted substantially twenty-eight years. He became a member of the Quorum of the Twelve October 6, 1933. He went back to the mission until a successor could be named. His successor was LeGrand Richards. President Callis died suddenly on January 21, 1947 in Jacksonville, Florida, while there organizing a stake. It seems very fitting that he should have died and his spirit taken its flight in the beautiful, sunny southland which he loved so much and where so much of his life's service had been given.

After he was released to become a member of the Quorum of the Twelve, he and I were very good friends. I used to go to see him quite frequently in his office in the Church Administration Building, never dreaming that some day I would occupy as an Assistant to the Quorum of the Twelve, the very room which he occupied for some thirteen years as a member of the Twelve. It became a very sacred privilege daily for me to kneel in that hallowed place, to offer up my prayer of gratitude and faith to my eternal Heavenly Father.

While I was bishop, I asked President Callis to officiate in the ground-breaking exercises for the construction of the Garden Park Ward meeting house. We also had him come and talk to our sacrament meeting on several occasions, and we have entertained him and Sister Callis in our home many times. He was a great influence in my life, as he was in the lives of thousands of other missionaries and other members of the Church.

Heber J. Grant:

One of my favorite hymns is "We Thank Thee, Oh God, for a Prophet," and it has been an exciting experience to me to have had to this point six presidents of the Church as personal friends. While these friendships were also a kind of father-son relationship, they also have been a great inspiration in my life. The first President of the Church that I knew personally and fairly intimately was Heber J. Grant. He, with his two counselors, J. Reuben Clark, Jr., and David O. McKay, singed my bishop's certificate which was dated September 17, 1936.

I was ordained a bishop by George Albert Smith and set apart by him with my counselors to preside over the Garden Park Ward in Salt Lake City, which was two blocks wide running from 11th East to 13th East and four blocks long running from 9th South to 13th South. One of our first duties was to find a building site on which a ward meeting house could be built. There was only one site in the entire ward which was suitable, and that was the old John C. Howard estate in the very center of the ward. That is, if you were to draw lines diagonally through the ward from its four quarters, it would center in the John C. Howard Estate.

However, the chief executor of the estate was antagonistic to the idea of having a church located on this beautiful piece of property. He was also antagonistic to the Church as some of his family had been excommunicated. This ground adjoined the lot on which his own home was built and he indicated very definitely that he would not sell it to the Church for any amount under any circumstances. Because there were no other vacant lots, we considered the possibility of tearing down enough houses to make a space on which the church could be properly located, but that would have been very costly and even then no suitable place could be found. We then examined the idea of building the meeting house outside of the ward limits, but that idea was also abandoned as impractical and very undesirable.

We called on this objecting chief trustee many times to try to persuade him to let us have this land, as to locate a church here was, in our opinion, the highest use to which this land could be put. Under our continual pressure and friendship, he began to soften and finally he said: "There is only one way that I would ever agree to let the Church have this land, and that is if Heber J. Grant himself would come down here to my office and ask me to let the Church have it."

We reported this matter to President Grant, and before we had finished telling him about it he had on his hat and was on his way. The 2.32 acres of land was bought for $24,321.68 and President Grant said that that was too much for us to pay, and the Church would sell the land to us for $14,250.00

President Grant worked very closely with the bishopric in the erection of the building. He laid the cornerstone, he came to our ward two or three times to talk to us about it, and finally on April 2, 1939, he dedicated the meeting house. And it was the good pleasure and great honor of my wife and I to entertain him at dinner in our home.

He used to talk to me at great length about his association with Colonel Haws and President Buckner of the New York Life, and the fact that he was general agent for the New York Life in the very early days. When any New York Life officials would come to town, President Grant was always very glad to meet them. Not only was he very cordial to them, but they were always very complimentary to him. Vice President Van Schaick, who was formerly Superintendent of Insurance of the State of New York, attended the opening session of conference on April 6, 1939 and after hearing President Grant's opening sermon said of him, "Rarely if ever does one see a man of his years of such driving force and vigorous utterance." Some statements made about President Grant by Dudley Dowell, President of the New York Life, are recorded on pages 93-94 of this book.

George Albert Smith

When Heber J. Grant passed away on May 14, 1945, he was succeeded in this highest office in the Church by George Albert Smith. For ten years I had lived almost as a next-door-neighbor to President Smith. I had been in his home many times and he had been in mine. I had ridden to work with him on several occasions. It may be that there has been a kinder, more sympathetic man someplace than President Smith, but I do not know who he was. He had been a great scout official, a great church man, and a great human being. I had had a number of intimate visits with him and I knew him to be my very good friend. I had a number of great experiences with him that are a little too intimate and confidential to relate here. But I have been uplifted and inspired by the thought that he was my brother, my leader, and my sincere friend.

David O. McKay

President Smith died on April 4, 1951 and his counselor, David O. McKay, who was also the senior member of the Quorum of the Twelve, became the President of the Church. Every President of the Church has been different from every other one, with a different set of virtues and abilities. President McKay was noted for his great love of people, his great human interest, his great ability as a speaker and for his influence with people. He had great enthusiasm for righteousness and a great love of life. He had an ideal relationship with his family. He had been a great football player in his college years. I was appointed by him to be the vice-president of the Deseret News, where I served for ten years. I had a very satisfying contact with President McKay, and on April 9, 1954, I was set apart by him to be an Assistant to the Quorum of the Twelve. President McKay, the members of the First Presidency and the members of the Quorum of the Twelve all placed their hands upon my head. President McKay then ordained me and set me apart as an Assistant to the Twelve with all the powers of the Holy Apostleship except the giving of second blessings and the ordination of patriarchs. (See page 140 for the blessing he pronounced upon me.)

I greatly enjoyed the friendship, the great warmth of personality of this great man on very many occasions. On several occasions he was a champion of my cause. I have been honored by him in many ways, and have retained several dozen of the personal letters that he has written to me over the years.

Joseph Fielding Smith

President McKay passed away on January 18, 1970, at age 96 and Joseph Fielding Smith, age 93, became President of the Church on January 23, 1970.

I had also lived as a close neighbor to President Smith. We lived in the same ward, and I had been his bishop for nearly ten years. President Smith seemed to most people to be more than ordinarily stern. Certainly he was greatly devoted to the work of the Lord. He was very proud of his father, who had also been President of the Church, and of his grandfather, who was Hyrum Smith, the brother of the Prophet. But President Smith had a great love in his heart for people. He had a great sense of humor, but his undeviating sense of righteousness was probably his most outstanding trait.

Before he was President of the Church, I asked him as his Bishop to lead the Special Interest Group in the M.I.A. We often asked him to speak in sacrament meeting or in some other place, and he always responded with the greatest good will. He was married to Jessie Evans while I was bishop, and she was also a great friend. Sister Smith loved to sing, and on many occasions we enjoyed her rich music and her rare humor in our ward. President Smith was very complimentary to me about my radio programs and on several occasions mentioned them in our General Authorities' meetings while he was President of the Quorum of the Twelve.

On a great many occasions I accompanied President Smith on his conference assignments, and had many very interesting experiences with him and Sister Smith. On several occasions my wife and I have taken them to dinners or some other social or religious engagement in our automobile.

He became a member of the Quorum of the Twelve in 1910 and thus served as a General Authority for 62 years. During that time he preached thousands of sermons. He has written hundreds of newspaper and magazine articles, and he has left a great literature to the people. During his lifetime, in addition to his speaking, teaching, newspaper and magazine articles, he has left twenty-two books.

I am very grateful to the Lord for my very close association with this great man. I have in my permanent file many choice letters that he has written to me personally, one of which I am including herewith. It was written while I was serving on the high council a few months after I had been released as bishop. It was eight years before I became a General Authority of the Church and 24 years before his death. It is as follows:

"Dear Brother Sill:

"I hardly know how to write to you, words fail me. This morning we received your wonderful letter containing sentiments that touched us both, and which we fear are not altogether deserved. However it makes us both happy to know that there are those who feel towards us as you have expressed yourself. It is not often that a person receives such a letter at least it is not often in our case, although letters of appreciation have frequently been received, but not such a letter as this one from you.

"It is, however, expressions of this kind that buoy us up and help us to be what we ought to be. The encouragement coming from true and tried friends; the confidence which they have in one, is an impelling force to keep one in the path of duty. This is how your kind expressions make us both feel. When we think that there are those who care and who have confidence in us, we realize that we cannot fail. No one but a coward or a knave will betray a confidence, or destroy the faith in a trusted friend.

"One thing that has impelled me onward is that I am justly proud of my ancestry. The Lord once said of my grandfather Hyrum Smith: 'Blessed is my servant Hyrum Smith; for I, the Lord, love him because of the integrity of his heart, and because he loveth that which is right before me.' Then the Lord permitted him to become a martyr because he held jointly with his younger brother the keys of this dispensation. How can I betray him? Then again my father past through a life of hardship and deprivation until middle life and in later years was abused by his enemies as few men have been abused, because he loved the truth. How can I fail him? Then again, the Lord has permitted me to hold a position of great trust and responsibility among a host of a million people, how could I betray that trust? And then when friends are kind enough to show their love and confidence as you have done, there is only one course open, and that is the path of steadfast integrity to the truth. I cannot afford to betray one friend who has confidence in me. The same is true of Jessie Evans Smith. So, you see, Brother Sill, we are compelled to take the narrow way; our friends will not permit us to do contrary. For this I am thankful.

"And then, when all is said and done, the fact remains, that we owe to our Redeemer the duty of being true and faithful to Him, for he bought us with a price, a price which we can never pay, and to him we are forever indebted for life and redemption both from the grave and from our own sins, if we will be faithful.

"Well Brother Sill, thank you for your kind sentiments and likewise for the wonderful basket you sent us and which we greatly appreciate. Again, I say, words fail us in expressing our gratitude.

"May the Lord bless and prosper you, we humbly pray.

Sincerely,
Joseph Fielding Smith
Jessie E. Smith"

He died quietly in his chair Sunday evening July 2, 1972, after listening to the Sunday evening broadcast from Temple Square, given as a part of my Sunday radio series. He was preceded by eleven months by Sister Smith in death.

Harold B. Lee

President Harold B. Lee became the President of the Church on July 7, 1972, and died suddenly on December 26, 1973, at age 74. Outside of the Prophet Joseph Smith, his death took place at an earlier age than any of the other Presidents of the Church and his tenure in office was the shortest, as it lasted only fifteen months.

The average age at death of all of the presidents between the Prophet Joseph Smith and Harold B. Lee is 80 years and their average tenure in office has been 12 years.

President Lee was a great student of the scriptures and he had a substantial ability as an executive. He introduced a large number of new programs in the Church.

Some few months after my appointment as a General Authority, I had a very friendly expression from him in which he said:

"Dear Sterling:

"When I returned from my Mesa appointment I found your kind letter of December 30, on my desk. To feel the assurance of your faith and confidence with respect to my humble efforts is an uplift which will give me the courage to continue trying for the sake of those like you who have confidence in me. My constant prayer is that I will not fail those like you who have devoted themselves to the work of the Lord.

"May peace be in your heart and give you the joy of your work. I want you to know that I feel in you the strength of a powerful man with a background of admirable training which when transferred to the work of the Lord would be of tremendous benefit. May you be continued long with us.

Faithfully yours,
(s) Harold B. Lee

Spencer W. Kimball

Spencer W. Kimball became President of the Church on December 30, 1973. President Kimball became a General Authority of the Church in 1943. I became a General Authority eleven years later, and I have had a very pleasant and extensive association with him. I have also traveled with him to several stake conferences and assisted him in the reorganization of several stakes. President Kimball is a man of great kindness and love of people. He has espoused the cause of the descendants of Father Lehi.

He himself is a kind of miracle. He has had most of his voice box removed because of cancerous growths. He has had open heart surgery. He has had heart trouble for many years, and yet on his eightieth birthday he seems more vigorous than he has been for a long time. He is one of the Church's greatest examples. Those great qualities of industry, devotion, spirituality and faithfulness are so apparent in him.

The Prophet Joseph Smith once said, "Every man who has a calling to minister to the inhabitants of this earth was ordained to that very purpose in the grand council of heaven before the earth was." This means to me that Spencer Kimball and all of his predecessors and associates, not only in the leadership of the Church, but in every other office, were approved in heaven for their callings here. And I know of no one in the Church who is more devoted or who is willing to give more of himself or of his resources than is Spencer W. Kimball.

I am overwhelmed when I think that it has been my privilege to have this intimate knowledge and association with some of the men who have not only been among the noble and great of this earth, but who surely were among the noble and great in the antemortal existence and will also be among the noble and great hereafter. And I look forward to an association with these brethren in eternity.

David W. Evans

There are a great many other people to whom I am very grateful. Two of the most appreciated of these were my two counselors in the bishopric, David W. Evans and Joseph W. Bambrough. Though they were very different in some things, yet they were very similar in their devotion.

My first recollection of David Evans was when I met him at an Exchange Club meeting in 1933. I was impressed with his genial smile, his apparent great intelligence, and his friendly disposition. Later when I was asked to nominate two men as my counselors, the first name that came to my mind was that of David W. Evans. I told him that I had been asked to serve as the bishop of this ward to be created and asked him if he would be willing to serve as my first counselor. He said, "I don't know if I would like to be your counselor or not, but I would be glad to talk with you about it." I was a little bit let down as I had expected a little more enthusiastic response. I said, "Would you tell me what the reservation is?" And he said, "Before I could tell whether I wanted to be your counselor or not, I would need to know what kind of a bishop you are going to be." He said, "If you are going to be a preaching bishop, I would not like to be your counselor. However," he said, "if you are going to be a working bishop, I would be delighted."

I said to him, "I will tell you the purpose that I would like to have you serve in the bishopric. To begin with, I would very much like to be a good bishop. I can't think of anything I would like more than to be a good bishop. But I have some blind spots, and I don't always see myself as others see me. If you would agree to give me a kind of guarantee that you would make a good bishop out of me, I would like that very much." He said, "Would you like to talk about it right now?" And so we sat down and took a piece of paper and he outlined what in his opinion would be required if we were going to make the most of our bishopric (meaning he and I and Brother Bambrough). "But," he said, "there are certain things that we must do." He had already had some successful bishopric experience, and besides that he was older, wiser, and smarter than I was. And I also felt that if I could have his frank and personal interest that we could have a great bishopric. I was perfectly delighted in the things he pointed out that must be included in our leadership, and I never changed my opinion of him even for one minute during the next ten years that our bishopric existed. I have included on page 179 of this book a statement by David W. Evans himself about our bishopric experience.

Joseph W. Bambrough

Brother Bambrough was also a great counselor, while very different from Brother Evans. Brother Bambrough had a steady, dependable faith that could move mountains, and did. Brother Evans said of him, "Joe Bambrough is one of the most unselfish, dependable, sincere, and kindly men I have ever known." And I count these two men, outside my own family, as two of my greatest benefactors.

Henry H. Blood

Another of the great men in my life was Henry H. Blood. I knew him primarily in the roles of stake president and Governor. I met him on one occasion when I was very young when he was visiting our ward. I just happened to get in the aisle at the right time, as he came along. He stopped and shook my hand and asked me what my name was. Then he asked me what my father's name was and he said he knew my father. I suppose this interview lasted for a total of one minute. But in that minute something wonderful happened to me, inasmuch as I determined that some day I would like to represent in my person some of those traits that I could feel in him. That is, in order to communicate with other people, you don't always need to express yourself verbally. People can feel things. If you love someone very much, you don't always need to tell them about it. And while we ought to express ourselves in this direction more frequently than we do, yet they are able to feel that in your presence.

Some time later I found some verse that reminded me of this experience, and I would like to include it here because this is probably the experience of every other person. On one occasion Thomas Curtis Clark said:

> I saw him once, he stood a moment there,
> He spoke a word that laid his spirit bare,
> He clasped my hand then passed beyond my ken
> But what I was I shall not be, again.

Everyone has had the experience of being ennobled and lifted upward by the good example and encouragement of someone else. And the corollary of this idea is also true, that everyone in the next thirty days will have the opportunity of changing the lives of a great many other people. It may be just a pat on the back, or a word of encouragement, or a little friendliness, or the conveyance of some interesting idea. And yet for good or for evil we shape the lives of those around us.

Daniel B. Harris

Daniel B. Harris was my first bishop. He was born October 30, 1848. He was ordained a bishop and set apart to preside over the North Kaysville Ward, which included all of the area now known as Layton, on September 9, 1889. He was released as bishop of the Layton Ward in 1910 after a tenure of twenty-two years.

The ward then met in a frame meeting house built in 1907. Bishop Harris presided over this vast territory from his home up on the edge of what used to be known as the Sand Ridge, which is now the entrance to Hill Field.

When I was a very small boy, I was employed by him to pick tomatoes. I do not remember how long I worked or what terminated the employment. I do remember that he was indebted to me in the amount of 35 cents, which apprently he did not have. I remember occasions when he came to our house to make his ward teaching visit he would say, "Is this the little boy that picked my tomatoes?" After I assured him that I was, he would say, "I wonder if he will ever get his money." I was not so sure about his last question and I don't remember whether I ever did or did not, so I suppose I did.

James E. Ellison

I have had some other wonderful bishops. James E. Ellison is one of those who stands out most prominently in my memory. He was bishop of the Layton Ward from July 18, 1915, until May 6, 1934, and it seemed that he was a very good personal friend of mine.

I used to walk to church and I always used to get there early. Very frequently he and I would do the janitorial work of dusting off all of the seats and similar things before the other people arrived. I later became his stand-in in the priests quorum and he was a great inspiration to me all of his life.

Lawrence E. Ellison

Lawrence E. Ellison was my banker. He made me a loan of $25 when I was fifteen years of age. He loaned me money with some regularity until the time of his death. I don't think he ever required any security and he never asked me to have anybody sign my note, even when I was under age and legally was not obligated to pay it back. I was honored by him to be the speaker on his eightieth birthday celebration at the Farmington Oak Ridge Country Club, and his family honored me again by asking me to speak at his funeral.

Because so much of my life has been spent in my occupation, the men who have been my associates and those who have been responsible for my training and supervision come high on the list of my great benefactors. Fred A. Wickett, of course, leads the list because of the very close association which we had over such a long period and because of my great admiration for him. (See page 75.)

Frank Satter

One of my great experiences came in the person of Frank W. Satter. In 1940 I became the inspector of agencies of the intermountain department and one of the offices under my supervision was the Montana Branch office, with headquarters at Butte.

In the early part of 1940, I attended the annual spring meeting of the Montana Branch held at the Finlen Hotel. At the luncheon I sat by a young man who was then a clerk in the office, which position he had held for nine years. He was a very likely looking young man some ten years younger than I was and I encouraged him, telling him that he might do much better for himself and the company by getting out into the field and demonstrating his ability as a salesman. This he did, and it was not very long before he was running close to the top of the list of all the salesmen in the Montana office.

At a later date, I had the privilege of recommending him to serve as an assistant manager and later as a manager for the company. He rose steadily until he was the highest paid manager in the service of the New York Life. Then the company asked him to be Regional Vice President and have charge of the Northwestern Division with headquarters in Seattle, where he set some impressive company and divisional records.

Finally, after many years of outstanding service, he decided to go back into the field as an agent where again he made some phenomenal records, qualifying immediately for the Million Dollar Round Table. At the time of his retirement from the company's service, he began devoting his entire time to the service of his church. And I am sure that he will uplift and inspire the lives of a great many people. Here is a young man of very modest background and education who, on his own power, has risen to great heights in a business world where the keenest competition is one of the chief characteristics. But everything that he does he does superbly well. Above his occupational expertise, he is a great human being with a beautiful quality of friendship.

John McKenna, one of the outstanding "Horatio Alger" men that Frank Satter had developed, was telling me on one occasion of the thing that he would dislike to do more than about anything else. He said that the only way that he would possibly do that would be if Frank Satter asked him to. He said, "I owe my entire success in life to Frank W. Satter, and no matter what honorable thing he asked me to do, I would do it." What an inspiring situation it is when great human beings can have that kind of pleasure in their relationship with other people.

Frank and I have also had a wonderful relationship over many years. To me he is like a valuable jewel in my life's treasury. On one occasion he made a written statement of our relationship which I include here because his feelings toward me are fully reciprocated in my love and appreciation for him. He said:

"My friendship with Sterling Sill dates approximately 40 years, and I shall ever be grateful for the magnificent influence that he exercised over my life through his guidance, example, and inspiration!

"Let me review briefly and specifically several instances that support my claim.

"Sterling Sill appointed me as a general manager for the New York Life and the most valuable instruction he gave me at that time was that I need not be like some of the great leaders in the New York Life that were known to me, such as Dudley Dowell, but that I too had certain qualities and characteristics that would enable me to be a good manager if I would trust in my own abilities. This instruction gave me the help I needed, for I couldn't be a Dudley Dowell. I was a Frank Satter.

"Perhaps the next instance was when I went to visit Sterling and Doris at their home in Salt Lake City. Not only was I very much impressed by the lovely home, the manner in which they lived, the automobile they drove, but equally impressive were Sterling's accomplishments in his work, in his community, and in his church. In other words, he was successful—and that which gave him his success was the discipline afforded by his church and its application. Consequently, I resolved that through this example I, too, should more closely live to the teachings of my church.

"Then during one of the earlier years in my career, I had been extremely fortunate in coming up with a good performance record and I recall so well Sterling's commendation—a commendation which was given in the form of a bulletin. He had likened my business effort and success to the efforts and heroism of a self-sacrificing soldier and hero. This publication, of course, was not only recognition, but beyond that it led me to understand that I must have possessed some unusual capabilities, and so engendered confidence, which in turn led to new and more meaningful business records for me.

"Sterling has been, still is, and I'm sure always will be, noted for his communications in the interests of others. In these early stages of our association together, since he had the responsibility for guiding my business activity and that of a number of other New York Life managers spread over a vast geographical territory, he gave a great part of his instruction through bulletins, wherein he would outline the principles for successful management. I recall that at one time in a meeting together he was particularly complimentary about some idea that I had been using and he wanted to know where I had gotten it. Actually, it was an idea of his as set forth in one of his bulletins. However, he just hadn't recognized my interpretation of it. Then it was my time to offer direction so I told him that inasmuch as we were being motivated by his bulletins that if he wanted to keep up with the rest of the crowd, he was influencing, he would have to start reading his own bulletins and taking action on them instead of merely writing them for our benefit.

"Yes, I am at this time and ever shall be grateful to Sterling Sill for the influence he exercised over my life. To properly illustrate the example and the inspiration and guidance would require a book in itself—throughout these years a close friend offering encouragement, inspiration, and I know from my own experience, many, many, many, many others he has so affected. It was his profession, his performance, his promise that makes him 'a good man to know—a good man to be.'"

Dudley Dowell

Dudley Dowell and I were born in the same year. We were fellow managers of the New York Life together, I in Salt Lake and he in Butte, Montana. Later he was transferred to Seattle and then to the home office where he finally became the president of the company and, as such, probably did as much or more for NYLIC and its agency men than anyone in the company's history. He and I were almost completely different in temperament and personality, and yet we were very good friends.

I have been invited on four different occasions to be vice-president. Two of these requests came from Dudley Dowell himself. He told me I could either go to the home office or be a regional vice-president and I could pretty well have my choice of regions. But I liked Salt Lake and have never been unhappy that I chose to remain here.

At the time of his retirement he moved back to his native state of Arkansas and lived in the beautiful Eden Isle at Heber Springs. And we have kept in rather close touch ever since that time.

Several years after his retirement he wrote me the following letter:

"Dear Sterling:

"I find it difficult to tell you all that I feel and would like to say to you at this time since I just learned in a wonderful letter from our mutual friend, Golden Driggs, of the serious impairment of your eyes. Elizabeth and I are both shocked and distressed to hear about it. But knowing you as we do, we take comfort in the knowledge that whatever crosses God may send you, with Heaven's help you will shoulder them. Although the load may seem so great, how light to what Christ bore for our sake.

"In my retirement I have some time for reflection. In reviewing my years with New York Life, I often think of you and others who were so dedicated to our great Company, and who made such an impact on the lives of so many people.

"At one time I wrote an inscription on a picture of myself that I sent to you and it was something like this: 'To my good friend and our greatest recruiter, Sterling Sill.' (Dudley)

"The records of the Company through the years verify that appraisal I made of you about 20 years ago.

"In your 34 years of agency work with the New York Life, you were number 1 in 12 of those years in personal production of combined New Organization, and number 1 in 13 for the total office production in the same area. I note, too, that for 11 years in a row, from 1955 to 1965, your office totals ranked you at the very top of the list. In your career you were competing with from 110 to about 300 other offices. To my knowledge no one else has approached that kind of achievement. You and your fine team have a right to be proud of that record. What you have done has been well done and has the admiration of all our respective friends in NYLIC.

"Well do I remember the night of your retirement dinner in the Hotel Utah. At that time in my remarks I cited not only your outstanding service to the New York Life, but for your civic and educational and church activity. That has been a fine balance of a well-lived life, which I have tried, perhaps unsuccessfully, to emulate.

"Sterling, I hope you are well and are enjoying your continued constructive activity in your high church position, and in your writing. I have enjoyed reading many of your books.

"Elizabeth joins me in sending you and Doris our best wishes and affectionate regards.

Faithfully yours,

/s/ Dudley"

Golden K. Driggs

One of my closest and most productive friends has been Golden K. Driggs. Golden has had a great influence on many people in and out of the New York Life. He has done many things that have been helpful to me both in a business, a personal, and a religious way. And I am very grateful to him for his friendship.

After his company retirement he became president of the Shreveport Mission of the Church, and I was his supervisor for a short part of that period. My wife and I and Golden and Maude toured the Shreveport Mission in May of 1972, which was Golden's first year as mission president. We had a wonderful time together. But our friendship began long years ago in 1932, and I am sure it will continue to the end of our lives and beyond.

There are a great many other people who have touched my life for good, and I have of necessity left out many of those who have been most influential and constructive. Near the end of the life of Shakespeare's Brutus, he said, "I had no friend but that he was true to me." Will Rogers said, "I never met a man I didn't like." And so it is with me.

As I write this part of my biography, I have tried to think of those people who have offended me. And while I have had a few occasions when I have been disappointed in people and I have had people who I thought have taken unfair advantage, yet I do not know of one single person whom I actually dislike or who has offended me in any serious way.

Neither have I ever had anyone who has ever tried to lead me astray in my religion or involve me in any immoral or unethical practice.

But it has certainly been wonderful to me that I have had a personal and intimate relationship with nine men who have served as president or chairman of the board of the world's tenth largest corporation. This in addition to having known and been known by six Presidents of the Church, as well as many other noble men and women who must have been among the noble and great in the antemortal council of God. And in my heart I express my gratitude for these wonderful men in my life.

Chapter Eleven

My Religious Life

It's difficult to tell the story of one's life when it is made up of so many strengths and weaknesses in so many fields. This is especially true when so much of it still lies in the future. It seems to me that our lives resemble the various strands of a rope, or different wires of a cable. It is sometimes helpful to examine them one at a time. Then one can go back to its beginning, follow it through towards its end, and make any desired changes to strengthen one's life generally or in any particular part. But regardless of the excellence or mediocrity in one field, or in one period of time, as a usual thing each area and each period transfers some of its strength or weakness to the other. In planning for life's improvements, where should the primary attention be given?

Thomas Carlyle tried to answer this question by saying that "a man's religion is the most important thing about him." That is what he thinks about and believes in and works at and fights for and lives by. I am persuaded that of the various cables that run through my life, the most important area is found in the region of my religious life—it is more or less like a backbone that connects and gives strength to all other parts of the body. However, it is sometimes a little difficult to tell which experiences are religious, which are occupational, or educational, or cultural, as they all tend to merge into and depend upon each other.

Since beginning the writing of my autobiography, I have developed a little better appreciation of what Jesus may have felt when He said, "To me, all things are spiritual." (D&C 29:34.) Certainly this would apply to our industry, our human relations and our general success. The dictionary says that religion is a service and adoration of God as is found in accepted sacred writings, or declared by recognized teachers while one is in pursuit of a way of life.

Definition number two says that religion is a state of life of a religious person. It is a profession or practice of religious belief. The greatest fact in the universe is the existence of God. He is our Eternal Heavenly Father. He is the giver of all good things. He is the world's greatest business man and chief advisor. How grateful I am for that part of my existence that I refer to as my religious life!

I was born into a family supported by several generations of great religious background and tradition. As one of the first experiences in my life, I was taken to church and held in the hands of several good men, and was given a name and a blessing. I was taught to pray at my mother's knee. Sacred prayers were said before each meal. I began attending religious services and was taught the principles of religion as soon as I could talk.

I was baptized when I was eight years old and my duties were held up in clear outline before me. I was ordained to the Priesthood at age 12 and began a long series of Priesthood elevations. I became a Sunday School teacher at age 14 and was placed in charge of a scout troop at age 18.

At age 20, there began one of the greatest experiences of my life when I was called by the First Presidency of the Church to go to Alabama to be a minister of the gospel of Jesus Christ, with authority to preach and teach, baptize and administer in other sacred ordinances.

Sometimes people complain about life by saying how difficult it is for one to live his religion. They say it is difficult to be honest and sober and moral. But it is just as easy for an honest man to be honest as it is for a dishonest man to be dishonest. It is just as easy for a sober man to be sober as it is for an alcoholic man to be alcoholic. As a usual thing, a person burns up many times more energy in going to hell than is required to take him to heaven.

The Lord said about the Word of Wisdom that it is adapted to the capacity of the weak and the weakest of all Saints who are or can be called saints. (D&C 89:3.) And that description might well apply to every other principle of the gospel if we just make up our minds about it.

Jesus voiced the greatest success formula that has ever been given in just two words when He said, "Follow me." From the time I was baptized until the present, I have been engaged in helping to carry forward the work of the Lord, which has given me greater strength in every other field. That is, the strength that I developed in my religious life has carried over into every other activity.

For example, in 1932, before being given a promotion in my business, I was asked to come to New York to be interviewed by the head of the agency force. Among other things during the interview, he said, "Sterling, are you a Mormon?" I indicated that I was. He said, "Do you keep the Word of Wisdom?" I told him that I did. Later on when I knew him a little better, I reminded him of this experience and asked him what possible difference these questions could make to him. He said, "As you know, I smoke a little and I drink a little, and I do some other things that would not be approved of by your church. But," he said, "I would never hire you if you did those things." I said to him, "But you know the Word of Wisdom is true just as well as I do. You know that the New York Life Insurance Company last year paid out many millions of dollars in drunken driving accidents, lung cancer deaths, emphasema and heart disease." He said, "I know that, and I think the Word of Wisdom is wonderful. Everybody in the world ought to strictly obey it. Just think what a world we would have if they did. But I believe the Word of Wisdom is just a great idea, whereas you think it is the Word of the Lord. If I break the Word of Wisdom, I am just using bad judgment. But if you break the Word of Wisdom, it is a sign that you lack character, and how could anyone trust you or anybody else who posed as a member of the Church and yet disobeyed its principles; that is, if you would not keep the Word of Wisdom, even when you believe the Lord Himself had commanded it, how could I expect you to obey the New York Life merely because the officers of the company had asked you to?" This is good logic.

Many years later, just prior to my retirement from company service, I attended a company field management meeting in New York. For five days we had had a wonderful meeting, which was concluded on Friday. Friday night we had the big annual formal dinner preceded by a social hour, when hors d'oeuvres, drinks, etc. were served, and everybody visited pleasantly among his many friends such as one would in a college class reunion. In the group where I stood someone jokingly made some reference to the color of the tomato juice in my liquor glass. I responded in the same spirit by saying, "I've been coming back to these meetings for many years, and none of you fellows have ever tried to teach me how to enjoy all of this good, free liquor that is available." The president of the company, who is a very close friend of mine, said, "Sterling, if I should ever see you with liquor in your glass, it would break my heart." He said, "Each of us says a hundred times a year that one of the reasons that we are in the insurance business is to try to build up the homes of America. If we have properly done our job, then when the breadwinner dies, the mortgage on the home will be paid, the children can go to school, and the mother can stay in the home in order to hold it together. This gives us great power and a high motivation, and we tell that to people a hundred times a year. But everyone in this circle, with one exception, has in his glass this poison that does more damage to the homes of America than any other influence in the world. And if we were going to be consistent, we would either get out of the insurance business or quit setting a bad example to all of our agents and policy holders by pouring this poison down our throats." In substance, what the president of the company said was that the New York Life wants the same kind of people to run its affairs as the Lord wants to represent Him as members of His Church. And that is the kind of husband that every woman wants and the kind of friend that every individual wants.

One of the greatest experiences of my life were these twenty-seven months that I spent in teaching people that the Son of God had reappeared upon the earth and restored the Gospel of Jesus Christ for all to benefit from.

When I came home, I became Assistant Superintendent of the Sunday School and I also went back into my old job of Scoutmaster, teaching the Scout laws and the Scout Oath, with a daily good turn thrown in, which should be an important part of the religious life of every American. If I learned what I taught, how could I miss?

On May 10, 1931, five years after I had returned from my mission, I was appointed a member of the High Council of North Davis Stake under President Henry H. Blood. Henry H. Blood has been a great influence in my life. In 1932, Henry Blood was elected Governor of the State of Utah. At the same time I was appointed manager of the New York Life Insurance Company.

On October 1, 1932 both he and I moved our places of residence to Salt Lake City. He was released as Stake President, and I was released as High Councilor. But seven years later, while still Governor, Henry Blood appointed me a member of the Board of Regents of the University of Utah. And thus, another very pleasant experience for nearly twelve years of my educational life came out of my religious life.

I have already pointed out on several occasions that life to me has been very pleasant and it has been made up of some really great experiences. One of the greatest of these is the nine years, eight months and two days that I served as Bishop of the Garden Park Ward.

Mention has been made elsewhere of the difficult time that was encountered in obtaining the building site, which was the only suitable one in the ward. But it was a delightful place of beauty and peace with its trees, its flowers, its lawns, beautiful stream, and the very comfortable adequate building which was erected in which to worship God. Of course, the most important thing about any situation is the people who make it up. And we had a wonderful set of people from every point of view. We had some very important business and professional people. We had people of great culture and refinement, and great spirituality. I have already indicated that my two counselors were two of the greatest of the many bene-factors that I have had during the entire period of my mortality.

Herbert B. Maw, Governor of the State of Utah from 1941 to 1949, had his home in our ward. Joseph Fielding Smith, long-time President of the Quorum of the Twelve, and later President of the Church, lived in our ward. In addition to President Smith, Richard L. Evans from our ward, was sustained as one of the First Council of Seventy on October 7, 1938. He was ordained an Apostle October 8, 1953, and continued to live in our ward until he died on November 1, 1971.

But, in addition to those two members of the Quorum of the Twelve, Adam S. Bennion, former Church Commissioner of Educa-tion, was ordained a member of the Quorum of the Twelve on April 9, 1953. Hugh B. Brown was ordained and set apart to be an Assist-ant to the Quorum of the Twelve on October 4, 1953. And Sterling W. Sill was ordained and set apart as an Assistant to the Quorum of the Twelve on April 9, 1954.

From one point of view, therefore, it might be said that five General Authorities of the Church were appointed in consecutive order from this one small ward. In addition, Bruce R. McConkie and Bernard P. Brockbank lived in this ward before they were made General Authorities, but their appointment did not come in consec-utive order with the ones above listed.

Ernie Pyle, the late war correspondent of World War II, once said that "nine-tenths of morale was made up of pride in your outfit and confidence in your leaders." I have never known of a Church unit which had such a high morale as was enjoyed by the people of this ward.

During this period, Presiding Bishop LeGrand Richards said he knew of no ward where the lot was purchased, the money was raised for the building, and the building completed and dedicated in such a short time. And during this time, the statistics, the friend-ships, and other indicators of high morale went up at a very rapid rate. Each year the Bishopric made a voluntary, detailed report of ward activities, one copy of which was submitted to the Stake Presidency. Another copy was kept to note the gains and possible weaknesses to the ward leaders themselves. A record was kept of twenty-seven main items, such as percentage of Sacrament Meeting attendance, percentage of attendance at the various quorum meetings, auxiliary organizations, percentage of subscriptions to church magazines, fast offering payments, and other important matters which could be represented by statistics. And in the last year of our Bishopric, Garden Park Ward had first place in Bonneville Stake in twenty-one of these, second place in three, third and fourth place in three, with a composite score which led the Stake and the entire church according to the comparative report that was sent out monthly from church headquarters at that time.

In this entire period of ten years, there was not one case of any immorality in any member of the Ward that was reported, confessed or suspected. During this period, there was not one case of disciplinary action, either taken, threatened, or contemplated; nor, was there any known case of antagonism or trouble between any ward member or between the leadership and any ward member.

On May 19, 1946, I was released as Bishop to serve on the High Council of the Bonneville Stake. I was given charge of the Aaronic Priesthood work in the Stake. At that time, Aaronic priesthood level of activity was very low in our Stake, and I was instructed by the Stake President to put the Aaronic Priesthood record of activity up at the top of the Church, and I felt that I knew how to do that.

In any desired accomplishment, all we need to do is to find out what the law is governing that particular success, and then follow it strictly. In recruiting the members to serve on the Stake Aaronic Priesthood Committee, I had them make some commitments to faithfulness and personal worth, which I knew in advance, would, if followed, bring about the accomplishment asked for by the Stake President. This program was followed to the letter by us according to our commitment, which each one of us made individually, and the following letter later received by me from the Stake President, indicates that the goal was accomplished.

June 3, 1950

Sterling W. Sill
1264 Yale Avenue
Salt Lake City, Utah

Dear Sterling,

I have just received a copy of the April report and note that our stake ranks high principally because of the fine work of the Aaronic Priesthood.

As I recall the statistics, you are leading the Church in every comparison of activity. We desire to express our appreciation for your very energetic and successful leadership in this important activity of the Church.

We have noticed substantial and steady improvement as the months have passed, and we commend you and your committee for this outstanding achievement.

Sincerely,
/s/ Owen Reichman,
Stake President

The experience on this stake committee, and position attained of leadership excellence was another of those great experiences of my life. And our stake continued as the leading Aaronic Priesthood stake in the Church as long as I had any knowledge of it.

In 1951 I was asked to serve on the Sunday School General Board and, therefore, was released from the Bonneville Stake High Council. Soon after my appointment to the Sunday School General Board, I was asked by Superintendent Hill to rewrite the Sunday School Handbook. This was also a great experience as it forced me to make some determination about what I thought the program of a religious organization ought to be which had been given the responsibility of teaching the Gospel to all the members of the Church.

Then on April 6, 1954, I was called by David O. McKay to come to his office. He informed me that I had just been called to be an Assistant to the Quorum of the Twelve to take the place of George Q. Morris, who was being advanced to the Council of the Twelve, to fill the vacancy left by the sudden death of Matthew Cowley.

I was very pleased at this honor, especially in view of the great love and devotion that I already felt for President David O. McKay. He told me that I was to keep my employment for the time being. I was ordained and set apart on April 9, 1954 by President McKay, participated in by the other members of the First Presidency and all members of the Quorum of the Twelve. His line of authority and mine are as follows:

Sterling W. Sill was set apart as an Assistant to the Council of the Twelve, April 9, 1954, by David O. McKay.

David O. McKay was ordained an Apostle April 9, 1906 by Joseph F. Smith.

Joseph F. Smith was ordained an Apostle July 1, 1866 by Brigham Young.

Brigham Young was ordained an Apostle February 14, 1835 under the hands of the Three Witnesses, Oliver Cowdery, David Whitmer, and Martin Harris.

The Three Witnesses were called by revelation to choose the Twelve Apostles and on February 14, 1835 were "Blessed by the laying on of the hands of the Presidency," Joseph Smith, Jr., Sidney Rigdon, and Frederick G. Williams, to ordain the Twelve Apostles. *(History of the Church,* Vol. 2, pp. 187-188.) Joseph Smith, Jr. and Oliver Cowdery received the Melchizedek Priesthood in 1829 under the hands of Peter, James, and John. Peter, James, and John were ordained Apostles by the Lord Jesus Christ. (John 15:16.)

President McKay's prayer was as follows:

"Brother Sterling Welling Sill, dear associate and fellow-laborer in the Cause of Christ: By virtue of the Holy Priesthood and the authority vested in us as a First Presidency and the Council of the Twelve, we your brethren, unitedly lay our hands upon your head and set you apart as an Assistant to the Council of the Twelve Apostles in The Church of Jesus Christ of Latter-day Saints and confer upon you every authority, power, privilege, and key pertaining to this high and holy calling in the Melchizedek Priesthood.

"We bless you that you may go forward and represent the Council of the Twelve in setting in order the affairs of the stakes and wards, quorums, organizations, and missions throughout the Church.

"We confer upon you the authority to perform sealings in the temple, excepting second anointings, and the ordaining of officers throughout the priesthood in all quorums excepting the calling and ordination of patriarchs. These two authorities and privileges pertain to the Council of the Twelve Apostles. Other sealings and ordinances pertaining to stake presidencies, high councilmen, high priests, seventies, elders, priests, teachers and deacons, we confer upon you.

"We bless you that the spirit of this ordination, representing the Council of the Twelve in all parts of the world, may come to you in rich abundance, that you may feel the increased power and also the increased responsibility which comes with this ordination and setting apart. May you feel the responsibility of apostleship upon you and may you go forth with increased power in setting in order every condition, every authority, ordaining and setting apart every individual who may come under your jurisdiction and upon whom you must confer ordinations, settings apart, and authority. May the spirit of this calling be yours.

"May you radiate this power wherever you may be in counsel with individuals or groups, or speaking before audiences, that you may represent the authority now placed upon you in dignity and power conveying a convincing of the truth to the hearts of those who are earnestly seeking it.

"We bless you that in your travels by land, sea or air you may be protected.

"To this end, then heed the promptings of the Holy Spirit to which you are entitled. May you hear more definitely than ever before the whisperings of the Still Small Voice given through the Holy Ghost. It will protect you from harm and evil, seen or unseen, and furthermore, it will prompt you what to say and what not to say, that the word of the Lord may be given and that his purposes may be consummated through your administration.

"We bless you too with increased power and influence in your business affairs, that when you meet with non-members, counsel with them, they may recognize a power and intelligence and a dignity and authority which are not recognized in men who do not hold the apostleship as you hold it.

"Our Father in Heaven, we pray thee to be with this thy servant. Thou knowest his integrity in the past, his devotion to thy work. Thou knowest the scores of people whom he has blessed, the young people whose feet he has placed upon the path of virtue, and how many he has blessed through them and their families. Continue to inspire him in this great work and bless him exceedingly as he now goes forth with increased authority to bless the groups in thy Church and out of the Church to which he may come.

"We bless you that you may be wise in the conservation of your health, that your energy may continue, that you may radiate that life and activity which will inspire others in outside interests to follow your wise example in making contributions to the Church of Jesus Christ, that this work may spread throughout the world, that men who influence others in business affairs and political affairs and social affairs may be influenced to throw their financial interest, toward the advancement of the Kingdom of God.

"These blessings we seal upon you through your faith and faithfulness in the name of the Lord Jesus Christ. Amen."

I continued my full double responsibility until the end of 1958, when my business office became the largest office in the entire company in actual sales volume. But both of my assignments together were getting pretty heavy. I was spending three days a week attending stake conference. It only took two days in Salt Lake, but it took four days in Beaumont, Texas, or Calgary, Canada, and seven days in New Zealand and other foreign places, so that on an average, it required three days a week.

I was receiving two or three requests every day to make talks before educational groups, sales conventions, business organizations, etc. I was doing about fifteen hours of counseling a week. I was writing a leadership article each month for the Improvement Era (which were later put into two volumes on that subject by Bookcraft Publishing Company). I gave a series of radio lectures in 1953 and 1954 and on April 17, 1960, I began another series made up of two separate broadcasts. One was thirty minutes in length with about fifteen or sixteen minutes of speaking time. The other was a fifteen minute program with about five or six minutes of speaking time. With almost no effort at promotion, this broadcast grew to include about 370 radio stations with representation in every state of the United States. Both of these programs were continued every week for over seventeen years.

These required a preparation time between thirty and forty hours per week. This was in addition to touring missions, working with missionaries, etc. But in spite of my lessened business time, as if in fulfillment of President McKay's blessing, my business continued to grow phenomenally. And from 1954, my first general authority year, my business office led all other offices of the New York Life in recruiting and training without single exception for the next eleven years. The Church also made a miraculous growth.

At the time of my appointment as an Assistant to the Twelve, the Church was made up of 212 stakes. As I write this particular chapter in 1979, the Church is made up of over 1,000 stakes. To properly handle this great growth, the First Quorum of Seventy was organized and implemented. All of those serving as Assistants to the Twelve were made members of this Quorum on October 1, 1976. On that date I was given an additional ordination and setting apart by the First Presidency and the Quorum of the Twelve, Apostle Howard W. Hunter being voice, as follows:

"Dear Brother Sterling Welling Sill, we your brethren, who love you, surround you and lay our hands upon your head by the authority of the Melchizedek Priesthood and the appointment from the president of the Church; and we ordain you a seventy in the Melchizedek Priesthood of The Church of Jesus Christ of Latter-day Saints and confer upon you all the powers and authority of that office. We also set you apart as a member of the First Quorum of Seventy in The Church of Jesus Christ of Latter-day Saints and give you all of the power and authority that pertains to membership in that quorum. We bless you in all of the ways that you need blessing, particularly do we pray to the Lord that he will give you health so that you will not be impeded in your work. Oh, Father, we pray that thou wilt bless this, our brother, to the end that he can continue his effective work in thy kingdom. And now, Brother Sill, we bless you with all of these blessings together with all others necessary for your good and benefit and we do so in the name of the Lord, Jesus Christ. Amen."

In the 25 years that I have served as a General Authority the Church has been presided over by four presidents, David O. McKay, Joseph Fielding Smith, Harold B. Lee, and Spencer W. Kimball. When I was appointed there were 33 General Authorities. Today, in 1979, there are 68.

It has now been 149 years since the Church was organized upon the earth in this dispensation and it seems to me that our time is getting very short as the Lord has said that the message of the gospel should go to every nation and kindred and tongue and people. However, in some cases we have not yet gotten it down to the end of the block on which we live.

When the Lord made His time allotment to our world, it was patterned after the seven days of creation, except that one day with the Lord is a thousand years with man, so our time was given us on the basis of seven periods of a thousand years each. The Lord labored six days in the creation and rested on the Sabbath. Our world accordingly has been given six thousand years to get the main work of the world done. This period will be concluded by the glorious second coming of Jesus Christ, who will come with His mighty angels in flaming fire to cleanse the earth of its wickedness, and institute upon the earth the millennial period of its seventh one thousand years, when Christ will reign personally upon the earth.

During this period the earth will be changed from a telestial earth to a terrestrial earth where its paradisical conditions will be restored as in the Garden of Eden days. During this period, temples will cover the land. Both mortal and immortal people will labor here upon the earth to finish binding the human family together and to prepare the earth for its condition as a celestial sphere, which change will come about at the end of the millennium.

The Lord has indicated that no one knows the day or the hour of His coming. Not even the angels in the heaven know, but He has given us certain signs by which we may know that His coming is near. These signs are all about us, which should give us a great sense of urgency about doing the job that we have been assigned to do.

It is reported that the population of the earth is presently increasing at the rate of approximately forty million per year, whereas the entire Christian population of good and bad is increasing only at the rate of about four million per year, so that even the entire Christian community is falling far behind the population increases of the earth generally. This would be even more extreme if applied merely to The Church of Jesus Christ of Latter-day Saints, as membership in the Church has increased only one million in the last seven years, which would be an average of something more than one hundred forty thousand a year.

In 1830 when the Church was organized, the population of the earth was one billion people, all but six of whom were non-members of the Church. Today we have nearly four billion people, so that we have living upon the earth nearly four times more non-members of the Church who should have the message of the gospel than we had the day the Church was organized. And though our rate is accelerating in total membership, many of these are not properly prepared for that great experience that our earth will have at the second coming of Christ.

Certainly none of us have yet lived the greatest days of our lives because they are yet ahead of us. And how important it is that we try to better prepare ourselves for those important events which may be at our very doors.

In one of His greatest statements, the Master said, "Only he that endureth to the end shall be saved." Sometimes we build up a great devotion in our souls by our labor, and then take upon ourselves some kind of partial retirement whereby we discontinue our whole-souled service. Tennyson has his character Ulysses give us a picture of this situation when he returned to his home state of Ithica. After his 20 years of absence on account of the Trojan War, because he was considered too old to continue his service as the king of the little Greek state of Ithica, he said, "how dull it is, to pause, to make an end, to rust unburnished, not to shine in use." But Ulysses was not a quitter, he was not tired, he was not lazy, and in contemplating other adventures, he said, "Tis not too late to seek a better world. My purpose holds to sail beyond the sunset and the baths of all the western stars until I die. It may be we shall touch the happy isles and see the great Aquilles whom we knew, though much is taken, much abides and while we have not now that strength which in old times moved earth and heaven, yet what we are we are and equal venture of heroic souls made weak by time and fate but strong by will to seek, to strive, to find, but not to yield."

And may God bless us with this spirit that we may continue to the end, to strive, to seek, to find, but not to yield, that we may never quit, that we may never give up; but that we may always go forward.

Chapter Twelve

The Contours Of Life

Many people during their lifetime have the need to work with some kind of contour maps. Field engineers draw lines showing elevations and depressions from which one can determine the general topography of the land, including the locations of the mountains, hills, and rivers. It also shows where the valleys and the swamplands are located.

We also make a kind of contour map for businesses, like a graph showing the ups and downs of the stock market over a long period. By this process we also show booms and depressions in our general economic affairs. But it is likely that the most profitable contour map that anyone could make would be one showing the ups and downs of one's own personal, spiritual, mental, moral, physical, and financial prosperity. By this process he may teach himself how to live his life in the highlands of success rather than in the swamplands of failure.

I know one mother who keeps a measuring board for each of her children. When they are born, she marks their height and weight upon this measuring board, and then each year on their birthday they are again measured and weighed and the results are marked down. While it is true that physical growth takes place at a fairly average rate for the age involved, yet that is not true of mental or moral or spiritual development. Sometimes the contour lines of our lives might show us as walking along the mountain top at one time and then, like the leading character in John Bunyan's book *Pilgrim's Progress,* we find ourselves deep in the slew of despondency and failure at some other time.

Through her teaching, this mother also had some other kinds of measuring boards, by which she taught her children not only to stand tall, but to think tall and smile tall and live tall.

An airplane always carries an altimeter to show the pilot when he is gaining or losing altitude, and one of the serious difficulties in life is that we sometimes don't know that we are heading downhill until we have a crackup. To aid us in making the contour maps of our own lives, the Lord of life has given us some excellent basic rules to go by. If one wants to enjoy his occupation, or his marriage, or his citizenship, or his church responsibilities, and make them as productive as possible, he must learn to do them well. This is a basic fundamental law that cannot be ignored, bypassed, or violated. The business of life is to succeed. God did not create us in his own image, and endow us with a set of his attributes and potentialities, and then expect us to waste our lives in failure. We should make our lives successful and happy every day. This itself furnishes us with our best guarantee that we will live on the mountain tops. No one ever gets tired or bored while he is winning, and no one ever quits while he is ahead. No one ever does well what he does not enjoy doing.

Shakespeare said,"...No profit comes where there is no pleasure taken." We don't live very effectively when we are bored with life, or hate our job, or live our religion spasmodically, or engage in continual quarreling and disagreements in our marriage. We ought to have some very definite ways of making each part of life pleasant and successful, and of increasing the number of those contour lines in our lives which indicate a high satisfaction that we get from things that we are doing. We should so run our contour lines as to show a continually increasing profit from our endeavors. When the contour line begins to drop, we had better know the reason and determine what should be done about it.

Aristotle once said that we never know a thing until we know it by its causes. Every success has a cause. Every failure has a cause. Indigestion has a cause. Overweight has a cause. If we know what causes overweight, we can eliminate the cause. If we know what causes happiness, we can reproduce it in our own program. Just suppose, for example, that we kept on the wall of our marriage living room the equivalent of a great thermometer ten feet tall indicating the satisfactions that came from our marriage. If the indicator was at 100° centigrade representing the full potential when the marriage began, and we see it drop steadily month by month, we had better start doing something about it long before it gets down into the frigid area.

The story is told of an airplane pilot who cracked up in the Arctic. He knew that beyond the hills nearby he would find food, warmth and safety. And so he started on foot in that direction, but before he had gone very far, he began feeling very tired and drowsy. He thought that if he were to lie down in the soft snow for a few minutes he could get enough rest and refreshment to enable him to reach the hills. But just as he was about to drop off to sleep, he was struck by the awful thought that he was in the last stages of freezing to death. This so startled him that he jumped to his feet and began running for the hills as though his life depended upon it, as indeed it did. His great fear would not let him rest and soon his heart was pounding and hot blood was churning through his veins and soon his life was out of danger, providing he kept going at sufficient speed in the right direction.

When the thermometer of our marriage starts to drop because we have allowed sluggishness and boredom and sin to get into our marriage, we had better start running for the hills as if our lives depended upon it, if we want to avoid an awful crackup.

We should also keep the barometer of our business success out of those zones that signal danger. One of the best ways to do this is to see that we always maintain some wise planning procedures supported by an effective industry and a real enthusiasm for what we are doing. There is a great line which says, "eternal vigilance is the price of survival." Many marriages and businesses and lives get out of control before we notice those contour lines that predict the danger ahead. And we can keep these lines of excellence and success from dropping by continually manifesting those great traits of courage, righteousness, planning, and hard work. Certainly everyone ought to give himself the thrill of seeing his own accomplishment.

I am very grateful that my business and my marriage and my religion have been a great and continual source of pride and delight to me. One of the things that, in my opinion, has been most helpful is that I have kept good records. These records have served me as a dependable stimulant to support my enthusiasm, and I have been greatly motivated by them. There is an old proverb that says, "Nothing succeeds like success." Certainly nothing motivates like success, and nothing rewards like success. There are few things that motivate a farmer like a good crop. Not very many things are as pleasant to a good teacher as appreciation from his students and the knowledge that they are doing well. Robert Louis Stevenson once said, "I know what pleasure is, for I have done good work." Every successful person should have the feeling that his work is productive and that his life itself is showing a profit.

When God was creating man in His own image, He put into his fundamental makeup a great motivating power. We refer to it as a competitive instinct, and we ought to spend a lot more time and energy than we do in developing its maximum power. Reed Smoot once gave us a great boost toward the mountain top of life when he said that an ambition to excel is indispensable to success. The enthusiastic competition and desire to win on the football field gives one the strength and power to do things that would be unthinkable if done under any other circumstances. Certainly when one joins the Church of Christ or is in the service of the Master, he ought to do his work better, and be a finer person than those engaged in less inspiring enterprises.

The picture of the little spray of roses painted by Whistler started him on his way. I had a similar business experience when in my second month with the New York Life, I won a contest and the motivation thus started has lasted throughout my lifetime. To build up this power, I have kept all of the annual agency reports of my company showing my work in comparison with all others. We frequently lose the benefit which our failures shame us into when we crumple up the reports of our poor work and throw them in the wastebasket so that they can be forgotten. When you keep the report, and know that you are going to have to live with it, a great motivation is developed to make the record one that will give you pleasure instead of embarrassment.

Everyone knows the pleasure and motivating power that comes when those in charge of our work pat us on the back and commend us for the excellence of our performance. But it is very risky to always depend on other people for the commendation that our souls need and hunger for. Sometimes those who could help us by a pat on the back are thoughtless or unobserving or out of town or too greatly engrossed in their own problems to give us the attention we need when we need it. It is a much safer and more profitable procedure to learn to give ourselves a pat on the back by the records that we ourselves make.

No one needs to remind a successful basketball player which team won the game, or how many points he personally contributed to the victory. The score makes the game. If the football score is six to seven and we are on the one yard line with one minute to play, everybody is excited and on his toes. If the score is fifty to nothing, some of the players may have lost interest and bored spectators have gone home. If we are poor competitors and fail to provide ourselves with a good set of statistics, we become bored with the game of life, with disastrous consequences. Certainly we must not waste the motivation that is available in our successes.

If you want to be a high jumper, laying a bamboo pole across two measured uprights and jumping over it is a much better success technique than to merely go out onto the field and jump up into the air without knowing your score, or whether or not you are getting better or worse, or whether you are performing as a champion or a third-rater. When someone writes a great poem, or paints a beautiful picture, or when his business indicates an increase, he ought to use the record of that excellence to stimulate his future success.

Once each year NYLIC gets its agency managers, field leaders, and executive officers together for a five-day educational convention and fellowshipping association, and a written detailed report of the year's accomplishments is kept. Here these men from all around the country get together in some central place and stimulate each other and increase their friendship for each other. This association also lays a solid basis for friendly rivalry during the coming year. Because everyone is playing on the same team, the success of each uplifts the others. And because these agency leaders have more than an ordinary amount of hero worship and competitive rivalry, they tend to greatly stimulate each other.

I have just turned through the report of the meeting held at the Waldorf Astoria Hotel on January 30, 31, and February 1, 2, and 3 of 1950. The general meetings were held on the beautiful Starlight Roof of the Waldorf. Those in charge of the meeting had added to the stars that continually twinkle in the roof of this great convention hall by suspending ten large ornamental plastic stars from the ceiling with numbers printed on them running in reverse order from ten to one. The first meeting of each of these annual conventions was given over to the acknowledgment of records and giving proper honor and credit to those who had made the best showing for the company in that year.

In the other departments of our lives such as our marriage and family association, we could do a great deal more in honoring outstanding accomplishment, in each other, than we do.

Sometimes we don't acknowledge excellence in education, church work, government leadership, and other things as we should. People are more inclined to criticizing and scandalizing and belittling than they are to extending praise and appreciation. As a consequence, they miss a powerful motivation because achievement is not recognized. There are a great many places where we should never be guilty of "withholding the applause."

The officer conducting this New York Life meeting would take various categories of agency accomplishment and read the figures of the ten men who ranked at the top of the list in that particular activity. He would first call the name of the man who ranked tenth and have him come from his place in the audience to stand under the star labeled number ten. No one in the hall knew in advance what the accomplishment figures were for anyone except himself, and, therefore, no one knew who the leaders would be. Everyone was excited at the thought of discovering who had made the outstanding records and won the top honors. These figures not only indicated the honors that a particular leader had won, but they also determined what his compensation would be for the coming year. And the whole program of acknowledgment, companionship, and honor, was designed to make everyone not only want to win but also work to the very limit of his ability. By this process people may get into other accomplishments the spirit of the game and the spirit of success that has done so much to make our great American athletic contests what they are.

While the tenth man was coming up, the orchestra would play some tune indicating his location. If he came from New York City, the orchestra might play, "The Sidewalks of New York;" or if from California, it might be "California Here I Come." Someone from the South might have "Dixie" as his theme song. Then as each man came up, they would play this song most appropriate to him, to make him feel the full joy of the honor. The men would be called beginning with number ten and going up the list until the one who made the top score would stand under star number one. Then the awards would be given, and they would go back to their seats and the process would be repeated in the second category of awards.

Over the years when I have been recognized, the theme song may have been "Utah Man," or "When It's Springtime in the Rockies," or some other significant tune. However, during this 1950 convention, I was called up eight times out of ten possibilities, and the music played by the orchestra to represent my theme song as I walked from my seat in the hall to the platform was "The Old Master Painter from the Far Away Hills." The lyrics of this song are as follows:

> The Old Master Painter from the Far Away Hills
> Painted the Vi'lets and the Daffodils.
> He put the purple in the twilight haze,
> Then did a rainbow for the stormy days.
>
> He dreamed up the murals on the blue summer skies,
> Painted the twinkle in my darling's eyes;

Captured the dreamer with a thousand thrills,
The Old Master Painter from the Far Away Hills.

Then came His masterpiece, and when He was through
He smiled down from heaven and He gave me you.
What a beautiful job on that wonderful day,
The Old Master Painter from the hills of far away.

And while those words may not be very appropriate, yet the motive was sincere and the intended honor was greatly appreciated. In my first trip to the front of the hall, I was asked to stand under star number four. In my second trip, I stood under star number one. As Vice-President Johnson announced my record, he said (as recorded in the official convention report on pages 18-25), "And again that master agency builder, Sterling Sill, carries off top honors." My third trip to the platform was to stand under star number three. My fourth trip was to stand under star number one, and Mr. Johnson said, "All of the top personal records on the Class of 1949 would have gone to New York City agency men if it had not been for that omnipotent gentleman from Utah, Sterling Sill. Anyway, I know Vice-President Don Parker and Inspector of Agencies, Joe Shirmer, are proud that four of the five leaders this year hailed from New York City."

After the awards were made, we returned to our seats, but in the fifth group, I was also asked to stand under star number one. Then we came to the awarding of the two principle trophies. One was given for recruiting salesmen, and the other was given for effectiveness in training.

L. Seton Lindsay Trophy:

Mr. Johnson said, "In 1944 on the occasion of the retirement of our former leader in the Agency Department, L. Seton Lindsay, and because of his great interest in Agency Building, the Lindsay Trophy was established, a beautiful sterling silver loving cup to be awarded annually for five years to the New York Life Manager making the most outstanding record in career recruiting. This is determined by selecting the manager who has the largest volume counting for recruiting credits.

"This trophy has been won by some Master Agency Builders who would have been leaders in this or any other company:

Frank W. Satter	in 1945
Chase Wickersham	in 1946

Luther Byrd   in 1947
Sterling Sill   in 1948

"And now for the final year, for 1949, the winner of the Lindsay Trophy is once again, the Old Master—

Sterling W. Sill, Manager of the
Intermountain Branch

"Sterling, will you please come up to the dias and I am going to ask Dudley Dowell, Vice President in charge of Agency affairs, to make the official presentation on behalf of the Company." I received the cup and returned to my seat.

Griffin M. Lovelace Trophy:

Then Mr. Johnson said, "In the same year that Mr. Lindsay retired, our former Vice President, Griffin M. Lovelace, also retired. Because of his interest in the field of education and training and his leadership in the movement to professionalize life underwriting and to increase the effectiveness of all agents, new and old, the Lovelace Trophy was established. This beautiful burnished metal plaque is awarded annually for five years to the New York Life Manager showing the greatest increase in Quality Production Credits over the previous year.

"This trophy, too, has been won by some great New York Life Agency men:

Chase Wickersham   in 1945
Bethel Walker and Dick Stewart   in 1946
Turner Munsell   in 1947
Vernon Van Leuven   in 1948

"But before I announce the winner for the fifth and final year, I would like to say that nothing like this has happened since Bobby Jones, the Atlanta Golfer, won the 'British Amateur,' the 'British Open,' and the 'American Amateur,' and the 'American Open' golf championships all in the same year. I am sure you have guessed it by now. The 1949 winner of the Lovelace Trophy is Sterling W. Sill, Manager of the Intermountain Branch. Sterling, if you will come forward once again, once again I will ask Vice-President Dowell to make the presentation."

Then in addition to these awards, each year the company gives out a number of beautifully prepared certificates which might be framed and hung in one's office, indicating the honor that he has been recognized for in the previous year. The first certificate went to Sterling W. Sill, the second went to Sterling W. Sill, the third certificate went to Sterling W. Sill, the fourth certificate went to Sterling W. Sill, and the fifth certificate went to Sterling W. Sill. These were all presented at one time with one trip. So during this award meeting, I made eight trips from my seat in the hall up to the platform and I received first place honors for ten events, fourth place once, and third place once, and each time, the orchestra played the tune, "The Old Master Painter from the Far Away Hills."

It may seem to some a little bit indelicate or immodest for anyone to mention any honors which he himself has received; and, of course, in keeping one's own score, it is not necessary that he mention this recognition to anyone else. But we are concerned here with that important success principle of motivating accomplishment. One great man once said: "If it be a sin to covet honor, I am the most offending soul alive." All history has been said to be autobiographical, and many great things have been lost by our generating of that false modesty which leads to failure, where we train ourselves to belittle excellence in our occupations which ought to be sacred to us. There are others who are ashamed of outstanding accomplishment even in such important things as the gospel of Jesus Christ itself, or our own comparative excellence in it.

The story is told of an industrious high school female student who got an "A" on her report card. One of her companions said to her, "It probably won't hurt you very much if you just don't let the news get spread around." When someone does well in his church work or in his life, we sometimes actually belittle his accomplishment. We call him a "goody-goody" or a "mama's boy." By these and other processes we tend to put people on the defensive against their own success.

And thus by shunning excellence in ourselves and depreciating it in others, we orient ourselves to lives of mediocrity. I believe it is a serious mistake to leave the high points out of the picture of any one's record of good and bad. There are some people who, under the guise of modesty, do themselves and the world great damage by trying to be average or ordinary. They usually make a record of only their mediocrity and failure and thus destroy the motivation that could have resulted otherwise. There are some people who follow the destructive course of remembering and emphasizing only their weaknesses, and so they fill their minds only with the mistakes that they have made.

One man kept referring to the D.F.T. file as being the largest file in his office. Someone asked him what those letters meant and he said this file was filled with a memorandum of the Damn Fool Things that he had done. But that is not a good success procedure. Certainly one would be very foolish to fail to capitalize on the great experiences in his life. The honors that he receives give him confidence in his ability. They also make other accomplishments easier and help to establish a higher standard for other people. At one time, no one could swim the English Channel. Then one day Captain Webb did it, then Gertrude Ederle did it; and since people have known it could be done, dozens of other people have done it.

I am very grateful for the inspiring business meetings that I have attended over many years put on by my employer company in attempting to build up the power of those who have the company's destiny in their hands. These meetings served not only to encourage industry, loyalty, and greater accomplishment, but also to recognize deserved honors and to give pleasant pats on the back to those who have earned them. At these meetings, the company also tries to give its employees the highest kind of occupational instruction and extends to each one the personal friendship of all of the others playing on this great cooperative team.

My first New York Life Convention was also my honeymoon. I have attended an average of more than two company conventions each year for over forty years. In addition, I have usually attended the meetings of agents as well as the meeting of the managers and general officers of the company, with a few special conventions thrown in. From each one I have come away with some substantial values for myself and a greater ability to serve my company's interest.

The New York Life is the tenth corporation in size in the world from the point of view of assets. With the vigorous competition of our present business world, to get that near the top, a company itself must have great leadership, morale, and teamwork. Both Calvin Coolidge and Herbert Hoover have served as members of the Board of Directors of the New York Life Insurance Company, with other great national corporation leaders serving on the Board and as officers of the company. The meetings are held at attractive convention places and are very educational, motivational, recreational and colorful. There has usually been a vigorous singing of the Star Spangled Banner, the Pledge of Allegiance to the Flag, and company songs which serve the company's interest in about the same way that patriotic songs serve the national purpose. The various territorial subdivisions of the company have had beautiful, colorful flags on long graceful poles ornamenting the convention hall. And there has been a parade of the flags carried by their particular winner for that year.

Many other things have been done to quicken the spirit and enliven the interest that those present take in the meeting. This meeting is a time of great fellowship and sincere good will developed among all present from the Chairman of the Board down, so that the convention is more or less like an old college class reunion where spirit, ambition, and love of each other flourish throughout a week of rest, education, and recreation.

Here is a chance each year for the key men of a great corporation and the newest company manager to eat together, go swimming together, play golf together, enjoy entertainment together, enjoy a colorful formal dinner, a formal dance, and do many other interesting things in some key American city.

I have treasured these convention experiences and find in them some of the important contour lines of my life.

Chapter Thirteen

Meetings and Publications

It has been my privilege to have been on the program of a great many national managers' and agents' sales meetings during the years that I have been with the New York Life. This has been very pleasant and of great benefit to me in many ways. I mention it here with the hope that those who read this may profit from the ideas presented. Those things mentioned in this chapter have given me a feeling of belonging and responsibility. This participation has also helped me to be more effective personally by inducing me to prepare, as there are few things that stimulate someone as much as being put on the program. It is a very old principle that the teacher always learns more than the student.

The New York Life Insurance Company is probably one of the greatest sales organizations in the world. It is the tenth corporation on this earth in actual volume of assets. One of the companies outranking the New York Life Insurance Company in assets is an oil company, one is a telephone company, three are banks, one is General Motors, and three are life insurance companies. These three life insurance companies between them last year had 928 million-dollar producers (Equitable, 388; Prudential, 277; and Metropolitan, 263), whereas the New York Life by itself had 1,080 million-dollar producers. To feel that one is an important part of such a big-time championship team has many advantages. We are helped to be big by thinking big and feeling big, and being in the presence of big people. In preparing to teach somebody else, we increase our own abilities.

At the 1938 meeting held in St. Petersburg, Florida, I was asked to be on the program. After the meeting, Thomas A. Buckner, long time company president and Chairman of the Board, wrote an article in the NYLIC Review of February 1939 in which he said in part:

"The prepared addresses by members of the conference were unusually forceful and convincing. These addresses marked in my opinion a higher standard of instructive and informative ideas and plans for the agent in the field as well as for the agency men than I had hitherto heard. This was particularly true of Agency Directors Boyer, Derryberry, Driggs and Sill."

It is, of course, a very stimulating experience for a very young man to be complimented in public and in writing by the chief officer of his company. There are very few things as motivating as the consciousness of a high skill which an individual may possess. Mark Twain once said that he could live for two weeks on a compliment. Back in those days, a compliment from Thomas A. Buckner always lasted me for a much longer period.

The following year I was again asked to be on the program, and after I returned home, I received 58 letters asking for copies of the material which I presented. Several of these letters were from Inspectors of Agencies who reproduced my material and sent it to those managers under their direction. At that time, there were 142 offices in the company, which means that I had letters from forty-one percent of all of the offices in the company personally, in addition to those where the Inspector of Agencies represented a number of offices. Some excerpts from some of those letters are as follows:

Fred Munsell, in charge of the Atlantic Division headquarters in Philadelphia wrote:

January 20, 1940

My Dear Mr. Sill:

If you have a copy of the chart you used on the blackboard at the Agency Directors' Meeting, I will be very glad indeed if you will send me one or if you have them multigraphed in quantity, I would like enough to send to each Agency Manager in my Department—say about fifteen.

I liked the way you set that up and presented it.

Again let me congratulate you on your deserved promotion.

Sincerely yours,
/signed/ F. S. Munsell
Inspector of Agencies

Inspector of Agencies Dudley Bates from San Francisco wrote:

January 29, 1940

Dear Sterling:

Thank you very much for your letter of January 24, and I have received under separate cover the most interesting and constructive NYLIC charts that you so well explained at the convention. If you have no objection, I would like to keep these charts to use at our spring meetings beginning the first week in April, but if you would like them returned before then, please don't hesitate to let me know.

The points you so well made were so pertinent. Thanks for allowing me to borrow your constructive ideas.

Very truly yours,
/signed/ Dudley S. Bates
Inspector of Agencies

Walter T. Buckner, Manager of the Memphis Office wrote:

January 16, 1940

Dear Sterling:

I wonder if you have a copy available of that splendid chart on which you made your talk at the Meeting. This plan of yours certainly sells the NYLIC contract in a big way, and is different from any I had seen before. I don't want you to go to a lot of trouble, but thought possibly you already had a copy available that you could send.

There was also mention made that you were going to list the main things you had in your agency book. If you have already made this list, I would like to have a copy of it. Or, if you plan to make it in the future, put me on the list to receive a copy.

Always enjoy hearing from you at the Meetings as you always give us some constructive ideas.

Hope your business this year is starting off in a big way.

Cordially yours,
/signed/ W. T. Buckner
Agency Director

In the many years that followed, as well as those that had gone before, I was permitted to have a prominent part in many of the company's national meetings for the executive officers and the field management of the company. Without exception, these were very profitable and very stimulating experiences to me. Of course, a talk goes over much better if it is backed up by a personal record of high accomplishment, and so each year I worked harder during the year that I might speak with greater authority and confidence when meeting time arrived. And to have this recognition and participation is a good way to build up one's ability as well as his devotion to his company.

I have been honored far more than is my due in being asked to participate on so many of the company's educational programs. At the meeting held in the Palm Beach Biltmore Hotel, January 26 to January 30, 1960, in Palm Beach, Florida, I was given the following introduction by Raymond C. Johnson, Executive Vice-President, who for a number of years had the assignment of conducting the Manager's meeting. He said on that occasion,

"Our next speaker is Sterling W. Sill, Inspector of Agencies at our Utah General Office. On Tuesday afternoon you heard Sterling recognized in our Hall of Fame ceremonies for his many outstanding achievements in agency building. This happens just about every year, as you well know. His Utah office paid for $40,102,000 worth of business in 1959, more than any other office in the entire company has ever paid for in company history. You may not know that Sterling's office paid for almost $9,000,000 of business in the month of December alone. I believe that this is the largest amount any NYLIC General Office has ever paid for in a single month.

"Sterling also has another unusual record. He has remained in the same office for twenty-seven years. In order to do that, you have got to live right. When he took it over back in 1933, as I well remember the day, the office paid for less than two and a half million. From two and a half million to forty million is what I call growth with a capital 'G'."

In introducing me at another agency meeting just prior to my retirement, Paul A. Norton, C.L.U., Senior Vice President in charge of marketing said: "Sterling is the greatest agency man I have ever known. He is one of the greatest individuals I have ever known. He has created an image for our company and for the insurance industry that has contributed greatly to the success of both. As an agency man I have tried to emulate Sterling, as have others. I know no one in our business with greater ability or finer character or who has worked harder. We are all the better for having known him."

And what a thrilling experience life offers each one of us as we take hold of our share of the work of the world and minister to the needs of our fellow men that we may learn to do it with excellence and honor, that we may build these contour lines of our lives to put ourselves in the purer air that goes with honorable labor and effective accomplishment.

These managers' meetings have also served several other useful purposes in my life:

1. They have given me a much more intimate contact with some of the finest men in the insurance business and some of the finest people in the world, from whom I have learned a great deal. That is, five days out of each year have been spent by me in the environment of this managers' meeting under the most pleasant and productive circumstances. Some people, both in the home office and in the field, have specialized knowledge which can best be received in person rather than by written communication. That is, if one wrote a letter to the home office asking for some information, he might get back two or three paragraphs in the letter; but if you sit down personally with this man and have an interview for a half hour, you get not only the desired information, but you get the person and his background and his enthusiasm and his faith as well. You may talk with somebody from the field and get a point of view that would not be appropriate in the letter.

2. These company leadership meetings are as though one is immersed in the great spirit that cannot be had from just one or two other people.

3. Some lifetime friendships are made which become like growing plants and continue to stimulate you even after the person himself has long since passed away.

4. These convention meetings also give a change of scenery, a change of spirit that has a great purpose. Many people go on vacations by putting on their casual clothes and go around sightseeing in the company of their family or one or two friends. However, in a business such as those just referred to, one meets with several hundred of his friends, not in casual cothing out in the hills, but he frequently dresses up in formal clothing with the atmosphere that goes with it. And instead of loafing, he is doing useful work and receiving a great personal benefit from it.

5. The proceedings of these meetings are always recorded so that the spirit and information given may be preserved long after the people themselves are no longer present. And it is a great thrill to me now to go back over the talks given by myself and others at these meetings over this long period of my life.

There is another item that is very closely connected with this function of participating at these educational and motivational meetings. In the insurance business, like most other businesses, there are a great number of magazines published by the company and by other organizations to supply salesmen with information, ideas, procedures, etc. And if one is outstanding in his work, he will be solicited by various sources for articles to be put in the magazine, because if a magazine can get some good material, it will increase the magazine's prosperity. But if someone is not regularly asked to write an article for a magazine, that may be because someone thinks that he hasn't anything worthwhile to contribute, and that should therefore be a suggestion to him to do something about it. That is, he ought to change his success ingredients to a point where the magazines would want him to say something to their subscribers through their columns.

But before his ideas are marketable, they must be well thought out and well said. In our regular speech we usually don't select and arrange our words as carefully as we would if we knew they were going to be read by a lot of people. On one occasion, Regional Vice-President Dudley S. Bates came to visit me in Salt Lake. In the course of our discussion, I made an explanation of some things with which he was impressed, and he asked me if I would write the discussion out and send it to him. I readily agreed as this was material I had given on many occasions and with which I had an almost word-for-word familiarity. I thought it would merely be a matter of saying into the dictaphone what I had said to him.

When the material was typed from the dictaphone, I almost let it go to him without reading it, but I thought that maybe I had better check it for possible misunderstandings, or typographical errors. When I read it, to my horror I found it had a lot of very noticeable grammatical and other kinds of mistakes. The wording in many cases was not very good. I had become so used to it that it seemed perfect to me, except when I had to read it back and see it as somebody else would see it. I had to go over it several times correcting it, which made me a lot more cautious about the fact that it doesn't always sound to someone else as it does to the one who is giving it verbally.

Someone has made the stimulating observation that an idea always sounds a lot better as it comes out of your mouth than it does while going into somebody else's ears.

In the thirty-four years that I had been engaged in management training, I had written a weekly sales bulletin for most of that time. I am sorry to say that all of these have not been preserved by me, but a great many of them have. I am also sorry to say that I have not kept all of my published magazine articles, but some few of them are as follows:

Article	Published In	Date
How to Develop Your Ideas	Managers Magazine	July-August 1944
How Do You Rate	Managers Magazine	Jan.-Feb. 1944
Pigeons and Personal Planning	NYLIC Review	December 1946
Sell Yourself to Yourself	NYLIC Review	August 1946
How to Get an Idea	NYLIC Review	July 1947
Sell Yourself	Best Life Edition	September 1, 1948
Learning From Others	NYLIC Review	December 1948
Make Your Presentation Live	Managers Magazine	January 1950
The Recruiting Interview	Managers Magazine	January 1950
Imperturbability	NYLIC Review	December 1950
Give Way to the Illusion	NYLIC Review	December 1951
In Quest of Gospel Scholarship	Instructor	December 1953
Front Cover	Utah Alumnus	May 1953
Your Gallery of Art	Instructor	June 1953
Free Agency—A Challenge	Instructor	February 1953
Lead with Conviction That Ye Might Bring Souls Unto Me	Primary General Conference	April 1955

A great many other articles have not been published. In addition to the magazine articles, the company published in booklet form a part of a talk which I once gave at a manager's meeting entitled, "Selecting Your Life's Work," which as of this date in 1979, has circulated in excess of a million copies, and the number printed each year is still increasing. This, of course, is in addition to 25 published books, two weekly radio broadcasts per week for seventeen years or over 850 weeks, plus other talks which would probably average better than ten per week. The resulting study that must be done in these circumstances should help to keep one a little more on his toes than might ordinarily be the case.

One never knows who will be influenced by what he writes. A letter received as this autobiography was in preparation reminded me of the unseen good that one's books and writing can accomplish. Written from Salt Lake City on March 9, 1979, it said:

Dear Elder Sill:

I cannot let another day go by without telling you what a great influence for good you have had in my life.

I'm a convert of 38 years to the Church. During these growing and stretching years, your books and sermons have had a profound effect for good upon me and subsequently my family.

As the wife of a 30-year Retired Army Colonel, I have had countless opportunities to see and hear how you have influenced others throughout the world. A case in point took place in Germany in 1974. As advisor to the CINC, USAREUR for family affairs, I addressed many areas of the military community.

On this particular Sunday I listened to a chaplain (colonel) address his congregation at a military chapel. The content of his sermon was excellent and had a very "familiar sound." Later, upon congratulating him, I said as much.

Taking me into his study, carefully closing the door, he confided that for the past 20 years, the bulk of his sermon material had come from the books of one man. As he reached into his shelves to show me, he said with emotion, "I consider this man to be the greatest minister the world has produced in the past quarter of a century."

The man, the author of all those moving sermons? *Elder Sterling W. Sill.*

You will never know the countless lives you have touched and buoyed—the lives that have changed in a positive way because of your spiritual insight, your wit and wisdom that can be assimilated—digested and put to practical use by both young and old.

May God bless you always as you always bless others.

Affectionately,

Lucile Johnson

To date I have copies of twenty-eight talks published by the Brigham Young University under the title *Speeches of the Year.* In the years between 1948 and the present, I have had thirty articles published in the Improvement Era. Thirty-three articles have been published in the Instructor and other Church magazines from 1953 to the present. There have been 152 articles that have appeared in the Church News from 1963 to 1966, and many others since that time. I am very grateful for this privilege as it has stimulated many to think about these important ideas.

Chapter Fourteen

My Literary Life

My literary life has been a very broad, expansive, and pleasant one when compared with what might have been predicted by the activity of my early years. My literary experiences have also been extended in many directions and have taken me to points far beyond the places to which I have gone in my own actual personal life.

In the experiences gained through books one may march with Napoleon or philosophize with Socrates. He may go to the Mount of Transfiguration with Peter, James, and John and see Jesus transfigured as he appeared in shining garments in his deliberations with Moses and Elias. Through the great literature one may suffer with the apostle Paul during that long cold winter spent in the uncomfortable cell of his Roman dungeon, or he may visit the hundreds of miniature worlds acted out by the characters of Shakespeare as they teach their various lessons upon the stage created by one of our world's greatest literary masters.

Through those books that I have chosen to be my companions, through those long pleasant hours of reading on airplanes, while waiting in airports, and during the evenings spent by my own fireside, I have been able to take an intimate part in the affairs and activities of many of the most noble people who have lived upon the earth in all ages of time and place them in contrast for my own comparison and appraisal with some of those whose lives have been engrossed in lethargy and sin, as a consequence of which they have become most miserable and profitless. The many vicarious lives that I have lived through great literature have held for me an intense fascination. Their wide variety and contrasting intensity have given me an appreciation and sympathy which has added greatly to the breadth and pleasure of my own existence.

Someone has said that the greatest gift that God has ever given to man is an imagination. In the imagination we can go backward or forward through time or space with greater facility than we could get out of our easy chair. In a very personal way the imagination helps us to enter the personal domain of the most interesting and productive men and women, and enjoy a communication and friendship which was rarely experienced by even their closest friends in their own day. In fact, in our imagination we can actually replace them while we act in their stead, enjoy their love of life, and feel the joy of their attitudes and the honor of their accomplishments. Edgar Allen Poe said, "Literature is the noblest of the professions."

The word literature itself can make a satisfying and inspiring atmosphere to everyone of its devotees. The dictionary says that this word literary pertains to learning, or letters, or literature, and applies especially as the pleasure of that learning may be transmitted to us by books, writing, or the work or ideas of learned men. One may be occupied with literature as a profession, or as an educational process, or as the highest kind of enjoyment, or as a means of acquiring those vicarious experiences that will be the most helpful to him in carrying forward his work, building up his personal accomplishments, or building up those satisfactions that he desires most.

I do not fully understand the beginnings of my absorbing interest in literary things. I think the seeds of my interest must have been carried over from an antemortal life. From my earliest recollections I remember, as I suppose every child does, the interesting fairy tales, the myths, and the stories with their constructive morals that so much fascinated me during my youth. A little later in my life I taught reading for two years in the seventh and eighth grades. The texts that were used in all of the upper grades at that time were books called *Studies in Reading* compiled by J. W. Searson, a Professor of the English Language of the University of Nebraska, and George E. Martin, President of the State Teachers College of Kearney, Nebraska. These books were made up of some of the greatest poems and the greatest short stories ever written by the greatest authors. When I left this teaching assignment, I obtained a set of four of these books and have kept them with me ever since. Though these were published for the use of children in the fifth, sixth, seventh, and eighth grades of grammar school, yet in my opinion they are adequate for the wisest men and women. And while literary interest and activity has lain partially dormant for many years at a stretch, I am grateful that the germ of interest continued to remain alive to serve me when it was called back into activity. I have memorized a great deal of the material therein presented, and the personal compensation has been tremendous.

As a freshman in high school, I also took a class from my beloved high school principal, Leo J. Muir, where we read many interesting things from the great literature. The literary accounts of the lives of the people involved were fascinating experiences to me; the great emotions of these plays I shared with the principals themselves. It was, of course, not uncommon for people to weep, or despair, or exhalt, or become, as they enjoyed a community of interest with those they read about. The interest of these vicarious events was heightened in my heart by the love I had for Leo J. Muir, who is one of the great idols of my life. We closed our mortal association when I was one of the speakers at his funeral.

I have often thought of the Bible class which at one time was taught by the dramatic actor, Charles Laughton, wherein he merely read the Bible for an hour each week and charged the people $3.50 who listened to him. Someone asked one of these students why he would pay $3.50 to hear Charles Laughton read the Bible when he could read it himself for nothing. The reply was that when he listened to Charles Laughton read the Bible, he not only got the Bible, but he also got Charles Laughton. And to have *Enoch Arden* read by Leo J. Muir, I not only got Alfred Lord Tennyson and the life's experiences of his great characters, but I also received a full thrust from the personal power and spirit of Leo J. Muir. I think it would be a great experience to me even to hear Leo J. Muir read the dictionary or the telephone directory or any other thing which would expose me to the radiations of his scintillating and provocative personality.

The four books edited by Searson and Martin containing some of the greatest poems, the finest statements of loyalty, the great examples of faith that are known in the world, have also made a tremendous impact on my total life in all of its departments, including the deep broad grooves that have been made through my mind. The encouragement I received from Adam S. Bennion for me to adventure into a systematic study of the great classic literature has been recounted elsewhere. And I have in my notebooks the potent passages and interesting phrases copied from 987 of the world's great books, which is the literary concentrate of some of the world's greatest men.

Of course, towering above all of these books and writings in their influence upon my life are the Holy Scriptures. It has always been an inspiring thing to me that I may read the word of the Lord Himself, as recorded by his holy prophets, and run through my mind the very ideas which have been produced by the all-important agencies of the divine.

I have often wondered about what the result would have been upon me if I had had more formal academic exposure to the great literature from professional teachers. But I have tried to console myself that at least to some extent all learning is self-learning, that learning comes more from within than from without. Someone once asked these questions: Which political science department has an Abraham Lincoln to its credit?" The University of Pennsylvania never produced a graduate equal to Benjamin Franklin who, without great academic learning, was instrumental in establishing the University of Pennsylvania. Who taught Brigham Young to be a colonizer? Or how did Abraham become the father of the faithful? Or how did Joseph Smith become the first prophet of the greatest and final dispensation?

I am sure that most of my limitations were manufactured on the inside of myself and did not come from any outside influence or lack of it. Our great virtues and abilities are also born within ourselves. Certainly we learn to do by doing; we learn to read by reading; we learn to write by writing; we learn to appreciate by appreciating; we learn to worship by worshipping. And when we put all of these together, we greatly compound our advantages.

For most of the years of my life my job has been to try to help some life insurance men increase their ability to make sales. I have attended a great many sales classes where, when something has been said which was thought by those who listened to have value, the request has frequently come, "Could we have a copy of that?" In trying to teach salesmanship, or any other thing, I've found that the idea can be gotten over a lot more readily if it is given with the assistance of an enthusiastic personality, and then if a written copy is available to help the student with the recollection to make alterations in his own presentation and to assist him to reinforce those ideas in himself by his own practice and drill.

Tennyson once said, "I am a part of all that I have met." He said, "I can no more remember the books I have read than the meals I have eaten, yet each is a part of all that I am." And certainly everything that we read, or think, or do, becomes a part of us and we become a part of it.

Previous to my entry into the insurance business, I attended three lectures given by one of those men who go around the country selling ideas of self-improvement. This man's name was W.K. Brausch. I was very impressed with what he said, and after the meeting I bought three little books in which he had written the ideas that he had given us orally.

Later, when I went into agency work, as a part of our training we used to have a Monday morning sales meeting at which I attempted, through my own efforts and the performance of those that I selected, to do for the agents attending what W. K. Brausch did for me. To supplement the oral presentations, I began writing down ideas and sending them out so that the salesmen who heard them could remember them and have the other advantages of having them recorded in writing.

I tried to persuade these agents that if they would take at least one good sales idea each week and thoroughly master it by memorization and practice, it would not be very long before their skills would be greatly increased and available to help them to push themselves a little higher up the ladder of accomplishment. That is, sales knowledge must be available not only in his sales brain, but sales skills must also be available in his sales muscles. There are a lot of people who know how to play basketball in their brains who would make a horrible display of themselves on the floor because they did not have the skills in their muscles. A skillful basketball player can make baskets almost automatically with very little help coming from his conscious mind. This is also true of a good salesman.

For some twenty-five years or more I sent out a weekly sales bulletin. If it did not do anything else, it was a great benefit to me, because I had to develop the habit of getting ideas and then organizing them into a presentable form which could be profitably used by someone else. If it was good enough to help somebody else, the learner, it would help me, the salesman. Certainly the best way to learn is to teach. It has been demonstrated many times that if you take two salesmen of equal ability, they might be selling life insurance or appliances or whatever, but if you sell one the business and give him the responsibility of developing the ideas, attitudes, and skills of those under his direction and generating the industry of excellence in them for making more sales, it will not be long before the one in charge may be making sales doubling those of his former companion. If anyone can develop enough quality and enthusiasm in his ideas to lift someone else up, he cannot help but raise himself higher.

I have had some very interesting experiences through these sales bulletins. When I became Inspector of Agencies in 1940, in addition to sending these sales bulletins to my own agents, I also put the managers of the offices under my direction on my mailing list. The bulletins usually were reproduced by them for the agents in their office. Then one of my assistant managers attended a training school at the home office and took some of these sales bulletins back with him, which he showed to his roommate. The roommate asked if he could have his name put on the mailing list, which was done. In turn he showed them to his manager, who wrote me a letter asking if he also could be put on the mailing list. Then some other Inspectors of Agencies and later Regional Vice-Presidents became involved, and some of them were republishing these bulletins and sending them out to the members of their departments or divisions. Because of this, my mailing list increased in quantity by leaps and bounds.

Then, at a manager's meeting in San Antonio, Texas, Romney Campbell had a meeting of the managers of the eastern division. He discussed these bulletins in his meeting and suggested to each of his managers that they get me to put them on my mailing list. This was the straw that broke the camel's back, as my postage bill was already costing me a great deal, and I was using up a year's paper supply and then some every month. And so I discontinued sending them to everyone except our own agents and the managers under my direction.

I have had a number of other interesting experiences in this reading and writing combination. Early in my career as a General Authority, the Church asked me to write a series of articles on leadership to go in *The Improvement Era*. After they had been running for a number of months, Marvin Wallin, the manager of Bookcraft, put them in a book which he published entitled *Leadership*. The royalties from this book were given to President McKay to help provide some funds to send out special missionaries. Many thousands of copies of this book have been printed. Two years later, Marvin Wallin published another set of these articles entitled *Leadership No. 2.*

My writing and speaking experiences have caused me to make an interesting discovery. There are enough ideas that go over or through one's head every day to fill a book, but because one has no immediate use for them they vanish and are forgotten before they are actually born. But when you have need for them, you run up a kind of mental antenna so that the ideas come down into the machinery where they can be utilized. After many years of writing and speaking, I have a literary reserve of usable ideas a hundred times greater now than I did when I began.

I have at least as many additional talks in preparation as the total of those I have already given. The fact that most of these will never be given is unimportant. The important thing is that this study process may do something for the expansion and development of my mind and spirit. Many of these idea discussions already have a title, and the key ideas have already been recorded on paper. They're just waiting until I have time to develop and organize them.

At the end of a long, useful, and productive literary life, Victor Hugo said about his own production in history, verse, story, satire, ode, and song, "I have tried them all, and yet I feel I have not said a thousandth part of what is in me." He said, "When I go down into my grave I can say like many others, 'I have finished my day's work,' but I cannot say, 'I have finished my life.' My day's work will begin again on the next morning. Death is not a blind alley, it is a thoroughfare. It closes upon the twilight, it opens upon the dawn." And so it seems to me that while a considerable volume of ideas has come into me from the outside and an equal amount has gone out of me from the inside, yet in each case it represents only a small part of the possibility.

My radio talks were published in a little purple booklet sent out to those requesting it, and a mailing list of several thousand had been built up. At the end of each year the fifty-two talks were published in a book for that year, which has been an interesting challenge to me from several points of view.

Some time ago, I read in a minister's handbook that their rule of thumb for preparation was an hour per minute. That is, you spend an hour of preparation for every minute of presentation. If you are going to speak for sixteen minutes, you spend sixteen hours in preparation. I did not do that on the first one or the second one or the third one. Anybody could talk about his business, or his family, or his religion for fifteen minutes without making any preparation. But if you were going to speak interestingly and constructively on any one of these subjects to the same people for a thousand times, then you had better spend a little more time in preparation.

I have received thousands of letters from people all over the country who have talked about their conversions and their interests which has prompted them to seek more information and make greater investigation of the gospel subjects discussed in this radio program. I have had a rather extended correspondence with a number of ministers of other churches which has been very pleasant to me. And I have also had some great satisfactions out of this material which has been written down.

Before one can effectively write something down, he must get it organized, get his convictions in definite order and then so arrange his material that it will be interesting to other people and also exciting to himself. Writing also enables one to get his mental

power a little more formalized as a permanent and usable possession. If I have any mental, spiritual, or physical posterity who
may be interested, I would like to make all of my written and unwrit-
ten volumes a part of my biography.

We speak and think and write out of our own experience, and
everything we say or write is colored by the interests and activities
of our own philosophy.

Above everything else in the world, I am grateful for my life.
And I am also grateful for the lives of those other people who have
combined in me to make up my literary life. They are also responsible for the many vicarious lives that I have personally lived. I wish
that all of my lives were much better than they are, but I am humbly
grateful that they are not any less.

God is the giver of life, but we may acquire and give out some
of the ideas, the inspiration, and the motivation of which the whole
is made up. One important aspect of the most abundant life pertains
to that part of learning which is transmitted by books and the writing of our learned men. I am very grateful that God has permitted
me to appropriate unto myself so much from the lives and inspiration of others.

Chapter Fifteen

My Books of Letters

We sometimes have ordinary things that develop great value so far as we are concerned. One of these is a book, and one of the most valuable sections of my collection of books is my books of letters. These contain a written record of many of the events, the accomplishments, and the commendations of my life.

The most valuable thing in the world is life, and life is made up of individual attitudes, experiences, enthusiasms, and memories. It has been indicated many times that everyone ought to keep a biography. There should be a record on paper of the important events making up every human life.

Frequently we make a biography much as we do a financial budget. Many people make up a financial budget at the end of each month by making a list of where their money went. However, it has been found a lot more profitable to make a planned budget at the beginning of the month telling the money where to go. And so with a biography. Some people wait until the end of their lives comes into view and then write the history of where their life went. These are usually ancient and lifeless facts reconstructed out of a dead past. Other people keep a record of their life as it proceeds, while they can still tell their lives where to go and what should be accomplished along the way.

I was successful in keeping a brief written biographical account of my activities for a part of the time that I was on my mission. But life sometimes becomes a little humdrum and I soon discovered that every written page was just about the same as every other written page, with not much excitement pulsating beneath the lines. I discovered that even about exciting things dead statements of fact alone were not very interesting. If there are 365 days in a year and one is going to keep a diary for 50 years, then his diary would have the account of what happened during 18,250 individual days. However, for all practical purposes such a diary is likely to give a record of one day that has been repeated 18,250 times.

Many years ago, I discovered by accident what to me was a much better way to keep a diary, and that is to let other people write it for you. Their letters not only supply the necessary information, but they also provide a great deal of motivation which helps to bring to pass many of the desired accomplishments. We also know of the heart hungers. We frequently desire the loving sentiments that come to us from our friends which may not be present in our own writing. The value of the discovery of the written statements of our friends has also been made by other people. But, like me, they have not always taken full advantage of this valuable find. Someone has pointed out that very frequently we are being educated the most when we are not aware that we are being educated at all. Sometimes the moment of our greatest experience is like the moment of birth. That is, the moment of birth is an unconscious moment. We don't know that we are being born when that event is actually taking place. And we usually do not discover that we have been born until quite a long time afterwards. Sometimes we actually never do find out that we have been born. Someone said of an acquaintance, "he doesn't know that he is alive." Sometimes that is very near the fact. And so it is with our other great events. Before the importance of our great events dawn upon us, memories of them may slip away and become lost because the moment of impact skated too lightly through our consciousness.

Sometimes we need a little more perspective to know the real worth of what our lives may mean. As Henry Thoreau once said, "We must wait 'til evening to know how pleasant the day has been." We frequently also need some third party influence about the importance of the experiences that make up our lives.

While I was on my mission, I developed a vastly increased enthusiasm for the gospel. And I also developed a great love for my mission president, Charles A. Callis. I developed a kind of attitude toward him resembling hero worship. This feeling has served me very advantageously in many ways during my later years when my greatest understanding and gratitude came into being. My great admiration for Charles A. Callis gave him a more powerful influence for good over the balance of my life. Because I served for some eleven months as conference president, I received many personal letters from President Callis filled with instruction, commendation, and expressions of confidence and love. In between letters he paid several visits to me in Alabama in his attempt to train and motivate me and the other missionaries. He and I used to go for long walks during these visits and he used to preach the gospel of advice and theology and friendship to me with great power on his part and with great pleasure to me. His written messages have preserved for me in tangible form some essense of his great spirit which I loved and was always uplifted by.

After President Callis passed away, I discovered that his letters to me acquired an additional value they previously had not had. His message and signature became to me a kind of living presence, which continued to uplift my life in a very substantial way. But my attitudes of appreciation and hero worship have proven to be contagious and have also given my later heroes a kind of immortality of which I am the beneficiary. I therefore began saving all of my most important letters instead of merely those of my mission president, so that over the years I have actually accumulated letters from many of the great people who have touched my life. Their personalities have, through their letters, become stimulating and motivating influences, each of which delivers to me a blessing on every occasion of contact. It is very inspiring for me to estimate how much I have been built up by these letters in my business success, love of life, appreciation of my friends, and faith in the Gospel. These letters saved numbered only a few at first, but as time went on the volume of the stream, both incoming and outgoing, has been increased.

Then in 1975 I heard President Kimball say that everyone ought to write his autobiography, and he said particularly that he wanted every General Authority to write his autobiography. And because I like to do what the President of the Church suggests, I got started the next day.

But large sections of my experience had become a little bit dim and indistinct in my memory. Then I thought of these many files of letters which had been stored away and almost forgotten. And so I uncovered and went through them, and they were so full of my interest and so stimulating in their influence that I took them to the printing shop and had them bound in bright red binding in 32 great volumes so filled with my life that I imagined I felt about as much elation over them as must have animated the discoverer of the Dead Sea Scrolls, especially if the Dead Sea Scrolls had all been written about him. Therefore, I now have these 32 volumes of my biography "and the end is not in sight." These motivating excerpts of my life have been written by my friends, my associates, my Church leaders, and others who have had a part in the formation of my life's history, and have had a firsthand observation of its results.

I have attended many business conventions at the end of which I have received a number of letters in comment which make up a far better record of the convention and my part in it than I myself would have or could have made. I have also kept every one of the company agency reports for the 35 years of my agency activities. And so I find that I have a diary of my life written by others, plus the many bulletins and personal communications sent to me by company officers, church leaders, associates and friends. These are all very informative and interesting, and in addition they are as fresh as yesterday.

I have letters from every president of my company from Thomas A. Buckner to Dudley Dowell. I have letters from every president of the Church from Heber J. Grant to Spencer W. Kimball, including 38 from David O. McKay.

Many of the writers of these letters have now passed beyond. To read their letters now is like a message from another world and each time I read them they re-arouse the great feelings of love and emotion that I previously felt for these great men and women who were my heroes and my friends.

The tragedy of my books of letters is that I did not get started soon enough in this saving process. My mother wrote me regularly all the time I was on my mission, but only one letter from her has survived. Most of my brothers and sisters are not represented in my treasury by any letters, and I have no written communication of any kind from my father.

As my wife and I approach our fiftieth wedding anniversary, she has communicated to me the fact that she had saved all my love letters during our courting period and I finally prevailed upon her to let me read them. And while they may not rank very high as literary masterpieces, to me they are very inspiring, for they have rebuilt anew some very pleasant emotions, attitudes, and passions that I felt while writing them. However, I am filled with severe regret that I did not keep hers. This does not reveal any lack of interest on my part. Rather, it is a combination of pure thoughtlessness with a serious admixture of stupidity.

When I come to the end of my life, I think I will have some important feelings of comfort and consolation to know that a very real representation of my finest friends during my entire lifetime are standing by in the pages of my books of sacred memory, to render what additional service they can as I prepare to cross the boundary to where I expect to meet them all again. And I have some hope that it might be said of me what has been said of someone else;

Dead he lay among his books:
The peace of God was in his looks.

Chapter Sixteen

Great Experiences
A "Sterling" Friend

On February 14, 1975, I had lunch with Dave Evans at the University Club. I was telling him about the fact that on February 6, 1975 President Kimball had expressed his opinion that everyone should write an autobiography so that his children and grandchildren and others interested could be helped by knowing something about him. President Kimball had made a strong statement about his conviction that particularly every General Authority should prepare an autobiography.

I had planned that some day I would do this for myself, but had put it off until now. But because of President Kimball's nudge, I got started on it the next day. I suggested to Dave that he was now nearly eighty-one years of age, he had had a very constructive and full life, he had a large posterity, he now had some free time, and I thought he should also get started immediately to put some of these important things about himself down on paper. He told me that he had already started, and while most of the job was yet undone, he had written some things about his and my association together which he intended to include in the story of his own life. He told me that if I would like, I could have a copy of what he had written.

Because the experiences that he mentions are important parts of both of our lives, I am including some of his account herewith without taking any responsibility for the accuracy of some of his appraisals of me. This section dictated by him is entitled *A "Sterling" Friend* and he records as follows:

179

"No book about me would be complete without a tribute to my great and good friend, Sterling W. Sill. After knowing him for some twenty years, I wrote this to him on July 2, 1953 in response to an autographed copy of a set of sermonettes which he had just sent me.

"You are an amazing fellow. Even I who thought I knew you 'like a book' am astounded at the quantity and quality of preparation and production you make in so many lines."

"And now, some twenty years still later, I feel the same way about this great man. No one of my acquaintance has dedicated himself more completely to his objectives, whether they were to become the nation's 'best life insurance salesman'; 'the best bishop in the Mormon Church'; 'the best stake leader of an Aaronic Priesthood program'; 'the best and most persistent reader and student of the great works of sacred and profane literature'; 'the most prolific writer of inspirational books and broadcaster of faith-promoting radio sermons.'

"In a letter which Sterling wrote to me in 1967, he recalled the first time we met. It was at Exchange Club in the Hotel Utah. In his letter he said: 'I remember how friendly and warm your greeting to me was and I have carried a mental picture of you on that occasion ever since. I remember of no instance where this friendliness has ever failed. I wish I had written those lines to him first as I well could have done for that first meeting truly began an affair of 'love at first sight.'

"About the same time of this first meeting, Sterling and his wife, Doris, had moved into the Gilmer Park neighborhood on Yale Avenue near 13th East, just a block away from our family home on 12th East. Sterling and my brother, Richard, had married the lovely Thornley sisters from Kaysville, Doris and Alice. There is no doubt this family relationship had something to do with a quickening of our friendship, but it was by no means a chief factor. We liked each other; we trusted each other; we liked being together. At each weekly Exchange Club Meeting, we would try to sit together, but for some time that was the extent of our personal contact.

"It was not long, however, until an event occurred which was destined to bring us into daily and almost constant contact. It began in the summer of 1935, when rumors in our neighborhood and at the business office where I worked, were afloat that a new Church ward was about to be formed out of a portion of Yale Ward and LeGrand Ward. One of my close business associates at the time was a counselor in the Bonneville Stake Presidency. Since I had just recently been released from a six and a half year term as a counselor in a bishopric in Granite Stake, it was not unreasonable that my name, along with a number of others, should be mentioned as a possible member of the new ward bishopric. The truth or falsity of those rumors has never been confirmed and is not the point I wish to make. Whether true or false, I knew from recent personal experiences about the heavy responsibilities which rest upon bishoprics, and I didn't want to get involved again so soon. I was especially aware of the fact that forming a new ward of the parts in two dissimilar and somewhat incompatible wards would not be an easy task. Loyalties of the people who lived on the east side of the proposed new ward would belong to Yale Ward whose loyalties were strong for their present affiliation. To repeat, it was not a job I wanted. Not any part of it.

"One day at my place of business, when I was being probed for names of new bishopric material, I responded, 'I know a man who ought to be the new bishop; his name is Sill—Sterling W. Sill.' The reply to my suggestion was, 'I've never heard of him, does he live in our stake? Why doesn't he come out to church?'

"When I explained that Sterling Sill did in fact live in Bonneville Stake and within the boundaries of the proposed new ward but had retained his membership in Layton and was a stake high councilman in the North Davis Stake, I was asked if I could bring about an introduction of Brother Sill and the Bonneville Stake Presidency without letting him know the purpose of the introduction. After this had happened and the Bonneville Stake Presidency had investigated Sterling's church and business records, it was practically no time until he was asked to fill the position of bishop. As I learned later, he responded without hesitation, 'I'll accept the call if you'll grant me one request; let me have Dave Evans as my first counselor.'

"Joseph W. Bambrough was named as the other counselor; and thus began some of the busiest, most challenging, and most wonderful years of my life. As Elder Sill has repeated many times the rest of the story about my being asked to serve as his counselor, my reply went something like this, 'I will accept on one condition, and that is that we will be a working bishopric, not a preaching one.' And on that basis we three began the difficult job of bringing together the two halves of the new ward; of finding a suitable site for the building of a new chapel, and of organizing from scratch an effective team that would include both the poor and the rich; the humble and the proud; the active and inactive; and make out of them what I have immodestly considered one of the finest wards in the entire church. That took work and persistence, two characteristics which Bishop Sill had in abundance.

"The proposal to cut off part of Yale Ward, which was one of the elite wards in the Church, was not at first a popular decision. Some of the long-time members would be affected by this shift. A number of families would be separated and it would break up the close association of many neighbors and friends. Besides, the Yale Ward members felt that they were being 'moved west of the tracks' so to speak. A preliminary meeting of all Melchizedek Priesthood holders involved in the proposed new ward was held at the Yale Chapel on September 11, 1936. Vigorous and outspoken opposition was expressed by some of those who would be affected. One of these was Junius Romney, member of the stake high council. Stake President Joseph L. Wirthlin appointed him to speak for those who might be opposed to the change. Among the General Authorities present and supporting the proposal were Elders George Albert Smith and Joseph Fielding Smith, both members of the Quorum of the Twelve and later Presidents of the Church. Elder George Albert Smith reported that the proposition had the unanimous support of the First Presidency and the Quorum of the Twelve. After stating his reasons for opposing the move, Elder Junius Romney, while remaining firm in his opposition to the idea, declared in his usual spirit of loyalty to the Church, 'If it is the decision of the presiding authorities and in their best judgment that the division should be made, I will gladly vote for it for the good it will accomplish, and I counsel all others to do likewise.'

"On the following Sunday, September 13, all Church members living within the boundaries of the proposed new ward met in the Yale Ward Chapel. The new bishopric, which had been previously selected, were sustained. Also, C. Oscar Winkler was sustained as Ward Clerk. On Thursday, September 17, Bishop Sill was ordained by Elder George Albert Smith and the two counselors were set apart.

"Ward meetings were temporarily held in LeGrand Ward Chapel. Since the boundaries of the ward encompassed the choice section of the area which was familiarly known as Gilmer Park, the ward was first called Gilmer Park Ward, but later was changed at the suggestion of President Heber J. Grant for the reason that Mr. Gilmer, the original owner and developer of this tract of real estate, had won the land on a gambling debt, and was an unfriendly gentile member of the community. Our first regular sacrament meeting was held Sunday, October 11, in the LeGrand Ward recreation hall.

"Some time prior to the organization of the ward, a committee to select a new site for the chapel had been named by the Bonneville Stake President. Brother Sill had been a member of that committee.

The committee reported that it had failed to find a suitable site within the ward boundaries and the committee was released and the responsibility turned over to the bishopric.

"The logical site and the one which was eventually chosen, was the old LeGrand Young homestead which lay between Yale and Harvard Avenues just east of 11th east. The obtaining of this beautiful piece of property was not accomplished until March of 1938. The plot of ground and the large brick home standing on it had been planned and planted and the home constructed by LeGrand Young, a nephew of Brigham Young, and at one time general legal counsel for the church. The beautiful original winding walks of imported red brick, the massive ornamental wall capped by Italian terra-cotta with portholes at various points along the wall to give the passersby a glimpse into the magnificent estate inside were worked into the landscaping of the new church grounds. Entrance on the Harvard Avenue side was through a portal which was guarded by a massive wrought iron gate which had been added by the late John C. Howard and family. They had also built an ornamental stage with a walkway through a bower of lovely shrubbery and steps leading down to a beautiful outdoor swimming pool. A brook, whose origin was in the Red Butte Canyon several miles away, cascaded down gentle falls, bypassing the swimming pool through a subterranean channel, and flowed from there gently through a beautiful lawn ornamented with beds of flowers interspersed with some of the finest trees in the State of Utah.

"The spreading chestnut tree to the west of the spacious park was said to be unequaled for size and symmetry elsewhere in Utah. And the age and beauty of the lovely oak growths in the northeast corner of the lot was unsurpassed. One of the State's leading authorities on trees said of this grove of scrub oaks that they were at least seven to eight hundred years old. The tall native cottonwoods were also matchless. It would take a full century to replace them. These unique works of nature and man led me to write in a commemorative historical brochure published in 1961 to commemorate the twenty-fifth anniversary of the establishment of the Garden Park Ward these lines: 'Matchless trees, quiet walks, fragrant flowers, the running brook; still, clear pool; song of birds, the heavenly skies by day and by night—here is a sanctuary of peace and beauty to bring out the best in men. Here on these grounds and in this building are the memories of inspirational speakers, the stirring testimonies of men like President Heber J. Grant, Elders George Albert Smith, David O. McKay, Hugh B. Brown, Marion G. Romney, and other apostles and General Authorities and

Church leaders by the dozen. They have spoken from the pulpit of this chapel and have born burning testimonies that God lives and that he restored this church with its priesthood and power in these latter days.

"Yes, this ward is special—the people, the building, the opera seats in the chapel, the carpeted foyer, the pipe organ (the same make and quality of the Salt Lake Tabernacle Organ at the time our organ was installed), the grand piano, the duck pond, the trees, everything! As Bishop Sill said when it all started, 'We must *have the best and do the best* in everything.' And so it started, and so it continued during the ten years there was Sterling Sill presiding as bishop: and so it has continued since."

"Bishop Sill was not one to take all the credit to himself nor make decisions without counsel. He gave his counselors many opportunities to propose programs and set policies. One of the rules we scrupulously followed was to personally evaluate every eligible member of the ward for each specific job before making final appointment. This proved to be especially important in the new ward for the new mix of people. Prior performance or merit based on past faithfulness was not enough. We always looked for new or hidden talent. In this way we found great leadership which otherwise might have been overlooked. Also by involving new people, one of the keys to character and spiritual development, made possible by church activity was put into practice. A number of men and some women who had not seen the inside of a Latter-day Saint church for a number of years, unless it was for a funeral, were brought into activity. Some of these became our staunchest supporters and most able leaders. This policy was not unique with us, but we emphasized perhaps more than in most wards who didn't have an effective persuader like Bishop Sill to accept their first assignments—in some cases the first of a lifetime.

"In the nearly 18 months between September 1936 and March 1938, when this beautiful tract of land was finally acquired, many obstacles had to be removed which at times challenged the resourcefulness and faith of the most stouthearted.

"When the purchase had finally been effected, it was announced to the members at a rousing meeting in the LeGrand Ward recreation hall on March 13, 1938. President Grant was present and made the announcement. All members of the Bonneville Stake Presidency and Elder Joseph Fielding Smith, who was one of the charter members of the ward and one of the oldest residents of the area, were also in attendance. Dr. Adam S. Bennion was sustained as chairman of the finance committee, who were charged with the responsibility of the raising of funds for the purchase of the lot and the erection of the meetinghouse within the year's time.

"The first meeting of Garden Park Ward on the church grounds was on Easter morning, April 17, 1938. Immediately following the beautiful Easter services, the Finance Committee held its first committee meeting on the lot under the shade of one of the large cottonwood trees. During the first summer, many memorable outdoor meetings followed and on August 28, President Grant laid the cornerstone with appropriate ceremonies. On Easter Sunday of 1939, just one year from the date of the first announcement that this site had been purchased, President Grant again visited us and dedicated the building and the grounds and the project which had often been referred to as 'Wirthlin's Folly' became 'Wirthlin's Pride'—and Sterling Sill's. Joseph L. Wirthlin was President of Bonneville Stake at the time Gilmer Park Ward was established. About our new chapel Presiding Bishop LeGrand Richards said: 'Your new building is one of the very finest ward buildings in the Church. Beautifully designed, artistically decorated and furnished. It is wonderfully located on one of the very choice building sites in our city. In the history of the Church there probably have been few if any complete ward plants financed and built in such a short period of time.'

"In the preceding two and a half years some goals had already been set and some traditions established. First of these goals was friendliness. Garden Park Ward had already become known for its friendly bishop and its friendly congregation. Old timers, even some who were not members of the Church, felt at home when they attended socials or otherwise participated in Garden Park activities. How well I recall that Maurice Warshaw, a non-member but a next door neighbor of Elder Sill's accepted a 'call' from his Bishop to be chairman of the annual ward reunions.

"A second goal which Bishop Sill had set for Garden Park Ward was that it must be a ward for young people. Beginning with him, every Bishop since has put emphasis on 'youth' and youth has responded. This is now another Garden Park tradition.

"A third commitment of the Sterling Sill Bishopric was to the beautiful things of life; good music, good literature, good teaching; and fine artwork in the Church foyer and chapel, beautiful flower gardens; a lovely, clean, tidy interior; cut flowers (usually furnished by Brother Bambrough) decorating the hall on every occasion. The tradition for holding an annual reunion, which involved everybody living within the confines of the ward, also became a tradition.

"Because of the uniqueness of the grounds and the building of the Garden Park Ward, Church headquarters and some government officials often directed visiting notables to see the Church in action in Garden Park Ward. Life Magazine selected it as "a showcase of Mormonism;" took scores of pictures, although an inopportune newsbreak delayed and eventually eliminated this feature from publication.

"When the governor of Utah became host for a few days in May of 1944 to Lord Halifax, Ambassador to the United States from Great Britain, and Lady Halifax, the Garden Park Ward was selected as a sample of Mormonism. Nine hundred persons attended the meeting on May 14, 1944, at which he attended and participated. Governor Maw, Dr. Adam S. Bennion, and Richard L. Evans also participated. In the absence of Bishop Sill from the state, it was my privilege to preside at this memorable meeting.

"Among the numerous church and community leaders who spoke at the Garden Park Ward in the ten years in which Bishop Sill presided, it sounds like a Who's Who of the Church. The list includes Presidents Heber J. Grant, George Albert Smith, David O. McKay, and Joseph Fielding Smith; and Elders J. Reuben Clark, Jr., Richard L. Evans, Jesse R. S. Budge, Marion G. Romney, Charles A. Callis, LeGrand Richards, Sylvester Q. Cannon, Steven L. Richards, Joseph F. Merrill, Levi Edgar Young, Hugh B. Brown, Bryant S. Hinckley, Albert E. Bowen, Ezra T. Benson, John A. Widtsoe, Matthew Cowley, Joseph F. Merrill, and many, many others. On May 19, 1946, the Sterling Sill bishopric was released, but the traditions set then have continued to this day.

"The circumstances under which this change occurred were most unusual. Generally when the release of a bishopric is proposed by the stake president, ward members will recognize the reasons and accept them and the inspiration behind them without question. It was not exactly the case on this occasion. The Garden Park Ward members were not quite sure a change was due.

"In advance of the 'release' meeting, word got around that the change was to be made. Bishop Sill did his best to allay any opposition to the change and promptly conveyed the fact to the stake president that there might be opposition and offered to make a statement supporting the stake president in his decision. For some reason, Bishop Sill's offer was refused. On the night of Sunday, May 19, when the release was officially proposed, some questions were asked by the congregation and some outspoken opposition to the change was voiced by a number of the ward's finest and most loyal church members. The discussion continued for a considerable time and finally the release of the bishopric was accepted by the people though the vote was not unanimous. Bishop Sill had already been asked and had accepted an assignment on the stake high council and was placed in charge of the Aaronic Priesthood.

"In this new calling, he did a magnificent work in raising the standards of the Aaronic Priesthood activities and participation. He held this high council assignment for five years and then was appointed a member of the Sunday School General Board in 1951 and an Assistant to the Council of the Twelve in April, 1954.

"In the meantime, Elder Sill has performed many other useful and unusual services, both to the Church and the community. In 1951, for example, while he was a member and Chairman of the Board of Regents of the University of Utah, the request came to the board from Dr. Virginia F. Cutler, head of the Home Economics Department, for the purchase of a large home near the university to serve as a practice house for those majoring in home building and teachers of home economics in the Home Economics Department. Since there were no funds in the University's regular budget for this purpose, Chairman Sill offered to raise the funds independently. But after some investigation, it was thought advisable to build a new building rather than make an adaptation of an old building. This new building proved to be the first-of-a-kind family home living center in America.

"The architect, a Mr. Raymond J. Ashton, agreed to provide all the architectural services without cost if Sterling would raise the necessary funds to build it. Thus an $18,000 project eventually became a $350,000 project. In raising the funds for this project, Sterling Sill made over eight hundred personal contacts and also contributed considerable funds of his own. After the project had been finished, it was properly named, 'The Sterling W. Sill Home Living Center.'

"At the dedication of the Living Center on June 9, 1953 in accepting this building on behalf of the University, Mr. William J. O'Connor, then Chairman of the Board of Regents said this about Sterling, 'I've seen a lot of men in my life. I just want to pay a tribute to the dogged determination, the enthusiasm of a man who, by himself, in three years, went out and got the good people of this state to build this institution, the Sterling W. Sill Home Living Center. It is really an institution...I can't imagine anything better in education than to prepare a young woman to build a home or to make a living by intelligently teaching home building to others... having voted against the project to begin with, and with all the humility and pride, and with great tribute to the man, Sterling Sill, who is responsible, and the good citizens whose energy and enthusiasm he aroused, I'm very grateful to accept this building on behalf of the University of Utah.'

"After Sterling's chairmanship on the Board of Regents had expired, he received a much deserved honorary degree of Doctor of Laws from the school that he had so generously helped in so many ways.

"Turning the pages back to the years of the Garden Park Ward, I recall an experience which changed the whole life style of Elder Sill. It grew out of a lecture that Dr. Adam S. Bennion was invited to give to the adult members of the Garden Park Ward M.I.A. The time was World War II. Noting that some thousands of American prisoners of war were left languishing in enemy prison camps, Dr. Bennion announced as his subject, 'If I were a prisoner of war and was permitted to take ten books into a prison camp, what ten books would I want to have with me?' He then listed the ten of his choice beginning with the Bible. It was a fascinating lecture, causing all of us to reach for our pencils or pens and write down the names of those ten best books. But only one person in the class reaped the full benefit of that inspiring lecture. That person was, you guessed it, Sterling W. Sill.

"In addition to reading those ten books, Sterling marked in pencil the passages that most appealed to him. He also memorized long passages from each of them as he walked to and from work, day after day, month after month, year after year. He read and sometimes reread over nine hundred other books, and marked, memorized, and card indexed countless passages from all of them. Perhaps no man of his generation—at least none that I have heard of or met, has kept so well that 1943 resolution that made Sterling Sill an educated man, an inspirational writer, a popular speaker and radio commentator and a man who has more than met the challenge of leadership and scholarship among the big men of his day. It has been my privilege to check from time to time in the libraries and distribution centers of various missions of the Church in English speaking countries, and nearly always I have found Sterling Sill's books among the best sellers.

"On May 28, 1946, after he and I had been released from the Garden Park Ward bishopric, Sterling Sill wrote me a letter which I prize greatly. He said in part, 'When the ward was organized, there was a great deal of opposition to it, but as we give up our office, I feel satisfied that many people are as happy and contented and as enthusiastic about the ward as any group of people it has been my privilege to associate with.' Then the letter concluded, 'Life under the most favorable circumstances is not very long, and it is so tremendously important, it seems to me, that along the way we each have someone in whom we have perfect trust and confidence, and with whom we can discuss our problems, hopes and ambitions, as well as our mistakes and the places where we have not measured up, with some assurance that this confidence will abide and will not be adversely affected or blown about by every change of circumstance.'

"Actually, while he was trying to share some credit with me for the successes in that bishopric, he was really demonstrating a quality which I like best in him. As usual, he was giving credit to others, which he so much deserved himself.

"The natural humility of Bishop Sill and his desire to work as a team made our experiences together most joyful. I cannot recall a single instance when the three of us were not able to come to a complete agreement on every decision that was made. However, Bishop Sill was generous to a fault, giving credit to those who worked with him...he had some special qualities that made our team most effective. The one thing he had was persistence, and when it became difficult to get through the doors of some of our disgruntled members, that was just part of the challenge to Bishop Sill.

"One of Bishop Sill's strong points was to get things down on paper. One of the very first things he did was provide himself and his counselors with a little pocket-sized notebook in which the name of every family and every individual and the dates of birth, priesthood held, and other vital information was listed. He corrected these periodically. We never held a meeting or a conference without carrying with us the complete list of our members. Bishop Sill next made large maps in three sections on which every house in the ward and the address and the name of the family that lived in it was indicated. The members were shown in black and the non-members in red. He had the middle section personally to look after, I had the north section, and Joe Bambrough the south. When people moved in and out of the ward, the changes were noted on the map.

"Bishop Sill knew how to bring people together, the rich, poor, old, and young. He was a great mixer. He was also an effective driver, tolerant, generous in giving credit to others, with a rare type of humility which shows a willingness to take counsel. He was one of the great bishops in the Church, especially suited to the assignment and time in which he served.

"Like the super-salesman he was, he didn't take no for an answer when some of the rest of us were inclined to be discouraged over our failure.

"As I conclude this tribute to one of my truest and best friends, I do it with a note of sadness. Sterling is going blind. The reading he does and the correcting of manuscripts he continues to write must be done under the most difficult and discouraging of conditions. The letters on the printed page can be read only when illuminated with a special bright light and with the aid of a strong magnifying glass. The sermons he delivers at the stake conferences where he presides, or in the Tabernacle at General Conference sessions are all memorized. Even the large type on the teleprompter that some of the Brethren use gives him no help. But fortunately, the Lord endowed him with a superb memory which he has further cultivated through practice and he needs or asks no pity for his physical defiency."

Mileposts And Awards

1. Born March 31, 1903
2. Baptized August 27, 1911 by Frank L. Sheffield
3. Confirmed August 27, 1911 by Joseph A. Sill
4. Lived 60 days in Delta, Utah 1913
5. Ordained a deacon on the 24th of January 1915 by Levi S. Haywood
6. Ordained a teacher January 14, 1917 by Charles W. Robbins
7. Ordained a priest January 8, 1920 by Lucius D. Laudie
8. Lettered in football, Davis High School, 1920
9. School play, 1920
10. Graduated Davis High School, 1921
11. Attended U.S.A.C. Logan winter quarter 1920-1921
12. Patriarchal blessing, October 9, 1923 by James Henry Linford, Kaysville
13. Ordained an elder November 26, 1923 by James E. Ellison
14. Left on mission, January 4, 1924
15. Minister's certificate, January 8, 1924, Heber J. Grant, Charles W. Penrose, and Anthony W. Ivans
16. Letter of appointment to the Alabama Conference, January 15, 1924, Charles A. Callis
17. Letter of appointment as President of the Alabama Conference, May 8, 1925
18. Certificate of Honorable release, March 25, 1926
19. Taught school 1926, 1927
20. Agent of the New York Life Insurance Company, June 7, 1927
21. High School Teaching Certificate, June 26, 1928
22. Lead in play that won first place in the Church grand finals M.I.A. Drama Contest, 1928
23. Married Doris Mary Thornley in the Salt Lake Temple, September 4, 1929
24. Elected Layton Town Trustee, November 5, 1929
25. Ordained a high priest May 10, 1931 by Henry H. Blood

26. Became a member of the High Council, North Davis Stake, May 10, 1931
27. Eagle Scout, July 18, 1931
28. Re-elected town trustee November 3, 1931
29. Appointed Assistant Manager, Intermountain Branch, N.Y.L.I.C., October 1, 1932
30. For first nine months of 1932, ranked eleven in number of paid for applications among the entire agency force of 11,243 salesmen in the United States and Canada
31. First Utah Man ever chosen from the State of Utah to speak at a National Association Meeting. The 1932 convention of the underwriters was held in August in San Francisco.
32. Appointed Manager of Intermountain Branch, January 1, 1933
33. Elected Secretary-Treasurer, Utah Association of Life Underwriters, June 13, 1933
34. Elected to membership of Salt Lake Exchange Club, 1933
35. Re-elected Secretary-Treasurer, Utah Association of Life Underwriters, June 13, 1933
36. First Utahn to be awarded the CLU degree, September 27, 1934
37. John Michael Sill born December 12, 1934
38. Elected president, Utah Life Underwriters, June 11, 1935
39. Ordained and set apart as a Bishop, October 12, 1936
40. Original member of the Bonneville Knife and Fork Club International, 1937
41. Original member Social Security, 1937
42. President of Exchange Club during National Convention in Salt Lake City during 1938
43. David Sterling Sill born June 3, 1938
44. Graduation certificate from Utah Life Manager's Association, Life Insurance Sales Research Bureau, November 9-10, 1938
45. Graduated from Dale Carnegie course in Sales Training and Human Relations, New York September 27, 1940
46. Mary Carolyn Sill born July 2, 1944
47. Appointed member of the Bonneville Stake High Council, 1946
48. Appointed member of the Sunday School General Board, 1951
49. Vice-president of the Deseret News, 1952-1962
50. Voice on "Sunday Evening from Temple Square" from November 1, 1953 to February 28, 1954. (This was before I was made a General Authority.)
51. Honorary Doctor of Laws Degree, University of Utah, June 9, 1953

52. Ordained and set apart as an Assistant to the Quorum of the Twelve, April 9, 1954
53. Largest general office award of New York Life Insurance Company, 1958
54. Carnegie Hero Award, January 21, 1959
55. Voice on "Sunday Evening from Temple Square," second time, April 17, 1960 to July 17, 1977. Awarded First Presidency stainless steel engraved plaque mounted on velvet and wood in appreciation of over 17 years as spokesman for weekly radio program "Sunday Evening from Temple Square."
56. Weekly articles in Deseret News each week from March 9, 1963 to February 19, 1966.
57. John W. Yeates Memorial speaker by Los Angeles General Agents and Managers Association, 1968
58. Proclaimed a member of the Amalgamated Society of Trained Seals, Texas Tri-city sales caravan, February 21, 22, and 23, 1968
59. Appreciation Dinner, Zion's First National Bank, June 6, 1968
60. Honorary Retirement Plaque, September 1968 (New York Life)
61. Given distinguished service award, Ricks College, March 5, 1974
62. Awarded Ivan Johnson Award, May 8, 1975
63. Attended Area Conferences in Asia, August 6-18, 1975
64. Who's Who in Religion, First Edition, 1976-77
65. Who's Who in America, Thirty-ninth Edition, 1976-77
66. Keynote speaker at LAMP Meeting, 1977
67. Ordained a Seventy and set apart as Member of First Quorum, Apostle Howard W. Hunter, voice.
68. Classified as Seventy Emeritus effective January 1, 1979.

Clubs And Associations

*I*n 1933 I was invited to become a member of the Salt Lake Exchange Club. I remained a member until I became chairman of the Board of Regents in 1947, when a conflict of meetings made Exchange Club attendance impossible. I had a fine experience during these fourteen years, when each Friday about seventy-five men would gather together in the Junior Ballroom at the Hotel Utah and have a dinner and program. Here we would build friendships with each other and have a good social visit together. I made many important friendships during this period. I was elected president of the club for the year 1938 when our club was host to the National Association of Exchange Clubs which held their annual meeting that year in Salt Lake City.

It is a very interesting thing to sit down once a week with a group of men who you come to know rather intimately while you enjoy a fine dinner, then enjoy a program, and listen to the problems or triumphs of other men entertaining the same kinds of hopes and ambitions that you have. As members of the club we had such men as Will Folland, Chief Justice of the Utah Supreme Court, and Leroy Coles, whom I later nominated as president of the University of Utah. It was at an Exchange Club meeting that I first met Dave Evans, and I was very impressed with him. My good friend Maurice Warshaw was a member of the club; he was also my next door neighbor for a number of years. Maurice started out on the streets of Salt Lake with a banana cart. Later he set up a little fruit stand, and his business has grown into a very large and prosperous enterprise. Maurice's son Keith, became a victim of polio during his high school days, and has been in a wheelchair ever since, and Maurice has spent a good deal of his money to aid other handicapped people. Fritz Hinckley was also a great favorite of mine. There are many others, too numerous to mention, who gave me the benefit of their friendship and uplifting associations, and whom I came to like very much. I was able to rejoice in their successes

194

and be interested in their problems, as though they were a part of my family. Altogether my Exchange Club membership provided me with a very pleasant, total experience. This club sponsored a great many good things like sending boys to college, helping the handicapped, and sponsoring a lot of good ideas like "back to church Sunday" and other things.

On April 5, 1953 I joined the Timpanogos Club, which is made up of a number of prominent people. This club meets at 6:00 p.m. the fourth Thursday of each month in the President's Room at the Hotel Utah. The membership consists of a hundred men especially selected from the very most prominent people in the community. We have a couple of university presidents, a United States senator, and a great many prominent business, professional, and educational leaders. This group prides itself on the fact that it has no outside speakers. All of the stimulating ideas by which the members are entertained and instructed come from within the group itself. It was also my privilege to serve as president of this club. This was especially pleasant, and we have a lot of fun. My wife and I also attend a group to which we have belonged for many years made up of former Governor and Florence Maw, Dr. Raymond and Ramona Maw, Dr. Antone and Flora Cannon, Werner and Mercedes Keipe, and Dick and Leota Young, until Dick's death. We have enjoyed these wonderful associations very much. I also served a three-year term as a member of the Board of Directors of the United Way and as a member of the Executive Committee. I have also served several years as a member of the Board of Directors of Multiple Sclerosis. In addition, I have belonged to the Underwriter's Association, the CLU Society, and the Salt Lake Manager's Association.

During my lifetime I have lived in six homes. One was the house in Layton I was born in, the next was the little home on Easy Street that we lived in for a few years. We went to Delta in 1913 for two months, then we moved to Layton where I lived until I was married. After our marriage we rented a little house owned by Jim Morgan in which we lived until we moved to Salt Lake on October 31, 1932. For a few months we lived in the Kimball Apartments and then the Los Gables Apartments until we bought our home on Yale Avenue in early 1935, soon after Michael was born.

I have belonged to three Church Wards in my life: the Layton Ward from the time of my birth until we moved to Salt Lake, and the Yale Ward, from which the Garden Park Ward was split off in 1936. I still greatly enjoy my membership in it.

My wife and I also belong to four social groups. One is called "Trends," to which we have belonged for forty years. Some of the members are Marion G. Romney, A. Ray Olpin, David Romney, Rulon Clark, Bicknell Robbins, Alex Jex, and many others. Another of these groups was organized by Alvin Pack and his wife many years ago, and it includes Lynn Bennion, Alex Schreiner, John Boyden, Zora Reece, Junius Romney, Ferd Peterson, and Laurence McKay. Another of these groups is made up of Ted Jacobsen, Mark Garff, Dick Bird, Alice Evans, Bill Burton, Mickey Oswald, Jerry Smith, Lou Callister and Hal Beecher. For many years we have also belonged to the Cannon-Hinckley study group, organized over forty years ago by Edwin Q. Cannon and his wife. This club has in its membership all three members of the First Presidency and a number of other General Authorities of the Church. It also includes Dr. Henry Eyring, Harvey Fletcher, William F. Edwards, Carl Christensen, Dr. Russell Nelson, and other especially selected people prominent in the community. It is also true that some of those who are less prominent make the greatest contribution, but regardless of occupation, social standing, or Church membership, each puts himself into the club on a kind of united order basis, and each one shares in the friendship and association of all the others.

Before we were married, my wife and I belonged to a little group of four couples made up of ourselves, Gene and Florence Ammet, Ern and Francis Hurd, Bill and Melba Eldridge.

I have also greatly enjoyed being an American and also belonging to the human race. Some of my most pleasant and profitable associations have been my personal family, my NYLIC family, my community family, my social family, and my Church family.

I am very grateful for this gregariousness that God put into our lives where we associate together as nations, communities, churches, and families, and get so much out of each other.

Politics

$\mathcal{I}$f I were to say the word automobile, most people would just think of one thing. But recently on an automobile sales window I saw a statement saying that an automobile was 3,375 things. That is, an automobile is a carburetor, and a gas tank, and a steering wheel, and a rear bumper, and a radio. All are important. And if the most expensive automobile lacks a carburetor, all the rest is comparatively worthless.

The world itself is made up of parts. The scientists have discovered 104 elements in nature. There is nitrogen, and hydrogen, and oxygen, and carbon, and iron. These are nature's building blocks. Out of these elements in the right combinations and proportions, nature fashions all of the material things of the world. If you want to make a sack of sugar or a bag of salt, you put certain elements together in the right combinations and proportions. If you would like to make an ocean, you take two parts of hydrogen and one part of oxygen and put them together and you have an ocean. I am sure it isn't quite that simple, but that is the general idea.

Someone has said that the human personality is made up of fifty-one elements. There is kindness, faith, courage, integrity, righteousness, and ambition. These are the attributes of God himself. Put these together in the right combinations and proportions and you have what somebody called a magnificent human being.

But life is like that. Life is made up of experience. If we have enough great experiences, we have a great life. If we have too many inferior experiences, we have an inferior life. The most important opportunity that there is in life is to make of every experience a great experience.

One of the advantages of writing a biography is comparable to planting a flower garden. You can bring all of your experiences with their various interests, colors, and pleasures together where you cannot only be reminded of them, but relive and re-enjoy them.

On one occasion many years ago at a political rally in Layton of the Democratic party which I did not attend, I was named as a delegate to the Davis County convention. Because my father was a Democrat, someone assumed that I was a Democrat though I had not been active in either party. When informed of my appointment, I was a little bit ashamed that I had not taken as much interest as I should have done in the politics of my community. Actually, I did not know whether I wanted to be a Democrat or a Republican. Inasmuch as there was a Republican rally to be held a few days later, I decided to attend, more or less merely to see what went on. At this meeting I was elected precinct chairman of the Republican party. And thus I began my political career carrying water on both my Democratic and Republican shoulders. However, my political career never developed much beyond that point.

At a little later date, I was nominated and elected as a member of the Layton Town Council and served for a two-year term. At the end of that period I ran for re-election. At that time I was selling life insurance, and I was very interested in what the vote should be as I thought that would probably show something about my standing with the people with whom I worked. This election proved to be one of the great encouragements that I have received in my life, inasmuch as I led the ticket in number of votes so far as the members of the winning members of the Council were concerned.

My second term of office began on January 1, 1932 and would have run for two years until December 31, 1933, except that in the meantime I was asked by the New York Life to accept the job of Agency Director of the Intermountain Branch Office which required that I move my place of residence to Salt Lake City, which more or less signaled the end of my political career in Layton.

To that date Laurence Ellison had been the only mayor of Layton and served for many terms. One of the honors that I would have enjoyed very much in my life, that I have not received, is that I would have liked to have been mayor of Layton. At that time the salary paid the mayor was the same as it was to the councilmen: two dollars a meeting. We met twice a month, so that the compensation for my only political office was four dollars a month. I appreciated the four dollars, but I am also very grateful for my home town of Layton, as many of the most important events that took place in my life occurred there where I lived for the first twenty-nine years of my life. This is also where many of the men lived who have been most influential in my life.

In the year 1948, I had several delegations come to see me about the possibility of my running for governor of the State of Utah.

Of course, there were several other people who had that same invitation in that same year. My name also appeared in the press as a possible candidate for governor on several occasions along with other names. I received a number of letters about it. One of these, written by Roy W. Simmons is reproduced herewith:

January 5, 1948

Mr. Sterling W. Sill, Manager
New York Life Insurance Co.
Walker Bank Building
Salt Lake City, Utah

Dear Sterling:

I am continually sticking my nose into other people's business, and this time it happens to be yours. Today I was talking politics to a Republican leader in Salt Lake, (a man who was very helpful in our Dawson campaign before the primaries), and I asked him why we didn't try to get you to run for Governor. He has never had the opportunity of meeting you and would like to do so sometime.

I know that you haven't been too active in politics, and I don't even know definitely what party you belong to, but I do know that the Republican Party needs somebody who is of your type to lead them during the next crucial campaign, and I feel that you would definitely have a very good chance of receiving the nomination if we went to work for you.

I am leaving for Chicago Wednesday and will be away for two weeks, but would like to have your opinion of the idea when I get back.

Please forgive me for meddling in your affairs, but I feel that you are definitely the kind of man that I would like to go to work for, and I think that our success with the Dawson Campaign last year should prove that a good man with a clean record can win over organizations if his friends are willing to get out and work for him wholeheartedly.

Very sincerely yours,
/s/ Roy W. Simmons

I was interested enough that I took up with my company the possibility of obtaining a leave of absence from my work. They informed me that it would not be possible to have me engage in politics while on a leave of absence from the New York Life, as that may have some complications for the company and may constitute a conflict of interest for me and possible embarrassment to all concerned. They did make an arrangement, however, where they agreed to hire me back with the company at the conclusion of my term of office, if elected, at the same salary and conditions obtaining at the time I left the company's service with all of my seniority and pension rights fully reinstated. Anyway, I gave up the idea and did not attend any of the meetings leading to nomination, and probably nothing would have happened even if I had. And while I would like to have had a little more of a record for serving my fellowmen in a political way, yet I am sure that my personal interests were much better served by the course actually taken.

I have also had a little bit of regret that I have had no service in the military organization of my country. I was only fifteen when World War I ended and nearly thirty-nine when World War II began. I am very grateful that I live in America, and while I make no pretenses of any great bravery, yet as a part of my life I would like to have worn the uniform of my country.

Travel

One of the new conditions which was recently introduced into the lives of most human beings is that to some degree everyone has become a traveler. This is sometimes brought about by choice and sometimes it is a necessity. Many of these conditions were not present a few years ago. For example, J. A. Francis gives us an appraisal of the life of Jesus in his famous statement when he said:

"Here is a man who grew up in an obscure village, the child of a poor peasant woman. He worked in a carpenter shop until he was 30, and then for three years he was an itinerant preacher.

"He never wrote a book. He never held an office. He never owned a home. He never had a family. He never went to college. He never put his foot inside a big city. He never traveled 200 miles from the place he was born.

"While still a young man, the tide of popular opinion turned against him. His friends ran away. One of them denied him. Another betrayed him. He was turned over to his enemies. He went through the mockery of a trial. He was nailed upon the cross between two thieves. While he was dying, his executioners gambled for the only thing he owned, and that was his cloak. When he was dead, he was laid in a borrowed grave, through the pity of a friend.

"But since then, nineteen wide centuries have come and gone and today he is the very center of the human race. I am well within the mark when I say that all of the armies that ever marched, and all of the navies that were ever built, and all of the parliaments that ever sat, and all of the kings that ever reigned, put together, have not affected the life of man upon this earth as powerfully as has this one solitary life."

But times have changed, and travel has become one of our most important activities. Our highways are filled with automobiles. Thousands of airplanes carrying millions of people are spanning continents and oceans. Through networks of telephones, telegraph,

201

television, and radio our communications fill the air and encircle the earth. Thousands of people in the army, the navy, the air force, and in business and recreational pursuits go around the earth dozens of times during their lifetime.

In addition to our physical travel, we sometimes send our minds on excursions even while our bodies remain at home. We now have libraries filled with books on every subject that we can read to our heart's content, giving us full information on any subject and about any people. We have the opportunity of spending years in the most famous halls of learning, where we study the histories, activities, and ideas of people in every corner of the earth. And even without much wealth we can actually go to any part of the earth and see life as it is lived by other people who speak different languages and have different ideologies and a different color to their skin. A very large number of Americans change their place of residence and their occupation every year. We also go on frequent extended vacations.

My own travel experience has been very interesting and very broadening, though by nature and inclination I am a homebody. When I was twenty years of age, I went on a Church mission to the Southern States. And for twenty-seven months I traveled continually among other people. I lived in their homes, joined in at their meals, in their prayers, in their worship. Many of them opened their hearts and discussed with me their personal private problems, hopes, sins and ambitions, so that I not only saw many new territories, but also many new life situations.

When I was twenty-nine, I went into agency work for my company, where one of my assignments was to make a regular trip throughout western Wyoming, eastern Nevada, and the State of Utah, visiting and working with the company's representatives, recruiting and training salesmen, and looking out for the business of the company generally. When I was thirty-six, my territory was increased and I was given the additional responsibility of supervising the company's interests in Idaho, Montana, Wyoming, Colorado, New Mexico, Arizona, Utah, Nevada, and a part of Oregon. During this period I attended many company conferences in all parts of the country. At forty-seven, I began doing some traveling for the Sunday School General Board, and at fifty-one the territory was increased when I became a General Authority of the Church, so that every part of the earth became a potential travel target.

I attended the August, 1975 Area Conferences of the Church held in Tokyo, the Philippine Islands, Hong Kong, the Republic of China, and Korea. In the Philippines we saw the people planting their rice crops and using the ancient animal, the caribou. It was my privilege, to a limited extent, to go among the people in each of these areas, shake hands, extend greetings, and to some degree communicate with them, many of whom could not speak a word of English. And I could not speak one word in their tongue. But I could read a great message in their eyes, their clothes, their homes, and those attitudes which were plainly visible. Some of these people traveled for eight days in order to be at this religious conference. Some had gone without food in order to get the money to pay the necessary expenses of their trip to see the President of the Church, hear the various messages of the conference, and associate with a large number of fellow believers.

Through interpreters I heard many of my fellow human beings from Asia express their hopes and ambitions publicly and privately, and I felt a helpful feeling of companionship and brotherhood with them. My conviction was made more real that we are all the children of God and that we ought to cooperate in helping and encouraging each other.

I always have had, and still do have, a great feeling of enthusiasm and loyalty for the great country in which I live and the people who are my countrymen. But while in Asia, as I shook hands with large groups of young people dressed in clean white shirts and neckties with an excellent grooming, and as I learned something about their sacrifices and limited opportunities, I felt sorry for some of the people in my own land who may have lost interest in themselves and the better things of life, and are unwilling to make the sacrifices that are made by their less fortunate brothers and sisters in some other lands. I have also lived among the Maoris of New Zealand and lived in the culture of the Samoans, the Australians, and the peoples of Mexico, South America, etc. And I am very grateful to have had at least this limited acquaintanceship with my brothers and sisters living on other parts of our good earth.

But in addition to the physical travel which I have done in my lifetime, I am also grateful for the fact that I have done a great deal of traveling in many other ways. By means of the moving picture, I have climbed to the top of Mt. Everest. I have stood on the tops of the Alps in Italy. I have lived in the palaces of kings, and visited with the earth's great captains of industry. With the travel privileges granted me in books, I have lived a lifetime with William Shakespeare. I have campaigned with Julius Caesar. I have been with Moses on the top of Mt. Sinai for his meeting with the great God of creation himself.

Through the various scriptures available, I have attended the Council in heaven and heard the debate about the objectives of this life. I have taken a personal part in the war that followed, and then through the 76th Section of the Doctrine and Covenants and related scriptures, I have made an exploratory trip through the four great post-mortal kingdoms, in one of which all of God's children must eventually find their place of permanent residence. Three of these are kingdoms of glory; the fourth is a kingdom which is not a kingdom of glory.

I have also spent some time in those intermediate states of paradise and the prison house. I have visited that great eternal reform school—the divine institution sometimes known by such terms as hell, or the prison house, where, through suffering and education, those who were not able to cleanse their lives of their sins during their mortality, will have an opportunity to have those sins purged from them to make them eligible for the highest possible condition of which they are capable.

While I am very grateful for those opportunities which have enabled me to actually be in many parts of the earth, I am also grateful for my own fireside and my comfortable easy chair and the great books that have enabled me to understand other conditions and opportunities.

I realize that sometime in the fairly near future, I will be making a trip in which I will go beyond the borders of mortality to places where other great experiences await me. I will be asked to stand before the judgment bar of God, and I ought to engage in a great deal of contemplation about what the results of that particular experience may be. I will have the magnificent thrill of a literal bodily resurrection.

I have had some great enjoyments out of my physical and mental faculties in this life. I have known the sheer thrill of being alive, of being enthusiastic about life and feeling the surges of physical health. I have had the magnificent delights of the great senses of vision, sound, taste, smell, and touch and all of the combinations of these physical, mental, and spiritual joys. I anticipate a great amplification of these delights when I am resurrected, immortalized, and hopefully celestialized. I expect that the benefits of my travel experiences will then be greatly increased. I realize that the basis of my future privileges will be built on the record of my past attitudes and activities. For my future travel experiences, I am sure that my passport will be carefully examined by the emigration authorities of those jurisdictions which I have never yet visited. I truly hope for many other exciting adventures, including a reunion with friends and loved ones, as well as those who will follow after me.

In The Presence Of Imminent Death

On January 21, 1959 I had one of the great experiences of my life at the Hollywood Beach Hotel in Hollywood Beach, Florida. In this unusual experience I had all of the conscious sensations of drowning. Since that time I have been more than ordinarily aware that death is always hovering over us. Death is so closely connected with life that it is never very far from the center of our activities. There are other important events in life that come upon us unawares where we are unconscious of the fact that something important is about to take place.

This event happened on the second day of the five-day agency meeting at which some five hundred New York Life Company representatives were present. Included in this group were some of the directors and most of the top executive officers of the Company from New York as well as all of the field officers and managers throughout the Company. We had had a very interesting Company educational program the day before this event happened.

Much of the first day of these manager's meetings was given over to discussion of the records that had been made. The year 1948 had been a very good business year for me. In fact, it had been one of the very best in my life. When I had assumed the managership of the Utah Office of the New York Life, it was the 101st office in size out of 105 offices. In spite of the fact that we had been split up a couple of times, yet we had grown steadily in rank until in 1958 we had nosed out for first place the great San Francisco Office which had been the leader for several years. Los Angeles came in third place. But out of the fourteen major awards that had been given the day before, it had been announced that my office had won ten of them as shown in the annual agency report.

I had been on the program and had been given a great deal of favorable comment, which of course was very pleasant to me. These meetings were usually held at the latter part of January, after all the reports were in for the previous year's work, and they were usually held at some convenient resort hotel in Florida. The Hollywood Beach Hotel is a very interesting place and is located right on the beach. Because I liked to swim, and because there was not very much opportunity for exercise during these five days of meetings, I had formed a habit with a number of my friends of having a good swim in the ocean about seven o'clock in the morning, which is just the time the sun comes up out of the ocean in this part of Florida at this season of the year. And each of these ocean sunrises presents the sun as a giant red ball which in itself is something inspiring to behold.

As we were having dinner the night before, one of my friends said, "Sterling, are you going swimming in the morning?" And I said, "Harold, I go swimming every morning." And we talked a little bit about the fun we had had that morning. He said, "I think I will go with you in the morning." And in a joking mood, I said, "No, I'm sure you won't make it." He said, "What do you mean?" I said, "Well, if you can't even make up your mind now, I'm sure you won't be able to make it up in the morning before daylight while the wind is whistling around your window. And I don't think you have enough courage to get yourself out of your warm bed and go out there and dunk yourself in that nice cold ocean."

At his request, I had previously tried to help him with some of his office production problems and had a kind of fatherly interest in his success, and I said, "Harold, I think it would be a great idea if you could develop the enthusiasm to get out of bed and go swimming every morning during the entire convention. This courage routine would make it a lot easier for you to build up the business of your office." Half in joke I tried to be a little bit philosophical in suggesting what I thought would do him a great amount of good.

There was a young man sitting next to me by the name of George Redding, who was the son of our manager in Butte, Montana. Because his mother was unable to come with her husband to the meeting that year, his father had brought him, as he had done a very good job in his schoolwork, and he was giving him a wonderful reward by letting him attend this convention in Florida. Apparently George was impressed with my attempt to be philosophical and said, "Mr. Sill, can I go swimming with you in the morning?" And I said, "George, I'd be delighted. And I'm sure you'll be there. I think Harold is a little bit of a panty-waist, and he probably won't make it, but I know you will."

The next morning about fourteen or fifteen of us met down on the beach at seven o'clock. The waves were about three feet high. A greatly oversized sun came up out of the ocean with a flaming red glow and we dived into the waves and had a great time for probably a half an hour getting our exercise, getting our blood circulation going, enjoying the inspiration of this great ocean, and working up an extra appetite for the breakfast which we were going to eat. I had forgotten all about George, but just as we were going up the beach to go back into the hotel, here comes George down to the water. He had overslept, and I could see the disappointment on his face because he, of course, couldn't go out into the ocean by himself. And in a disappointed voice he said, "Mr. Sill, are you going to get out now?" And I said, "No, I'm going to go back in with you, and I'll stay as long as you want, and we'll have a lot of fun."

This was a fine, clean-cut young man, thirteen years of age, and I had great appreciation for him and his father and his mother, as well as his grandparents. So we went out and swam around and he was telling me what he was going to do when he grew up, but we got out a little bit too far. We became separated by fifteen to eighteen feet, too great a distance for those circumstances. Then he startled me by calling, "Help!" I was surprised, because he knew pretty well how to handle himself in the water. I thought he was just joking at first, but I could see by the look of terror in his eyes that he was in dead earnest about needing some help. And so I swam over to him. In his fear he grasped me around the neck.

I had been standing down on a sand bar just a minute or two before and I thought probably I could still touch the bottom, so when I reached him I thought I would stand down where we could talk a little bit more clearly about what the problem was. But when I tried to reach the bottom, I discovered that there wasn't any bottom and I went clear down. But he was hanging on, and when I tried to get back up above the surface with his 130 pounds on my head, I found it wasn't quite so easy. I guzzled a little bit of water, but finally made it to the surface. I switched him around onto my back. But instead of going west to the beach I swam south to where I thought this sand bar was. And again I tried to touch the bottom, and again there wasn't any bottom, and I had this same struggle to get back up onto the surface.

This I did four times, each time taking in a little water, but each time thinking that I was going to locate this sand bar, and each time being disappointed. Then I began to get a little scared and thought I had better start for the shore, which was quite a long ways away. But I felt that I was a pretty good swimmer, and even though he had a pretty desperate hold around my neck, I had him on my back and I thought I could make it all right.

I've heard it said that when you are trying to save someone who is frantic in his fear of drowning and therefore might drown you, that what you are supposed to do is to give him a good sock on the chin and knock him out and then you can tow him to shore more easily. I don't know that I could hit any one that hard even if I was standing on concrete. But out there threshing around in this slippery water, and having deliberately tried to tire myself out by this exercise through two different sets of swimmers, I don't think I had enough punch even to hurt him very much, let alone knock him unconscious.

But anyway, I decided that if I was going to save his life I had better get started for shore. But I hadn't gone very far before I felt myself going unconscious. The doctor told me later on that I had drugged myself by guzzling this dirty sea water in my attempts to locate the sand bar that I had been previously standing on. It was just a little after sunrise and we two were in that part of the ocean by ourselves. I knew that it would not be very long before I would be completely unconscious. Then, for the first time in my life as well as the last time up to now, I yelled for help. And what a desolate, hollow sound echoed out across that water, and it was a sound that I knew no one was hearing. I knew that in a few minutes I would be completely unconscious and completely helpless to a point where I would probably drown, even if I was only in eighteen inches of water.

I had heard many times that when one is in the presence of imminent death a panorama of his life passes before him. This now became my experience in great detail, and I was certain in my own mind that the end of my life had come. At that time I had two sons on missions, and I wondered whether they would come home to my funeral or stay in the mission field. I wondered how my body would be recovered, and how it would be sent home. I thought what a dirty trick I was playing on my company, who would probably have a couple of corpses in the lobby when they started their meeting in about an hour. Then, in this deathly panorama, I thought about my wife and what effect my death would have upon her. And I felt sorry that I would not be around any longer to finish the journey with my wife and help to get my children established. Then I became very upset with myself. I had been perfectly capable of saving this young man's life as well as my own. The task would have been comparatively easy if I had started for the shore originally instead of wasting my strength trying to locate a sand bar. And it was my error in judgment that was going to be responsible probably for both of our deaths.

Then I took a last look at the shore which seemed to be way off in the distance. I had no sensations of choking or suffocating. It was as though I were floating around on a soft comfortable cloud. The only unpleasant sensation I had was my feeling against myself for causing my own death as well as that of my good friend, George, when neither of us were ready for that event to take place.

Just before I lost consciousness, I heard a voice and I knew that someone was speaking to me. And his face was probably within a foot and a half of my own, and yet I could not see him. I did not recognize his voice, nor could I understand even one word of what he said. I was completely blind and completely unable to understand. But I felt this boy's grip relax around my throat and I knew that someone was taking him off my back. Then I thought maybe I could swim. So again I tried to work my arms, but they were completely exhausted and just refused to obey my command. And in addition, I had lost all sense of direction. I didn't know where the shore was or toward which point of the compass I was tending. And then I sank into complete unconsciousness. If I had been allowed to drown, I am sure I would have had no other sensation beyond this point. That is, I had had all of the conscious sensations of drowning.

A little while later I came to out on the beach. Some people were working over me to get the water out of my system. My first sensation upon gaining consciousness was a tremendous overwhelming joy that I was still alive. This was not only a great joy to me, but it was one that was completely unexpected, as I had been certain that my death was imminent. Soon, Dr. William Bolt, our chief medical examiner, arrived on the beach. Under his direction I was placed in a little cart and wheeled up to my hotel room. I was swished through the bath tub to get off the salt and sand and then put to bed. The doctor told me that I was to stay there and he would come back and see me a little later. I protested that I wanted to go to the meeting, but he would not hear of it and said, "You have had a far more serious experience than you can understand and I want you to stay in bed. I will be up to see you at eleven o'clock." At eleven o'clock I had a fever and he sent me to the local hospital to be treated for shock, exhaustion, and threatened pneumonia.

I suppose I was the worst patient they ever had in that hospital. I could not bear the thoughts of missing the meetings, nor could I get over the anger with myself that I had thrown my own life away. And while I had been saved, yet that didn't satisfy me because I had no part in it and could claim no credit for my good fortune of still being alive.

Coming down on the plane I had memorized Robert Frost's poem about the man who was out in the woods in the winter with his sleigh. He stopped to look at the beauty. He said he was watching the woods fill up with snow, but then realizing that he had much to do—it may have been that he was a doctor out making calls or someone else with important responsibilities—but he closed his poem by saying,

> The woods are lovely, dark and deep
> But I have promises to keep
> And miles to go before I sleep,
> And miles to go before I sleep.

And even though I had been saved from death, yet this poem kept going through my mind, that I also had promises to keep and miles to go before I could sleep. That is, I had children to educate, a wife to provide for, my life's work to finish, and I still owed the Lord a great many years of service. Since then many years have passed and I have not yet completely gotten rid of this self-censure that I then felt because of my bad judgment in throwing away my own life and the other valuable life that was at that moment in my charge.

I was released from the hospital just at the time the convention was over and did not have the opportunity of going back to the meeting, though a number of my friends came to see me each day in the hospital and reported on the meeting, and my condition was reported to the convention. I called my wife in Salt Lake so she would not hear about my trouble from someone else who would not know the particulars. Nor did I get to talk to George Redding again to find out what his problem in the water actually was.

A few days after arriving back home, I received a letter from him which I have preserved and this is what it says:

Dear Mr. Sill:

How are you. I am fine. I hope you had a good trip home. We had a good trip home. Thank you for saving my life.

Sincerely,
George Redding

Two or three months later I had a man call me on the telephone who told me that he represented the Carnegie Hero Foundation of

Philadelphia and asked if he could come and see me. When he arrived, he told me that an application had been made for Robert Mitchell for a Hero Foundation Grant and Award. Andrew Carnegie established the fund with a considerable amount of money in it so that if anyone ever saves the life of another person, he is given a hero medal. And if he himself ever gets in serious need, this fund will give him a grant of so much money a month to help him solve his problems.

He said, "I understand that you know something about this case, and I have been sent out here from Philadelphia to investigate as to whether this award to Robert Mitchell should be given or not." I said, "If you give awards to those who save other people's lives, then you ought to give Bob Mitchell two awards, because he saved two lives. One was George Redding and the other was Sterling Sill." After that part of our business was taken care of he said, "There has also been an application made to give you a hero award." And I said, "If you give awards to those who drown other people, then you ought to give me two; because my foolishness almost lost the life of myself and George Redding." But he felt that those in Philadelphia who were responsible for making the decisions could best judge the merits of that question, and all he wanted from me was what I knew of the facts. And, of course, he also interviewed all of the other people who knew anything about it. Anyway, I received a bronze medal about five inches in diameter and a half an inch thick, appropriately inscribed on both sides.

It happened that one of the managers in our group named Robert E. Mitchell, Jr. was a skin diver. He had an oxygen tank strapped on his back and flippers on his feet, and he had been out that morning in the ocean for some reason unknown to me, as it would have seemed to me that that is a pretty dangerous situation to be out in the ocean all alone. But he was coming back and arrived at our scene just at the critical time. He took this boy off my back and when he had gotten him to shore he fell down on the beach exhausted. George said to him, "You better go out and help Mr. Sill as he is in trouble." And Robert Mitchell said, "I just can't do it, I can't swim another stroke. If I try it, I will probably drown, myself." But finally after lying there on the beach for a few minutes he got the courage to try for me. And how he ever got me through that much water and those high waves, I'll probably never know. But I am very grateful to him and to the Lord for excusing my poor judgment and by saving my life and making it possible for me to stay around a little while longer to take care of all of my unfinished business and fulfill the promises that I have made and that have been implied by my life. But my good friend Robert Mitchell and I were written up in the official and permanent Carnegie report. Mine as case number 4345 and his as case number 4346 as follows:

4345 - Sterling W. Sill, aged fifty-six, inspector of insurance agencies, helped to save George A. Redding, aged thirteen, from drowning, Hollywood, Fla., January 21, 1959. When breakers in the Atlantic Ocean swept him off a sand bar into water beyond his depth a hundred and twenty feet from shore, George called for help. Sill swam forty feet to George, who placed both arms about his neck and swung onto his back. After being submerged several times, Sill attempted to tow George toward shore but made no appreciable headway against the current. At times submerged by breakers three to four feet high, Sill took in much water and steadily weakened. Robert E. Mitchell, Jr., who was in the surf in skin-diving attire, swam a hundred feet to George and Sill. George lunged toward Mitchell, who held him off. Mitchell then told George to take hold of the neck of his rubber shirt, which he did. Although George drew himself partly onto his back and impeded his movements; Mitchell swam seventy-five feet toward shore as breakers surged over him. Already fatigued, he obtained footing and waded to the beach with George. Sill, who had been unable to swim against the current and was being carried farther from shore, then called for help. Mitchell waded into the surf and then swam a hundred and five feet to him. Breakers surged over Mitchell, and he experienced acute chest tightness as he towed Sill, who then was inert, seventy-five feet to wadable water, from where Turner Munsell aided him in taking Sill ashore. Sill was hospitalized three days for congestion in one lung and recovered.

4346 - Robert E. Mitchell, Jr., aged thirty-three, insurance company general manager, saved George A. Redding and Sterling W. Sill from drowning, Hollywood, Fla., January 21, 1959. (See award No. 4345.)

My Several Immortalities

It has already been pointed out that life is the most valuable commodity in the universe, and it is our business to take care of and increase its volume and value. The most powerful natural law of our being is the law of self-preservation. We cling to life with everything we've got. In the days of Job it was said, "All that a man hath he will give for his life." There isn't anything we wouldn't do, there isn't any price we wouldn't pay, to prolong life even for a week or a month, even though we knew that that period would be filled with pain and unhappiness.

In the famous Cato's soliloquy it is said:

> It must be so. Plato, thou reasoneth well.
> Else whence this pleasing hope, this fond de-
> sire, this longing after immortality.
> Or whence this secret dread and inward horror of
> falling into naught.
> Why shrinks the soul back on itself and startles
> at destruction.
> 'Tis the divinity that stirs within us.
> 'Tis heaven itself that points out an hereafter
> and intimates eternity to man.
> Eternity, thou pleasing, dreadful thought.

And yet it is the natural law of life that death must come to all. And it is the common experience of life that almost before we have had time to learn to live and to accumulate the means of our greatest productivity, the sentence is passed out that life has been finished. And he who lives more than one life has more than one death to die. But as we have several kinds of death, we also have the possibilities for several kinds of immortalities. Actually, physical death is a kind of graduation day. It is a transition; it is a gateway to immortality. Our death is an important part of our progress. The progress we

213

make in this life must be converted through death into an eternal progression. That is, no one would want to stop his educational progress in this life and spend eternity in the third grade. Because of the rebellion of Lucifer, he and his followers were cast out of heaven and were denied the great privileges of the mortal estate. But those of us who were obedient in the first estate have been added upon for this life and those who are faithful in this life may have glory added upon their heads forever and ever. The reward of success in this life is not just one immortality, by a little good management, we may actually have several immortalities.

One of the great secrets of our mortal success is had as we explore the various possibilities of our auxiliary immortalities.

1. Providing one is a good parent and a good teacher, he may live on in his posterity, who inherit his genes, his personality, and his attitudes.

2. One may gain a kind of immortality of thought and feeling and attitude through his books. That is, over the years one may spread out his mind, his heart, his music and his convictions to form a great paper personality which may live on after his mind has become inactive and his body has become inert.

3. I have greatly loved the prophet Job, who is yet alive to me, as every morning when I open the holy scriptures this prophet gives me a transfusion of his integrity as he says to me, "While the breath is in me and the spirit of God is in my nostrils, my lips shall not speak wickedness nor my tongue utter deceit. Till I die I will not remove mine integrity from me. My righteousness I hold fast and will not let it go. My heart shall not reproach me so long as I live." (Job 27:3-6.) And we might shout "Hurray for Job!" as his enthusiasm and philosophy of life can be made to live on in us and in our children. But not only can integrity be made immortal by writing it down, but so can the combinations of industry, courage, and ambition. And we may see some of the fruits of our investments in our immortalities while we are yet alive.

4. I may live on through my work. The great insurance industry which has made up my life's labor is devoted to writing billions of dollars of life insurance on the life of the bread winners, so that even though their lives may be cut short by death, their children may still go to school and the income left may provide them with the necessities of life, including full time mothers. When a man marries a wife for time and eternity, he should give some thought to providing for her support during that same period, regardless of whether he should live or die.

5. One of the greatest blessings of life is that it provides us with the possibility of a kind of economic immortality. One may pay a

small premium to the life insurance company and in the event his life is cut short, the insurance company will pay to his family that amount of money which he would have paid to them had he lived. Therefore, economically speaking, he can guarantee to them that the support he has promised them will not die. That is, neither the meal in his barrel shall be wasted nor the oil in his cruse. (I Kings 17:12.)

Without life insurance or other means of financial security some men automatically add a limiting clause to their marriage contract which says to their partners, "I will provide for my family's needs only till death do us part." There is much better arrangement than this available. This better clause says of the policy owner about the finances of his family, "though he were dead physically, yet shall he live economically."

6. A good doctor deals in a kind of immortality when he provides himself and his patients with health and longer life.

7. The teacher helps the student live on a mental level much higher than one he would have attained for himself.

8. There is a great set of religious doctrines which Jesus made a part of his church philosophy, which are vicarious in their natures and benefits. One person may be baptized for and in behalf of someone who did not have that opportunity himself. People may stand as proxy marriage partners for their own ancestors or other people who lived when this family sealing power was not available upon the earth. The Prophet Joseph Smith once said that those who neglect to seek after their dead do it at the peril of their own salvation. And because my time has been usually limited and my other assignments very heavy, I have tried to accomplish this goal by transferring the fruits of my other labors to helping other people to do temple work. There are many people who would like to work in the temple, but are unable to do so because they lack the funds to provide for themselves in the meantime.

Therefore, over the years it has been my great privilege to make it possible financially for many people to labor in the temple and do the work for thousands of people so that they may have eternal life under the highest and most pleasant standards of living. The names of these deceased people for whom the work has been paid for by me are listed in the various years in my book of letters. But there are many other ways that our lives may be continued beyond their natural term.

While we have the specific responsibility of seeking out and doing the work for our own progenitors, yet the Lord expects us to give a helping hand to others who have no family members to do this work for them. That is, in this as in doing missionary work, no one is restricted to members of his own family. It is a great idea that through some kind of a trust or fund or foundation, one may provide the financial means which will make many eternal benefits available to other people even beyond the day of their own deaths. That is, one may accumulate his surplus earnings in a fund that will provide a perpetual and eternal interest income and secure for him a kind of economic immortality. Even reaching beyond his own life, the earnings from this fund can provide the benefits that he himself might have provided had he been permitted to live forever upon the earth.

9. One of the most inspiring and profitable of my life's experiences was to fill a mission for the Church. I worked on the farm to earn enough money so that I could send myself on a mission to the Southern States, where I was successful in converting a considerable number of people to the principles of the gospel. I later had the privilege of sending two sons on missions.

Because my mission meant so much to me, I decided I would like to help some others outside my own family to have the same privilege, and from then to now I have paid either half or all of the expenses for over one hundred missionaries, to spend two years of their time or a total of over two hundred years in all, in helping them to increase the value of their eternal lives.

After Charles A. Callis, my mission president, became a member of the Quorum of Twelve, he toured the Mexican Mission. When he returned, he was very concerned about the fact that many promising young Mexicans wanted to serve as missionaries, but were prevented from so doing by lack of finances. President Callis suggested that I furnish the money to help as many of them as possible. This I did.

Since that time nearly 30 years have passed and I occasionally hear some of these young men who have served their own people as missionaries, but at the same time have developed great leadership capabilities within themselves. At a recent mission presidents' seminar, one of these missionaries that I helped to go on a mission many years ago, by the name of Abraham Lozano, introduced himself to me. He had just been appointed the president of the Mexican Villahermosa Mission. He wrote me the following letter from the mission field:

Villahermosa, Tabasco, Mexico
July 9, 1975

Dear Brother Sill:

With respect and affection I send my greetings to you and your wife and the rest of your family. Now that I am officially in the mission field I feel again the incredible joy of being a missionary.

These missions in Mexico are the highest in baptisms per missionary in the whole world, and we will do everything possible to preserve this standing.

Brother Sill, as I have already told you personally in your office when I was there with my wife in the beautiful city of Salt Lake attending the Mission Presidents' Seminar, my gratitude toward you is infinite as you sustained me totally in my mission. It is greater than anything I have received in all my life. I have never forgotten President Pierce, my mission president, when he told me when I was 19 years old that you were paying for my mission.

May God bless you more than he already has, now and forever.

Sincerely,
Abraham Lozano

I like to think that I will live on in some fraction in President Lozano. I converted some of my toil into the medium of exchange which he used to qualify himself for his great career as a mission president.

Andrew Carnegie capitalized on this idea of immortalizing his own abilities. He took many millions of the wealth which he had accumulated and established the Carnegie Foundations. His trustees used the money which he had created to build libraries, provide educations, and do many other things for people long after Mr. Carnegie himself had passed away. Mr. Carnegie was born in Scotland in 1835 and he died in America in 1919, so that he has already stretched out one part of his life for fifty-six years beyond the day of his death.

William James, the great Harvard psychologist, once said that the greatest use of life is to spend it for something that outlasts it. There are many ways that we may stretch our influence, our abilities, and our assistance to others beyond the boundaries of this life.

Andrew Carnegie has built up an "economic immortality." He converted his industry, his intelligence, his ability to plan and think and organize into cash and then his trustees used that cash in an endowment for the entire world which may make Mr. Carnegie's intelligence, planning, and industry last forever.

Each one of us may do that same thing. Money is the medium of exchange. We may convert our labor into cash and then with money we may build temples, send out missionaries, endow hospitals, make educations possible for our doctors and teachers and philosophers and religious leaders. Our bodies and our brains will some day get old and worn out, but between the time of one's birth and his death, he may convert that industry, ambition and helpfulness into the medium of exchange as a kind of sinking fund for his life. The most effective machine will someday wear out, but a business organization may establish a sinking fund invested at compound interest so that when the machine is worn out, the funds are available to provide a new machine. When that is worn out another machine may be made available, and so on, ad infinitum.

But we may do the same thing with life. It was said of Sampson that in his death he killed more Philistines than he did in his life. Through the great privilege of economic immortality, it may be possible for us to do more good for others after our death than we did before our death. That is, we may take some of the toil that wears out our physical body and invest it at compound interest so that the service of our earning power may go on forever.

10. Then we come to the final immortality, the immortality of the soul. Life is made up of three great subdivisions—an antemortal life, a mortal life, and a post-mortal life. The first two must of necessity come to an end, but we may invest them so as to increase the glory, the joy, and the eternity of the third which will be everlasting. Someone has said that our pre-existence is the childhood of our immortality. Our mortality is the time of growing up, but our post-mortal life is eternal. There we may live with God under the highest standards of living that we have prepared for during the other periods.

As of this date, I have a mortal expectation of life of approximately ten more years. And while I hope to do a little better than that, yet in this final ten years I expect to provide some of the additional finances needed by researchers and those desiring to do temple work to bring joy and progress to a very large number of other people for whom this research and these ordinances are essential.

Victor Hugo once said that the most powerful thing in the world is an idea whose time has come. And an idea's time comes when one gets a harness on it so that it can do work for him and others. After Sir Christopher Wren built his famous St. Paul's Cathedral in London, he built a house for himself at a certain vantage point where he could look out upon his cathedral masterpiece. This seems to me to be a kind of miniature illustration of those lines in Genesis indicating that God looked out upon the earth that he had created and called it very good, and one of the most constructive joys of life is that we may do the same thing.

Robert Browning once wrote a poem in which he said:

> Grow old along with me
> The best is yet to be
> The last of life
> For which the first was made.

And as I enter this last lap of these tremendous mortal experiences, I hope to make it the most productive of the total. For example, I intend to put a harness on this trust fund idea so that it will work for me in a substantial way forever. And I have no doubt that my Heavenly Father in his goodness will allow me some little balcony from which I may look upon some of my postmortal immortalities, not only to inspect their progress but to be made glad by them.

The Sterling W. Sill Home Living Center

As my term as Chairman of the Board of Regents was drawing to its close, we had a meeting at which Dr. Virginia F. Cutler,
head of the department of home economics, appeared before the
Board and asked for an appropriation of $18,000 to buy a house on
North Wolcott Street owned by Edgar A. Bering, which she wanted
to remodel and use as a practice house for the girls graduating in
home economics. The proposed program was that they study the
academic part of homemaking, and then serve a kind of internship
by living in this house where, as far as possible, they would actually
do some of the things that would be required of them when managing a home of their own.

The University's budget for that year had been exhausted, and
so the request had to be declined; but I was impressed with the
program that Dr. Cutler was trying to carry out, and I told her and
the members of the Board of Regents that I would personally raise
the money to buy this house. I felt confident that I could get seventeen other people besides myself to put in $1,000 each. Then we
could buy this home and give it to the University to be used for this
very worthy purpose. I mentioned the matter to a few people that I
thought might be interested and soon had fourteen of the necessary
eighteen thousand dollars.

Then I called on Leland B. Flint, and he said, "I will give you
the $1,000; but," he said, "I think what you are doing is wrong." He
said, "If the University needs a building, what you ought to do is to
build it on the University campus and build it to suit the need to be
served. It is both expensive and unsatisfactory to remodel an old
building; and if you buy a home in this residential area, you will
probably have problems of parking and other public relations with
the neighbors." I said to him, "Lee, I know that's so, but a new building would cost a great deal of money which the University doesn't
have. It would also take a great deal of my time which I don't have to
spare, and even this makeshift proposal would be a lot better than

what they now have, as they are renting a place off the campus not nearly as suitable as this, and it costs the University a great deal of money every year. This makeshift proposal is something that can be done and is a great improvement over what is presently being done." He said, "That may be so, but if you can't do a thing right, then maybe you ought not to do it at all."

I could understand the logic of what he was saying, and I decided to discuss it with Dr. Cutler. I told her what Mr. Flint had said, and she said, "We're already off the campus with all the possibility of unfavorable public relations now. It will probably be a long time before the University has enough money to build us what we ought to have; in the meantime, this would be much better and much more economical." And she said, "If you don't want to raise the rest of the money, I will give you the other $4,000."

I thought if it was that important to her, who had the responsibility for this work, maybe I ought to help her a little bit; so I went to see Ray Ashton, the architect, and told him what had been done. And I said to him, "Supposing that as Chairman of the Board of Regents I asked you to build us a building, and because we haven't any money you wouldn't be able to charge us anything for it, what would you say?" He said, "If you will let me build the building the way it ought to be, I will do it for you without charge." He said, "All of my life I have been building prices, and just one time in my career I would like to build a standard. I would like to build something to fit a need and not to fit a price." He said, "I will go up to the University and find out what their need is, then I will go around the country and investigate how this need has been solved in other places. I will do all the drawings, supervise the construction, pay all of my own out-of-pocket expense, if you will pay all of the other bills." I said, "That would be wonderful. How much would it cost?" He said, "I don't know what it would cost, and I'm not going to talk about what it would cost. I'll build the building the way it ought to be, and you pay for it—whatever it costs." I said, "Look, you don't understand. The University hasn't any money, and I need to know what it's going to cost." He said, "That's your problem, and I'm not interested in that. I've made you a proposition: I'll build you a building if you will pay for it." Anyway, he scared me to the point where I didn't dare discuss it with him any further; and I thought possibly it may cost $25,000 or $31,000, but even if it cost $36,000 or twice as much, I could probably raise the money. So I said to him, "Okay, you go ahead and build the building, and I will pay for it." Then I made a few more calls and got a little more money.

Six months later when he got the plans drawn was the first time I knew the building was going to cost in the neighborhood of $400,000, and I had agreed to pay for it. By this time he had already spent $16,000 of his own money in expenses, plans, etc.; and I had the most awful feeling of calamity that I had ever had in my life. I had just finished reading Dale Carnegie's book, *How to Win Friends and Influence People,* and I didn't think it would make Ray Ashton feel very good, after he had gone to all of this much work and spent this much of his own money, if I now said to him, "I have changed my mind, and now I don't think I will go through with my promise." I had gotten myself into a jam that I couldn't possibly see any way out of, except to go through with it. Even though it was impossible, I had given my word and I *had* to perform.

I was reminded of a story I once heard of a desperate woman who was being taken to the hospital to give birth to her first child. She was very scared and generally unhappy about the whole situation and said, "I don't think I will go through with it." I thought there was a great deal of similarity in our situations, and I felt that I was under about as much compulsion to go through with my ordeal as she was with hers. I had to go through with it, and I was almost frightened out of my wits. There was no possible alternative.

I remember that out on the farm they always used to have side-blinders on the horses so that the horses could not look back or out to the side but only straight ahead.

I called up five men on the telephone and invited them to go to lunch with me one day. These were men that knew about this project and had a considerable amount of interest in it, and I thought that they might help me figure out some way to get this job done. I expanded my list of possible contributors until I had the names of 706 men who I thought could, if they wanted to, afford to give a minimum of $1,000 without hurting them too much. I decided not to accept anything less than the thousand dollars, or we would be forever getting through it. At lunch I went over with them all of the reasons why I thought this was a great project, and they agreed to help. I gave them my sales presentation which had worked pretty well for me in the money that I had already collected. I also had some copies made of this list of 706 prospective contributors, and we went down the list of names and each one checked off those names that he agreed to call on and ask for a contribution.

A couple of weeks later, I called each one of them to see how he was getting along with his collection, and each one said in turn that he had been too busy with his own business and had had no time to make any calls. The next week the answer was the same, and the next week it was still the same. I had some sympathy for them as I myself was very busy with my own business; but I had an advantage that they did not have, and that is that I *had* to do it and they didn't.

Therefore, after I had finished my own list of names, I took each of the other lists in turn, and in the next two and one-half years I called on 704 of these 706 people, some of them several times. Only two of the 706 hesitated about giving me the chance for an interview, and in both of these cases the problem came about because of my faulty approach. But I called on everyone of the other 704 who lived in various parts of the state between Spanish Fork and Logan. Out of the 704 people, 457 of them turned me down; and if anyone would like to have an interesting experience, he ought to get himself turned down 457 times in a row on the same proposition. But the other 247 who did not turn me down gave me a total of approximately $400,000.

Here again, I saw in action the operation of this old law of averages which I knew so well from my life insurance selling experience. Everything can be foretold on a scientific basis if one knows his own version of the law of averages. That is, if you throw a silver half-dollar into the air once, you do not know whether it will come down a head or a tail; but if you throw it into the air a thousand times, it will come down substantially five-hundred heads and five-hundred tails. After a salesman has kept track of his experience for a while, he can soon determine what his percentage of calls, contacts, interviews, and sales will be. He can determine in advance the average size of the case he will sell, just as the insurance company can tell how many people are going to die out of a given number at a given age.

I soon discovered that my own law of averages was two people turned me down and the third person gave me an average of $1500, this means an average contribution per interview of $500. Knowledge of this law of averages has saved the success lives of many salesmen. In my case, for example, I was not discouraged when two people in a row turned me down, because I knew on an average every third person would give me $1500. By this I could figure out exactly how fast I had to work to get the job done on time.

Anyway, I arranged to have the money come in fast enough so that there was never a time when construction had to be stopped because there was not enough money to pay the bills. And I felt again the old thrill that I have known many times before, that there is always a great joy goes with success in any worthwhile undertaking. I also learned what I had already known before, that when you have a job like this to do, it is likely to cut into your productivity in some other place. During these three years the results of my recruiting and training of new life insurance men fell off substantially, and there will always be a dip in my production graph pointing out the years that I was building the homeliving center.

However, in the collecting of this money I had some tremendous experiences. Once I had recovered from the shock and threatened hysteria I had first felt, and after I had realized that I could depend on my old friend the law of averages, everything went fine and was a lot of fun, except that it took time.

I had known that you can sell life insurance and depend on the law of averages, but when you ask people to give money and get nothing in return either of value, or praise, or prestige, that seemed to me like a little different proposition; and while the law of averages may drop for some particular enterprise, the law itself remains the same, and the more difficult the accomplishment the more exciting the success tends to be.

Many people have their greatest pleasure in going fishing. They like to get a sizeable game fish on the end of a line and then exercise whatever skill is necessary to bring him in. In my opinion, it is a lot more fun when you've got a man on the end of the line with his pocketbook in his hand. I make another comparison in these two situations, because a fisherman takes unfair advantage of his prospective catch by disguising the hook in some attractive looking bait; whereas in my situation, I let him see the hook immediately and warned him about what the possibilities might be if he listened attentively enough to my sales-talk. My presentation lasted twenty-five minutes. I had carefully prepared my logic, psychology and enthusiasm. I thought my presentation was pretty good and that I had the ability to give it convincingly; and I'm sure I had more fun extracting this $400,000 from people than any fisherman ever had in going fishing.

For example, the builder told me that in order to hook onto the sewer system I would need four manholes, and I thought it would be a lot better to have everything contributed that was possible instead of paying for them. So I asked him where these might be obtained. He gave me an address of a little foundry down on the west side of town. I found the shop which had weeds growing in front of the doors; the windows were all blackened with smoke. The place looked like there hadn't been a customer in six months.

I knocked at the door, and no one responded. By this time I had decided not to ask him for any money as his business didn't look prosperous enough to justify a contribution to higher education, and I didn't want to embarrass him. Therefore, I turned and started away, but I had gone only a few steps when the door opened and a head was poked out through the opening that had on it the saddest face that I had ever seen. He looked as though someone had dumped a whole washtub full of troubles in his face. He said, "What do you want?" I stammered a little bit not knowing just how to tell him that I had come down to ask him for some money that I was now not going to ask him for. Finally I said, "I came down here to ask you to give me four manholes for a building we are building up at the University of Utah. I am not going to do that, but I would like you to tell me what they would cost."

I had told him enough that my apparent indecision had aroused his suspicion, and he said, "Do you mean some people are giving you the material free of charge?" And I said, "yes, some are, but you don't need to. I have plenty of money, and I can pay you for them." And to allay his suspicions, I told him a little bit about what I was doing. I think the idea that I was not going to ask him for any money hurt his pride a little bit, and he said, "I don't want you to think that I'm so poor that I can't make a contribution." He said, "If others are contributing, I would like to contribute." He said, "Besides, I have a son who graduated from the University. My son is a man of character. If I could build a little character in someone else through my contribution, I would like to make it." Then he said, "The reason that my plant is closed down here today is that my men are all off drunk. They are not like my son. They do not have the same kind of character that my son has."

Then we sat down on an old iron pipe that was lying there, and he told me about his son and how proud he was of his son. His son was a teacher, trying to help other people to live more successfully, and his father wanted to be a part of this program of human betterment. During our discussion he was about to cry, and I was about to cry. Finally he gave me the manholes and I went on my way. And I am sure that on many occasions since that time he has taken his wife on a drive some Sunday afternoon past this building which he helped to erect.

I made everyone of these calls personally and alone with one exception. Leland Flint—who was most generous in the construction of this building and donated some $30,000 worth of refrigerators, stoves, etc., to equip these apartments—had a fellow electrical appliance dealer that he thought would be interested in making a contribution; and he suggested that I take him with me on the call, which I was glad to do. When we got to this man's place of business, they reported that he was out in the warehouse opening some inventory. We went out and these two appliance men talked shop for a few minutes about their products, and then this man said, "You didn't come to talk about this. Let's go into the office and you can tell me what you came to tell me."

On the way in Mr. Flint said to his friend, "Bill, how's your wife?" His friend replied, "Not very well. She's been up at the hospital for some tests, and the doctor thinks that she has a brain tumor. She's going into the hospital Thursday to be operated on." When we got in his office, I was invited to go ahead with the presentation. After I had finished, this man said, "No, I'm not interested in making a contribution to the University." He said, "I never went to the University. I had to work for my money, and I think everybody else ought to do the same." He felt that learning was a substitute for labor.

When he finished with his objection, I said, "Mr. Jones, I think what you have said about education is very interesting. As you and Lee were talking about those wonderful appliances out in the warehouse, I was thinking that I could make a lot of your kind of appliance sales with even a fifth grade education, or even with no education at all. I did not know before that anything like that was available. And while anyone would not need an education to sell that kind of appliances, the one who figured out how to make them in the first place probably had an education. And I would like to ask you a question: How would you like to have the agency sell appliances manufactured by someone who had never been exposed to a little schooling?" And he said, "I had never thought of that."

I said, "Mr. Jones, I was sorry to hear that your wife must have an operation for her brain tumor. Suppose when you got her up at the hospital Thursday they announced to you that the man who was to remove her brain tumor was a high school dropout. How would you like it?" He said, "I wouldn't like it." I said, "There are many important people who have never graduated from a university, but anyone of them would seriously dislike to live in a nation or in a community where no one had been to a university. That is, you can have a great many of the advantages of a university without ever going there personally. You can have the services of the most highly educated doctors, lawyers, engineers, educators, and a lot of other people who are very helpful in building our society even if you have never gone to high school. And one of those girls that will go to the university to study home building may marry one of your grandsons, and you might be grateful that she has had the best training, not only in the home building courses themselves but in the culture, religion, refinement, and other things that go with a university." He said, "I've never thought of those things." I said, "I am sure you haven't." Then he said, "What was the amount you asked me for?" And I said, "I asked you for a thousand dollars, but since this conversation I am going to raise it to $2500." He said, "Alright, I'll give you $2500." And he wrote me a check in that amount.

The University got the $2500, but I am sure that this man has a much better appreciation of the role of the university in the community and in his personal life, even though he has never gone there himself.

On another occasion I called on the Anderson Jewelry Company, and they made a contribution of $2500 in silver, crystal, and china. One time at a later date I went in to see Mr. Anderson about another matter, and he was waiting on a customer. This customer was talking about buying a dozen sterling silver fingerbowls that were highly ornamented and polished so that they shone almost like the sun. The price for these fingerbowls was $360 per dozen, and this customer was trying to get the price down to $325. Mr. Anderson was very offended. To him this beautiful sterling silver was almost like his own children, and he was scolding the man for wanting a discount. The conversation was very heated and highly interesting to me.

After the customer had gone, I said, "Mr. Anderson, I heard what you said to that man who was trying to get you to reduce the price of your silver; and if you had solicited my aid, I would have probably helped you throw him out of the store." I said to him, "Do you know what you ought to do with those fingerbowls?" And he said, "No." I said, "They are too beautiful to sell to any individual person. No matter what that man had paid for those fingerbowls he would probably have taken them home and locked them up in the cabinet someplace and very few people would ever have had a chance to enjoy their beauty. What you ought to do is to give them to the University so that all of these young women who go there will have a chance to learn to love and appreciate beautiful things." He said, "That's the best idea I've heard today. You take them." And while he almost threw one man out of the store for wanting a discount, he gave them to me for nothing because of an idea that he liked.

At a later date, a burglar robbed the Anderson Jewelry Store and took what Mr. Anderson appraised at probably a thousand dollars worth of his merchandise. This robbery was written up covering three columns in the newspaper. I later jokingly complained to Mr. Anderson that this burglar only got a thousand dollars and he gave him three columns, and I got $2500 plus some fingerbowls and he didn't give me any newspaper publicity at all.

And while most people wouldn't want to undertake the responsibility of raising $400,000; yet everyone of these 704 contacts proved to be an interesting experience, whether they gave money or whether they did not.

I used to know a great salesman who had a goal to make a sale on every call. He didn't mean that he actually intended to write up an order for everyone he called on, but he did expect to leave everyone he called on a little more sold on his company product and its service when he left than they were when he came. And I hope that these 704 people and their families will be a little more appreciative of the privileges of education and our other important institutions in the community than they would have been if I had not called.

He That Hath Eyes, Let Him See

It is very interesting to try to understand the fact that the greatest invention of our earth is us. The most important event that ever took place in the universe is described in that part of the Book of Genesis which says: "So God created man in his own image, in the image of God created he him; male and female created he them." (Gen. 1:27.) God has poured out great blessings upon us and has given us dominion over everything upon the earth. Not only were we created in the magnificent form of God, but we have been endowed with his attributes and potentialities.

It used to bother me a little bit to hear the evolutionists propound their theories that by a process of natural selection this magnificent potentiality which is ourselves evolved by some series of accidents to become what we are.

Of all of the miracles and wonders that I have heard about, nothing surpasses the miracle of eyesight, which beholds the glory of the sun or can reach out across the universe to the most distant star. Our eyesight can bring back to us all of the beauties and wonders of the world. It is very difficult to conceive that such miraculous ability could have been developed by some blind, irresponsible chance.

Or think of our potentially magnificent brain. It is 70 percent liquid and yet in it can be stored as much information as in a great library.

Through our ears we enjoy a great symphony of sounds—the music of the spheres, the glory of laughter and the magnificence of the voices of our friends. We have some godly senses of touch and taste and expression. Our nostrils bring us lifegiving air, the fragrance of the flowers and the odor of the earth after the rain.

Jesus made what was probably the greatest criticism of our lives when he said that frequently these magnificent abilities are allowed to go undeveloped and unused. He pointed out that some

229

of us have eyes that don't see and ears that don't hear and hearts that fail to understand. Because these gifts are granted us only on a kind of lend-lease basis, when we fail to use them, they lose their potentiality. Consequently our lives themselves are let down from the high place that the Lord intended them to occupy. These gifts are also sometimes taken from us by processes of aging or ill health.

After nearly 70 years of abundant good health the optometrist discovered in my eyes the seeds of retinal deterioration which would eventually rob me of my ability to read. It is a condition where the central vision of the eye loses its ability to function. For a number of years I have suffered the effects of this downward trend in my physical vision. One by one, some of the great pleasures of reading, the joy of seeing clearly the expressions on the faces of my friends and the light in the eyes of my grandchildren have been gradually taken away. Consequently, my life has become much more solitary than ever before. I frequently become very lonesome for the faces of my friends and for the pleasant associaton formerly had with my other friends living in the pages of our great literature. Much of my association has also been cut off with some of the ancient and modern prophets. And because my newspaper print has become so reduced in size, I miss keeping up-to-date on the happenings of our own age of miracles and wonders.

When the apostle Paul was imprisoned in his Roman dungeon to await his execution, he wrote a letter to a young man by the name of Timothy, in whom he had a special interest, requesting that Timothy bring Paul's coat to the prison to keep him warm through the long cold months of the approaching winter and also to bring him his books. And the great apostle reminded Timothy that he was particularly anxious to have him bring his beloved parchments. I'm sure that Paul felt if he had his coat to keep him warm and his great books to keep his mind profitably and pleasantly employed, he would get through the winter all right. What a great joy it would be to me if for an hour or two a day I could borrow from creation a couple of good retinas while I fed on some of the great philosophies, the wonderful poems, and the great scriptures of those enchanting books that have lost some of their ability to lift me up though they still occupy their accustomed places on my bookshelves.

About some of these wonders of creation, the poet has said:

> Every day in books
> Rip Van Winkle lies asleep
> Moby Dick patrols the deep
> Every day in books.

Tall windmills turn in Spain
Where across the empty plain
Rides a rusty knight in vain
Every day in books.

Falstaff laughs and Hamlet dreams
Camelot is all it seems
Kublai Khan in Sahnadu
Hears the rivers running through
Every day in books.

Marco Polo sails away
Mr. Pickwick has his say
Troy is falling every day
Every day in books.

I have no serious feeling of guilt or regret because of my present inability to read, as I have read a great deal and have enjoyed it very much. I have memorized many stimulating passages. But I miss the ability not only to explore but to reread. We usually like those things best that we are most familiar with. We like to sing the familiar songs. Children like to hear the same story over and over again. Its value increases as we know it better. We love to read the biographies of the people we know. We love to hear the great literature that is most familiar to us.

Shakespeare wrote 37 plays and staffed them with 1,000 characters, each of which is the personification of some personality trait. Some of these children of Shakespeare's creative imagination are among my finest friends. I love to go into the court room at Venice and hear Portia make her great plea to Shylock for mercy for the unfortunate Antonio. Or hear Portia's inspiring expression of her tribute of love to her betrothed husband, Lord Bassonio. Or listen to Henry V give his impassioned speech of arousal to his soldiers before the battle of Agincort, or to hear Julius Caesar give his great philosophies of courage. Caesar said: "Cowards die a thousand times before their deaths: the valiant never taste of death but once. Of all wonders that I yet have seen, it seems to me most strange that men should fear; seeing that death, a necessary end, will come when it will come."

I like to walk through the pages of Paradise Lost as I go with John Milton to the councils of heaven and the councils of hell and hear the impassioned pleas debated about the great issues involved in the war in heaven.

I have a particular interest in John Milton for many reasons. One is that he was blind for some 20 years before his great epic poem Paradise Lost was written. Someone has said that John Milton never saw paradise until he lost his eyes. John Milton said of his own blindness:

> Thus with the year
> Seasons return, but not to me returns
> Day, or the sweet approach of even or morn,
> Or sight of vernal bloom, or summer's rose.
> Or flocks, or herds, or human face divine,
> But cloud instead and ever-during dark
> Surrounds me, from the cheerful ways of men
> Cut off, and for the book of knowledge fair
> Presented with a universal blank
> Of nature's works, to me expunged and rased,
> And Wisdom at one entrance quite shut out.

John Milton's first wife died, and he married again after he was blind. He lived with his wife for many years but never saw her face. He often wondered what she looked like and wished that he could see her, but he was blind. And then one night, he saw her in his dream. He thought he had never imagined anything quite so beautiful. He said:

> "Vested all in white, pure as her mind,
> love's goodness, sweetness in her person
> shined so clear that nothing could have
> rendered more delight. But, oh as to
> embrace me she inclined, I waked, she
> fled and day brought back my night."

That is, when John Milton was awake, he was blind. Only in the nighttime did he have eyes. Contemplating this great loss, he said, "Light, the prime work of God in me extinct, with all her various wonders of delight." And then he prayed that inasmuch as physical light had been denied him that God would grant him the great gift of spiritual vision that he might see and understand the things of God. And then in concluding his prayer, he said: "So much the rather thou celestial light shine inward and the mind with all her powers irradiate. There plant eyes, all mists from hence purge and disperse that I may see and tell of things invisible to mortal sight."

I have another special common interest with the blind Greek poet, Homer, who lived nine centuries B.C. He wrote the great epic poems, "The Iliad" and "The Odyssey." The Iliad is a story of the valor and heroism displayed in the ten-year Trojan war and The Odyssey is the account of the Greek hero Odysseus and his ten year adventurous return trip from the battlefields of Troy through 300 miles of island-dotted sea, back to his Greek kingdom of Itheca. I love to read the potent passages of these great experiences because I feel a relationship and an intimacy with those who take part.

And most exciting of all, I like to devour the holy scriptures and live with the prophets and hear the work of God himself. I can stand at the foot of Mt. Sinai and to the accompaniment of the lightnings and thunders of that sacred mountain hear the divine voice giving those great laws called the Ten Commandments. Or in imagination I can go to the top of the Mount of Transfiguration and see Jesus dressed in shining garments with Moses and Elias as the Savior Himself was transfigured before Peter, James, and John. Or I may stand at the foot of the cross as the Son of God made the great sacrifice by which he redeemed all of mankind, including me, and made eternal exaltation possible on condition of our own repentance and good works.

Occasionally, particularly at Eastertime, I like to mingle with the Roman soldiers as they stood their watch before the tomb of Christ and hear that great earthquake and see the angel of the resurrection whose countenance was like lightning and whose raiment was white as snow, standing as the immortal gods before the tomb. It was in their presence that the Roman soldiers became as dead men. And then one shining shape rolled back the stone and the Son of God came forth as he instituted the universal resurrection upon our earth.

Sometimes our senses deteriorate with age or they lose their power because of disuse, sin or perverted interests. And so I would say with Jesus, "He that hath eyes to see, let him see and he that hath ears to hear, let him hear." And while we have minds and hearts capable of understanding, we ought to use them to the limit.

How grateful I am that though some things have been taken, yet many still abide. I can still hear the testimonies of my friends and feel their enthusiasm. I am very grateful that my secretary and the President of the Church, and my dentist and the Lord himself can still see. And I have an increase of gratitude for those other great gifts of God of which I have a full use. I still have a heart and a voice, and several times a week I am permitted to use my voice in some more or less formal expression of those important convictions that are stored in my own mind and heart.

My earnest prayer to my Heavenly Father is that my ears may hear and that my heart may clearly understand those important truths that are so necessary to our eternal success and happiness, and that I may be some small instrument in his hands in helping someone else to see those great truths on which our eternal lives depend.

The Case of the Poison Ivy

As we go along in life we sometimes discover that little things may come to be very important because of what they grow into, or because of some sentiment that they may carry with them, or even because of the error of ridiculousness involved. Arthur Conan Doyle tells of the experiences of his famous detective Sherlock Holmes by the case method. He wrote about "The Case of the Cardboard Box," the "Case of the Creeping Man," the "Case of the Mistaken Identity," the "Case of the Devil's Foot," the "Case of the Dying Detective," the "Adventures of the Empty House," and the "Case of the Illustrious Client." Doctors and lawyers and others also sometimes divide their occupational practice into cases. I would like to attempt to present a part of myself by that method, and I would like to begin with "The Case of the Poison Ivy."

During the period that I was courting my wife I had quite a bit of trouble with competition, and while I think of myself as a fairly good competitor in most things, there were times in my courtship when I seemed to be playing on the losing team. This stimulated me, as most other forms of competition do, to make a little greater effort.

My wife-to-be was a schoolteacher, and she liked to keep her schoolroom looking very attractive for her students. This is a quality that has carried over with her into her home. During the autumn preceding our marriage, she asked me if I would take her up into the canyons and help her gather some autumn leaves with which to decorate her schoolroom. The expedition was very successful, and we came back with a car loaded with attractive colored leaves.

The next day I was driving along the mountain road east of Layton, and I saw some of the most beautiful, brilliantly colored leaves that I had ever seen. I was delighted at the discovery, because I knew that these would please her very much, and as a consequence I expected my stock to go up in her estimation. And so with my pocketknife I cut a large armful of these magnificent leaves. I took them over to her house, and she was delighted. She found a large wicker basket that would show off these leaves at their very best.

At that time her family had a highschool botany teacher staying at their home. When he came home from school, he made a comment about the pretty leaves and asked where they came from. And then my prospective wife told him very proudly that I had found them and brought them to her. Without anymore comment he disappeared into his room, and in a few minutes came back with a botany book showing plates of some beautiful leaves just like these. This botany book identified my beautiful discovery as poison ivy.

I had handled them quite freely in cutting and delivering them, and she had done the same in arranging them in the basket. Her mother had also come in very close contact with them, and we all expected that we would soon break out in some kind of awful rash and sickness caused by this poison that I had introduced into their home. And so we began a long period of troubled, expectant waiting. I expected that when we were all the victims of my poisonous present that my love suit might go down like a leaden balloon, but fortunately no one felt even the slightest ill effects.

After my release from my fears, I think I must have felt a little bit like the apostle Paul as the boat on which he was riding was shipwrecked off the island of Melita. Those on the boat abandoned ship and swam to shore, and because they were very wet and cold they built a fire on the ground to try to warm and dry themselves. The scripture says that "When Paul had gathered a bundle of sticks, and laid them on the fire, there came a viper out of the heat, and fastened on his hand." (Acts 28:3.) When the natives saw this venomous beast biting him, they thought there was no hope, that he would soon swell up and fall dead of the viper's poison. But Paul shook off the viper and it fell back into the fire. Then Paul and the others concerned went through their own period of waiting to see the working of the poison. But after they had waited a great while and saw no harm come to Paul, they thought he must be some kind of superhuman being. (See Acts 28:1-6.) It seemed to me that my guardian angel must have been working in my interests in that same direction.

Of course, there is another possible explanation for our delivery from the effects of the poison, and that is that as poison ivy gets to the fall time of the year, its poison may lose most of its potence. I am sure Paul was very grateful for his delivery, and so was I. In the near half century that has elapsed since that time, I have achieved some little distinction that because while others come to court with flowers and candy, I came bearing a bouquet of poison ivy.

The Case of the Unsewed Trousers

$\mathcal{I}$t is very interesting that experiences are sometimes a mixture of good and bad. Very frequently those events that might tend to embarrass us have some element of good in them. In August 1932, I had been invited by the National Association of Life Underwriters to attend the national convention held at the Fairmont Hotel in San Francisco. I had previously been selected to be one of the speakers at that convention. The night before I was to leave, my wife had done what she could in packing my clothes, as there would not be very much time the following morning because I had to catch an early airplane out of Salt Lake. But the night before, we attended the North Davis Stake MIA-day at Lagoon.

During that previous year, the MIA had been trying to teach its members how to waltz correctly, and because dancing was one of the things that I did very badly, my wife saw to it that I took in as many of these lessons as possible. I was a little late getting home from work to dress to go to Lagoon. In those days I had two suits that I might wear, both of them were made of blue serge. One of them was new; this she had laid aside for me to wear to San Francisco. The other was old and had come almost completely unsewed in the seat of the trousers. Not knowing this, she had hung this suit up in the closet and in my hurry I put it on without knowing about the error. I did not discover the problem until we were at Lagoon when it was too late to do very much about it.

We went with some other friends and had dinner at Lagoon, and when I was sitting down, I was completely safe. However, one of the important parts of the MIA-day program was the dance that was given in the large Lagoon Pavilion, as the main feature of which the MIA was going to sponsor a prize waltz as a kind of culmination of what they had been trying to teach in this particular year. The large dance floor was very crowded, as it was largely attended. And as people were packed together for the dance, I had little fear of the embarrassment of exposure. Then they announced the prize waltz, and they gave careful instructions that they wanted everybody on the floor to begin with. Many judges had been chosen and they would pass among the dancers and indicate those that should remain on the floor for the next encore by tapping them on the shoulder.

When the prize waltz was announced, my wife and I were on the west side of the pavilion, whereas our gathering place with our friends was over on the east side. My wife suggested that we could do as directed and when the first encore ended, and we would be eliminated from the dance, we would be with our friends on the east side from which we could watch the progress of the contest. But during this first period I was touched on the shoulder, indicating that we should remain on the floor for the next encore. This was much more serious, as many of the people were eliminated giving a much clearer view of the individual dancers. But my wife gave it as her opinion that if I stood up very straight, my coat might shield me from embarrassment during the next encore, as there were still quite a number of people on the floor and we would be released the next time the music stopped. But again I was touched on the shoulder. This elimination process went on for several encores, and each time as the dancers became fewer in number, my situation became increasingly more serious.

During the MIA season as we had attended these dance practices, my wife with her sense of timing had counted out the step-reach-close, step-reach-close rhythm in my ear, so that if I followed her counting, I would be all right so far as the steps were concerned, and my unsewed trousers gave me a powerful motivation for a perfect posture by standing up straight. Anyway, we were tapped time after time until we were the only dancers remaining on the floor. We won the grand prize. For some considerable period after the decision was made and our names had been announced as the winners, the orchestra continued playing for us alone, and the vast crowd around the hall was watching and applauding us as we served as "Exhibit A" as the prime example of how to waltz correctly.

I have often wondered what would have happened if my wife had had to cough or had an attack of laryngitis which would have seriously endangered my rhythm, or if I had had a heart attack which I seemed to be very close to; I do not know what would have happened to my honor. Anyway, over the years, one of my important Sherlock Holmes' triumphs took place in "The Case of the Unsewed Trousers."

A prediction has been made about the success of our country, that things may get so bad that the Constitution would hang by a thread. And it seems to me that my success has been in a position about as precarious as that on a great number of occasions, and yet some of these humorous circumstances helped to give interest and color to my life.

The Case of the One Minute Speech

During the October 1960 General Conference, some of the speakers had gone over their time. When my turn came, the conference schedule was five speakers behind. Before the meeting began, I said to President McKay, "President McKay, you are five speakers behind. Why don't you just take me off the program and that will solve at least twenty percent of the problem." He was very appreciative and said, "If you don't mind, that is what we will do, and I appreciate your thoughtfulness."

The following October Conference history repeated itself. Again the conference was running considerably behind, and again before the meeting began I said to the President, "Why don't you just leave me off the program and that will help the conference to get back on schedule?" He said, "It seems like we did that to you once before." And I said, "You probably ought to do that to me every time, because I have two radio broadcasts a week which the other Brethren do not have." He joked a little bit and it didn't appear to me that he was going to do it. So I said to him, "The talk that I have prepared is fifteen minutes long. My first suggestion is that you leave me off, but if you want to call on me I can either give the talk I have prepared or I will say something much more brief and be through in one minute." Again he joked about it, and with the idea of helping out I said, "You have these three choices, and any one of them will be all right with me. You just do what you want."

After I had said it, it sounded as though I were trying to tell the President of the Church how to run his business, and he jokingly said, "Brother Sill, you have told me I can do just what I want, and that's just what I'm going to do." I felt that he was not going to take my suggestions, and so I put it out of my mind and decided to go ahead and give my prepared talk as planned.

When it came my turn, President McKay announced me as follows (*CR*, October 1961): "Elder Sterling W. Sill, Assistant to the Twelve, will now speak to us. I am going to tell you something.

Brother Sill approached me just before this meeting started and said he has one speech one minute long and he has another fifteen minutes long. He said, 'You tell me which you want.' I believe, Brother Sill, we will take the one minute talk. Elder Benson will follow him."

My fifty-three second talk was as follows:

"My brothers and sisters, I appreciate this semi-annual privilege of having a part with you in the general conference of the Church.

"Someone has said that the greatest invention of all time took place at Platea, 2500 years ago, when an obscure Greek perfected the process of marching men in step. When it was discovered that a great group of individuals could coordinate their efforts and focus them effectively upon a single objective, that day civilization began.

"The Master himself emphasized this important ability when he said to his disciples, '...If ye are not one, ye are not mine.' (D&C 38:27.) Then the greatest intelligence of heaven gave the most important success formula ever given, saying, 'Follow me....' (Matt. 4:19.) And every human soul must finally be judged by how well he obeys that single command.

"May God help us I pray in Jesus' name. Amen."

President David O. McKay then said, "I like a man who is true to his word!"

I have often thought how it would have enhanced my popularity as a speaker if I had always had President McKay to go around with me to tell me when to sit down. The story is told of a student who took an examination without knowing an answer to a single one of the questions, and so he merely signed his name and handed in his paper. To his surprise, when it came back, the teacher had given him a grade of twenty percent. This he could not understand, as he had made no response of any kind to any of the questions, so he inquired of the teacher the reason for the grade. The teacher said, "I gave you ten percent for neatness and ten percent for brevity." And a great many speakers could substantially increase their score if their speeches had a little more brevity.

Someone put this idea in a verse when he said:

> I love a finished speaker,
> Yes, indeed I do.
> I don't mean one that's polished,
> I just mean one that's through.

In addition to the cases above listed, I think I might write a Sherlock Holmes book filled with my other life's experiences such as

"The Case of the Farmington Flood," or "The Adventure on the Bamberger Electric." While some of these may not be equal to Sherlock Holmes' adventure in the "Hound of the Baskerville's," yet they have been just as exciting to me, and have added much to life's interest generally.

I Had a Friend

When Robert Louis Stevenson was once asked the secret of his radiant youthful life, he replied, "I had a friend." What a great experience that can be, even though we may not always recognize it at the time. In my own case, I had a wonderful friend in the person of my mother. In a little different way, my father was my friend. I had some other boy friends that were very pleasant, but we were not bound together by the hoops of steel that Shakespeare recommends.

As a senior in high school, I became very close to a student from Bountiful by the name of Walter Eldredge. I felt an attitude toward him which filled the specification of those hoops mentioned by Shakespeare. We were both guards on the football team and went on our football excursions together. We took many of the same classes. There are some friendships when one might be just as pleasant as another; but with Walt it was different, he was special. And while 57 years have passed since then, I still get a lump in my throat when I think of my friend.

This was something I had planned in advance and I had already arranged to graduate. After I left school, my intimate association with Walt was largely discontinued. I dropped out of school and became a farmer; he went on to the university. In the newspaper I was, after a fashion, able to follow his athletic and scholarship career at the university. I judged myself by it, as I felt that by and large I could have done as well as he did. Later, I went on a mission, and I returned home just a little while after Walt had graduated from the university, and I went back to work on the farm. Walt was a civil engineer and was given a very outstanding job with the American Canning Company. He was given an assignment to go to Hawaii.

Though our ways had been separated now for some five years, just before his departure for Hawaii he came up to Layton and came out to the farm to see me, to share with me the news of the good fortune relating to his employment. I saw him coming up the dusty road.

He had on a silk shirt which was blowing out in the breeze behind him. He had purchased a new Ford Roadster and the top was down. I watched him come, though at first I did not know who it was. He stopped in front of where I was doing some scraping with a team of sweaty, tired horses. When I recognized him, I ran to meet him and we put our arms around each other in a joyful reunion. I was delighted to see my friend and we sat down on a log while he brought me up to date on his progress.

Being covered with the sweat and dust of the farm, I must have presented something of a contrast with my friend with his good clothes, his silk shirt and shiny Roadster, who was just about to take off on what both he and I knew would be for him a great career. We had spent a great deal of time together our senior year and had never once come close to running out of some interesting conversation, but it was soon evident as we sat there on the log that we did not have quite so much to talk about as we formerly had. It was not that our love for each other had lessened—I am sure it had increased, but our ways were now separated. He was headed upward towards success. Educationally, I was still approximately where I had been 5 years ago when we had parted company. It was now fairly clear to me that I did not want to spend the rest of my life on the farm and because my education was made up of 4 years of part-time high school work, I was not qualified for any of the professions or any other thing that I knew of, and I felt that the distance between us was now very great, which caused me some serious feeling of unhappiness.

It seemed that my chance of ever amounting to anything in the world was now very dim and his was very bright. And yet I felt that I could have done just as well had I followed a similar course. Finally we parted. I walked him out to the car, and smelled the new paint. Then I stood and gazed after him as he turned the car around and retraced his tracks down the dusty road, and in a way, out of my life. Two or three times before he was out of sight, he turned around and waved his hand. And I waved back at him, out of a heart filled with love and yet crowded by a feeling of loneliness, desolation, and sheer despair because of the distance that had come between us, and the failure which I felt I had allowed to develop within myself. Then I went back and sat down on the log again, and as I had quit trying to restrain my tears, I opened the floodgates and let them come. When I had relieved the pressure, I put the lines of my horses back around my neck and continued my scraping job. To a little larger extent that day, Walter Eldredge went further out of my life.

I continued to do my ordinary jobs. A little later I taught school for a couple of years but I did not have a teaching certificate nor the necessary educational qualifications, and I thought I was too old to spend four more years trying to get to that place that my friend, Walter, had already passed.

Later I became a salesman, which did not require an academic education, and in some ways life began to pick up a little bit. But it took me quite a long time to get back in my mind that high place that I had held as a senior at Davis High School, when I felt a kind of equality with the others around me.

In the many years that have followed since that time, I have always held a favored place in my heart for my high school friend. When I was in the mission field and became the conference president, I had the responsibility for training his brother Jim to be a missionary. I was pleased to have him and I'm sure Walt was pleased that I was the one to give some direction to his younger brother. And while I have had many close friends since that time, no one has ever taken his place, and I think no one ever will.

One day in 1976, I received a telephone call from a relative of Walt's wife. For many years Walt and his wife had lived in Albuquerque, New Mexico. I had never met her and knew none of the other members of her family. After his sister-in-law had checked my identity, she told me Walt had terminal cancer and that on a number of occasions during his sickness, he had mentioned my name and his wife thought it might be helpful to him if I would write him a letter, which I was very glad to do.

In the letter, I talked a little bit about the old days. I sent him a picture that had recently been published in the Kaysville Newspaper of our football team of some 50 years ago, and recounted to him that that seemed to indicate that he and I were a little older than we were in high school days. I recounted to him some of my own infirmities of my deteriorating eyesight. I wanted to talk to him a little bit about death and I knew that he knew that he was dying and I would like to feel that I was there to give him some support and comfort. Both of us had known all of our lives that someday, the experiences of this second estate would be over with. And I told him that one of the things that I would like to do over yonder would be to spend a lot more time with him. A few weeks later I received the following letter from his wife:

"Dear Sterling,

"Walt asked me to write to you for him. It was one of his last conscious times that he reminded me to be sure to write.

"When your letter arrived, he was in the midst of a difficult time and it was over two weeks before he was well enough to have it read to him and to understand it. He wept and said how like you to remember him and to send him such a beautiful and thoughtful letter. He did not have many clear days after that time but each day that he knew what was around him, he would mention your letter. It left him with such a feeling of warmth.

"He passed away on December 21st. We buried him in Bountiful on the morning of December 24th.

"Our prayers were so truly answered in that he went without pain. He went quietly to sleep at home, as quietly and thoughtfully as he had always lived. How fortunate I have been to have shared his life for almost fifty years.

"Thank you for writing to him. It helped both of us at a time when we were so in need of help.

Sincerely,
Ann Eldredge"

I have his wife's letter as a part of my book of letters for the year 1977, and sometime when it comes my turn to die, my friend Walter will not be present, nor will he be able to write me a letter. But on the shelf I will have his wife's letter among my collection of treasures for that year written at the time of his own death. This will give me great additional comfort and companionship to help me over that important occasion. And I have no doubt that sometime after I have "crossed the bridge" I will again rejoice in the love and companionship of that long-ago friendship. And we may even talk a a little bit about the old days on the football field at Davis High School. In the meantime I will content myself with Robert Louis Stevenson's sacred thought, "I had a friend," and this is one of the greatest of life's possible experiences.

Chapter Seventeen

My Patriarchal Blessing

One of the great programs of the Church since the beginning of man has been that of providing blessings and encouragement for the people. Patriarchs are ordained that they might have special inspiration from the Lord to declare the lineage of members of the Church and give them a blessing based on their own faithfulness.

God, the greatest patriarch, has given a general blessing to everyone in the world when he said, "There is a law, irrevocably decreed in heaven before the foundations of this world, upon which all blessings are predicated—And when we obtain any blessing from God, it is by obedience to that law upon which it is predicated." (D&C 130:20, 21.) On this basis, each one of us may provide the conditions on which our life's benefits are based. But patriarchs are appointed to give individual blessings, and on October 9, 1923, when I was twenty years of age, Patriarch James Henry Linford of Kaysville, Utah gave me a blessing which reads as follows:

"A Patriarchal Blessing given by James Henry Linford upon the head of Sterling Welling Sill, son of Joseph Albert and Marietta Welling, born at Layton, Utah March 31st, 1903.

"Brother Sterling, in the name of Jesus of Nazareth I lay my hands upon your head and seal upon you a Patriarchal Blessing. You kept your first estate, and returned or came to the earth to receive a mortal body. You left an immortal state and came to a mortal world, that you might receive a body of flesh and bones, that you might receive the Priesthood which you are entitled to by birth and by accepting the Gospel in immortality.

"Your Heavenly Father has his eye upon you because of your sterling worth in accepting the plan of salvation of our Heavenly Father for the salvation of his children.

"You will in course of time receive the higher priesthood and if you are faithful you will be called as a missionary to the nations of the earth and in preaching the Gospel your tongue shall be loosed to your astonishment and you will live to see many great and wonderful things transpire in your natural life, and in your ministry you shall be given power to the convincing of the honest in heart and lead them to Zion.

"Great blessings await you through your lineage of Priesthood. Positions of honor and trust will be placed upon you. You shall become a leader of men and the powers of the evil one you shall have power in your ministry to rebuke and to leave.

"The blessings of long life upon the earth I seal upon you and that you may fill the measure of your creation and stand at the head of a numerous family.

"Hold up your head and rejoice in the Gospel and in its blessings to you and to your Father's household. You have received the Priesthood by lineage through the tribe of Joseph and Ephraim.

"All these blessings with the desire of your heart in righteousness shall be granted you. Prepare yourself for the positions in the Church that await you and I seal you up against the power of the destroyer until the day of redemption. If you are faithful you shall have the privilege to lead a companion to the enjoyment of the mansions prepared by our Heavenly Father for his faithful children and enjoy eternal life for ever and ever. Amen."

And while this blessing is personal and very sacred, yet I would like to share it with my family members and friends who are interested. I also have some wonderful non-member friends who I hope will read it. Some of the most sacred events in the life of Jesus himself he has shared with others for our general good. Also, the blessings that Jacob gave to his twelve sons are recorded in the scriptures for everyone to read. My patriarchal blessing is given here with the thought that it may be of some encouragement or hope to someone else. And I cannot think that to withhold it because it is sacred makes very good logic, as sacred things more than all others should be shared. So far as I am concerned, this is a marvelous document. I have divided it in twelve sections for the purpose of analyzing it and as I get nearer to the end of my life, making some determinations in my own heart about its fulfillment.

There is a great philosophy in the world which says, "count your many blessings," and to try to specifically analyze their fulfillment may sound immodest, yet it has to do with the greatest possession of one's life, which is life itself. And any blessings received

or striven for have more power when they are specific and individual. And this document now points out to me the fulfillment of many
miracles involving me.

One by one these phrases are as follows:

1. *"Your Heavenly Father has his eye upon you because of
your sterling worth."*

It has always been a thrilling, exciting idea to me that God is
our Eternal Heavenly Father. He is sincerely interested in us and
his consciousness is continually upon us. Everyone has a great
value in his sight. I am confident that God has a personal concern
with everything that I do. I believe that he is pleased when I do right,
and he is grieved when I do wrong. It is a very stimulating concept to
me that God is interested in each one of us because of our sterling
worth as human beings and our obedience to him in that long antemortal existence.

2. *"In preaching the gospel your tongue shall be loosed to
your astonishment."*

I do not know how my preaching may appear to anyone else,
but in my early life I was accompanied by a bodyguard of fears, inferiority complexes, and glooms which paralyzed my tongue and
made it of questionable value. I don't know that anyone in his early
years suffered more agonies in his attempts to express himself than
I, in spite of great effort that was expended to overcome it. And that
I can express myself at all with confidence and joy is astonishing
to me.

This fear continued with me in diminishing measure throughout my mission. But I have always felt very comfortable with the
principles of the gospel themselves. For eleven months I was conference president, and a lot of this time when there was an odd
number of elders, I traveled alone as I went from one pair of elders
to another. I held my public meetings alone, I led the singing and
sometimes the singing consisted of my solo. I did the preaching,
praying, and frequently sang the closing hymn alone. But I have had
great joy even in that activity. And while my gift of utterance may
not astonish anybody else, it has been a great source of astonishment and satisfaction to me.

It has also been my job to do a great deal of speaking in other
places. And while I have had no ambition to be anything very closely
related to being an orator, yet I am willing to say that this blessing

of at least partially acceptable speech has been fulfilled to my satisfaction. And I have been pleased with a great many testimonials
concerning the partial fulfillment of this part of my blessing, two
of which follow.

In 1932 I was invited to be the first Utah man to speak before a
national association of life underwriters. The meeting was held in
San Francisco at the Fairmont Hotel, and one of the great national
insurance magazines, *The Life Insurance Courant* gave an account
of my participation as follows: "Residing in a village of 600 inhabitants, Sterling W. Sill described fluently and with great poise the
value of high standards in field work. With serene modesty, yet
strong conviction, this young man exhorted others to build well
through improved, thorough-going workmanship. If the job in hand
is to cook an egg, he said, heat the water with a good fire to 212°
because the fire is wasted if the temperature rises only 211°!

"Chairman Duff was for some minutes powerless to restore
order in the convention hall, so noisy and demonstrative was the
ovation accorded Mr. Sill at the conclusion of his talk. When the
gavel's pounding was finally heeded, the sentiments of the entire
audience were reflected in the presiding officer's assertion that he
held no fears for the future of American life insurance with men
like Sterling Sill coming along. This well-named young underwriter,
still in his twenties, left an indelible impression upon this convention."

On January 24, 1949, Golden K. Driggs, then New York Life
Manager from Fresno, California, wrote to President David O. McKay
as follows:

"Dear President McKay:
"Last Thursday I returned from the annual managers' meeting
of the New York Life Insurance Company held in Hollywood Beach,
Florida. There was an event which took place on Thursday, January
13 in which I think you would be interested.

"Sterling Sill of Salt Lake, formerly bishop of the Garden Park
Ward, was the speaker at the morning session of the convention.
Sterling made the finest talk I have ever heard in a business meeting
and I have been attending them many times a year for more than
twenty years. I have never seen a group of men so moved by a speaker.
The applause following his remarks was the loudest and lasted the
longest in my experience. When Sterling finished, everyone in the
room arose and lined up to congratulate him. In the line right along
with the others were the president and vice president of the company and many more leading businessmen of the United States.

"One prominent Catholic of Chicago said, 'Mr. Sill is a giant among men—he just towers over every other man at this meeting. No one else could have given us the spiritual uplift that he has done.'

"There is no question but that Sterling is the outstanding field executive of the great New York Life Insurance Company. His Church and friends can all be proud of him. I felt sure you would be interested in knowing of the fine impression he made with these business leaders of the nation. Of course, all know that he is a Latter-day Saint and that he has served his Church as a missionary and as a bishop.

"With warm personal regards and asking the Lord to bless you in your tremendous responsibilities, I am sincerely your brother, Golden K. Driggs."

Regardless of the degree of its development in me, I am very humbly grateful for this God-given endowment of speech.

3. "You will live to see many great and wonderful things transpire in your natural life."

When I was born, the Wright Brothers had not yet made their famous sixty-second flight from Kill Devil Hill in Kitty Hawk, North Carolina. At that time, there was no radio, no television sets, no mechanical refrigerators. Horseless carriages had been invented but they had no resemblance to the automobile of our day and were not in general use. The telephone also had little practical value so far as any usefulness was concerned. Some time after I was born, Theodore Roosevelt went to his inauguration as President of the United States for the second time in a chariot drawn by horses. Some two thousand years earlier, Julius Caesar had gone to his inauguration in exactly this same way. Almost no progress had taken place in that period. Like the sower mentioned in the parable of Jesus, my father sowed his wheat a handful at a time and covered it up with his toe.

But within the space of one short lifetime, I now find myself in the very midst of the greatest knowledge explosion ever known upon this earth. Our entire generation is the beneficiary of the wonders and enlightenment that have come forth.

4. "In your ministry you shall be given power to the convincing of the honest in heart and lead them to Zion."

I have had great pleasure and considerable success in my work of teaching people the principles of the gospel and, again, I am satisfied with this great gift of convincing the honest in heart. On May 22, 1979, I received a letter from a high LDS Church official in which he said, "Anyone who has ever wanted to persuade—with tongue or pen—has tried to follow Sterling W. Sill." The only reason that my ability to persuade and convert has not been much greater is that I haven't developed it more.

5. "Prepare yourself for the positions in the Church that await you."

When this blessing was given, I was nearly twenty-one years of age. Because of financial reasons I despaired of ever going on a mission. But a few months after this blessing, I was called to the Southern States. A little later I was asked to serve as President of the conference and supervised those twenty-five elders doing missionary work in the conference area made up of the state of Alabama and the thirteen western counties of Florida. I have also served as a teacher, a scoutmaster, a Sunday School superintendent, a high councilor, a superintendent of M.I.A., a bishop, a high councilor of another stake, a General Board member, and a General Authority of the Church. During all of the fifty-five years since this blessing was given, there has been hardly a single day that I have not been serving in some position in the Church.

6. and 7. "Positions of honor and trust will be placed upon you, and you will become a leader of men."

Positions of honor and trust beyond my fondest expectations have been placed upon me, and my greatest concern in life is and has been to honor that trust and magnify my calling. I have been greatly honored in my educational work, in my Church activity, in my business and in my personal life. I played the lead in the Church dramatic cast that won the Church finals in 1928. I served on the Town Council of Layton. I was a Regent of the University of Utah and served as the chairman of the board, which is the ranking officer of the state university, for two terms of two years each. I was awarded an honorary Doctor of Laws degree by the University of Utah on June 9, 1953, and was awarded a Carnegie Hero Medal by the Carnegie Hero Foundation of Philadelphia, Pennsylvania on January 21, 1959. I have been in charge of stake Aaronic Priesthood work and that stake led the Church in boy activity at that time. I have been a sales leader. I was the first Utahan to receive the C.L.U. degree awarded by the Wharton School of Finance at the University of Pennsylvania. I have been a recruiting leader and trainer of salesmen, and a General Authority of the Church.

I was President of the Alabama Conference during the latter part of 1925 and the first part of 1926. During the year 1926 the Southern States Mission had only two less convert baptisms in the year than the next two missions put together. And the Alabama Conference had only 56 less converts than the next two conferences in the Southern States Mission combined. (See page 52, "My Educational Life.")

In my last year as a salesman, which was 1932, my exact position was number eleven in number of sales made among the entire agency force of 11,243 agents. Vice President Fred A. Wickett included the following paragraphs in his agency report for the year 1934:

"San Francisco, California
January 9, 1935
"To Agency Directors of the North Central and South Pacific Departments:

"Hats off to Sterling W. Sill of the Intermountain Branch who made the outstanding record in the three Pacific Departments, having exceeded his top allotment by 48.7%—and his new organization allotment by 263.6%—a great achievement and one to be sincerely proud of. Never before have we recorded a similar accomplishment."

At my retirement dinner, the President of the Company, Dudley Dowell, said, "Sterling started in agency work more than thirty-three years ago and in all of that time there have been very few years when he didn't lead all New York Life recruiters, both in number and new agents appointed, and in the volume that they produced in their first year."

In introducing me at the Fifty-fourth Annual General Manager's meeting of the New York Life Insurance Company held in January 1956 at the Hollywood Beach Hotel in Florida, Vice President Raymond C. Johnson said, "There is something different about our next speaker. In addition to his devotion to NYLIC, he has assumed a most prominent role in his church and in his community activities. For many years he served as chairman of the Board of Regents of the University of Utah. In his own lifetime, Sterling has become a legend among agency men. And now this legendary and phenomenal active figure is going to speak to us under the title, 'The NYLIC Spirit,' Sterling Sill...."

I have been blessed in receiving many such kind introductions by my fellow NYLIC family members, and I have appreciated all of the kind things they have said about me.

8. *"The power of the evil one you shall have power in your ministry to rebuke and to leave."*

Success in this field is a little more difficult to identify. I have been inspired and made very grateful for the miraculous success that has seemed to attend a great many of my administrations of the sick and needy. I can only hope that there is a little more good in the world and a little less evil because of my life in it.

9. *"The blessings of long life upon the earth I seal upon you, and that you may fill the measure of your creation and stand at the head of a numerous family."*

I appreciate this tremendous privilege of life in this greatest of all dispensations. The average expectation of life in Jerusalem in the days of Jesus was nineteen years. In George Washington's day in America it was thirty-five years. When I was born, it was forty-eight years. Today it is seventy-five years. And I am just at that point right now and look forward hopefully to many more years if the Lord so wills it. I have not only lived longer, but I have lived in a time when more things are happening per second than in any other period of the world's history.

I am also extremely grateful for my family, both that part of it which may be called my father's family, as well as that portion which includes my wife, my children, and grandchildren, all of whom I am very proud of and grateful for.

10. *"Hold up your head and rejoice in the gospel and in its blessings to you and to your father's household."*

One of the advantages of writing one's biography is that it gives him an opportunity to count his blessings. How grateful I am that when I was eight years old I was born again in the exact meaning of the term as indicated by Jesus. And I was confirmed a member of the Church of Jesus Christ of Latter-day Saints by my father. In the organizations of the Church, as well as in my own home and by my own study, I have become gradually more and more familiar with those great principles of life and salvation announced by the Son of God himself.

11. *"You have received the priesthood by lineage through the tribe of Joseph and Ephraim. Great blessings await you through your lineage of Priesthood."*

The family is the most important organization in the world. Those who followed Lucifer have become a part of his family. And what a thrilling blessing it is to be a member of the family of Abraham, the Father of the Faithful, to whom the Lord said, "Through thee and thy seed shall all of the nations of the world be blessed." (Gen. 18:18; 22:18; 26:4.) I not only trace my heritage back to Abraham, but also through his son, Isaac, and his grandson, Jacob, then through Jacob's favorite son, Joseph, and through Joseph's favorite son, Ephraim.

I am also very grateful to be a part of the family of Joseph A. Sill and Marietta Welling Sill. I have had no feeling of envy nor any wish that I could exchange my parents for those living lives of great fame and power. Nor would I like to exchange the humble cottage of my father, with calcimined canvas nailed up on the wall studding to take the place of plaster, for the luxurious homes of great people.

12. *"The desires of your heart in righteousness shall be granted you."*

What a thrilling promise and what awful consequences if abused. Some individual has said, "Be careful of what you want because you will get it." I am very grateful for the desire I have in my heart that I have always wanted to serve God and please him by helping to build up his Kingdom. I have a great desire to help other people, to add to the happiness of my family and friends, and make the way a little more pleasant for everyone.

I appreciate this great and good patriarch, James Henry Linford, for calling some of these rich potential blessings to my attention, and for the Spirit of the Lord that helps me to know that if I obey God's law, I will receive the promised blessings. I am also pleased that the Lord would give me every other desire of my heart in righteousness, both here and hereafter, providing only I was willing to obey those eternal laws on which the blessing is predicated.

Chapter Eighteen

"Coming Events Cast Their Shadows Before"

We sometimes have an interesting experience where we think, know, or feel that something is going to happen before it actually takes place. Some of our foreknowledge is inspired and comes from God, who knows the end from the beginning.

John the Revelator was permitted to witness the final judgment several thousand years before it was scheduled to occur. The prophets have even told us the names of many of the people who would influence the world for good and bad before they were born. There are other instances of foreknowledge where, by a process of logic and reason, we figure out in advance some of these things that later actually take place. Then there are other cases where, by pure guesswork, we hit the nail on the head by foretelling something that later actually occurs. It may be that in some situations we get a combination of these possibilities where we arrive at a knowledge of some fact before it takes place. This process acquires more than ordinary interest when we find ourselves personally involved in some of these predictions that later turn out to be true.

In May 1972, while I was touring the Shreveport Mission, one of the missionaries there was Richard Van Clay of Bountiful, Utah, who had been on a mission in Alabama at the same time I was there in 1924, 1925, and 1926. At one of the missionary meetings where I was not present, Elder Clay told the people that Ella Peacock, a member of the Church in Sink Creek, Florida, had foretold in 1925 that I would some day be a General Authority of the Church. I remembered the occasion rather faintly, but at the time had passed it off as an interesting pleasantry and well-meaning attempt of my friend Sister Peacock to be complimentary.

But after I started to write this biography, I thought about it again and remembered that some other people had foretold the fact, by one or more of the processes mentioned above, that I would someday become a General Authority of the Church. And so I wrote to Brother Clay and asked him if he would put down in writing what he had said to this group of missionaries or what he remembered about the occasion of Sister Peacock's statement. The following is the letter that I received in reply.

"Bountiful, Utah
February 26, 1975

"Dear Elder Sill:

"We were happy to hear from you, and want you to know that we love you and appreciate your friendship. We seldom miss listening to you on Sunday evening. You are one of our favorite speakers among the General Authorities.

"Sister (Edith) Clay and I have been home from our last mission a year and a half and seem to keep quite busy in genealogy and temple work, besides the ward activities.

"On the incident you inquired about, I remember it quite distinctly. We were having District Conference at Bristol, Florida. Apostle George F. Richards was the visitor....

"You were walking along the side of Brother John Rooks' house deep in thought, perhaps going over your planned speech for the morning session of conference. Sister Ella Peacock came around the front of the house toward you and spoke about what an outstanding conference president and missionary you were and also commented on your ability as a speaker. You blushed and made a humble answer of some sort. It was then that she looked directly at you and said, 'President Sill, you will one day be a member of the General Authorities of this Church.' You sort of laughed and tried to pass it off.

"At that time I was only about thirty feet from you trying to figure what I might say were I to be called on during the conference. The reason I remember it so well is, I was jealous. No one had ever suggested that I was a good speaker, let alone that I might ever amount to anything in the Church. I tried to forget it, but that moment of jealousy impressed it upon my mind so that I haven't forgotten those prophetic words...in my mind's eye I can still see the little three-cornered pen for the hen and her chicks you were standing by at the time.

"Many details connected with that first mission have slipped from memory but that one is indelibly impressed upon me so I remember it.

"You encouraged us young elders to memorize the scriptures 'Word Perfect,' and because of that I am able to this day to quote many important passages as they are called for in gospel discussions.

"You were an inspiration to all of us elders and we all admired and loved you. We are pleased and proud to have served with one who later has become one of the Church's stalwart leaders....

"The Lord is blessing us in every way. We have just enough aches and pains to make us appreciate the good health we have. We love you and pray that the Lord's choice blessings will attend you and Sister Sill always.

Love,

/s/ Edith and Van Clay"

In addition to the above, several other people have mentioned this matter for a long period before the event took place. When Patriarch James Henry Linford gave me a patriarchal blessing he said, in part, "Positions of honor and trust will be placed upon you, and you shall become a leader of men." And then after he had finished expressing that thought, as though there were something yet unexpressed, he said, "Prepare yourself for the positions in the Church that await you."

For many years before this Church appointment took place, Vice-president Wickett of the New York Life Insurance Company had told many non-members of the Church in different parts of the country that I "would someday be a principal of the Mormon Church." This was also a prediction by Mr. W. H. Danforth of St. Louis, Missouri, who was the founder and owner of the Ralston-Purina Company. He was made a director of the New York Life Insurance Company and took a very friendly, personal interest in my welfare and showed me many kindnesses which I greatly appreciated.

I have in my files two letters from Golden K. Driggs, who was also a great admirer of Mr. Danforth, and who spent a great deal of time with him while at conventions and elsewhere. He said in one of these letters, "While attending the managers' meeting in Florida, Mr. Danforth and I were sunning ourselves on the beach. You were swimming. He talked to me about you and he said, 'That Sterling Sill is one of the greatest young men I have ever known. I wish I could steal him from the New York Life to help me run my own company. He is a model Christian gentleman. He would be an ideal for the Ralston-Purina family.' He told me about the dedication of one of his mills up in Idaho where you went with him in his special railroad car and you had offered the dedicatory prayer at the opening of this new plant. He said, 'There are altogether too few men who are dedicated first to a Christ-like life and at the same time are forceful and successful in their business lives.' "

The other letter from Golden about Mr. Danforth tells of a meeting in the early 1940's where Mr. and Mrs. Danforth and Mr. and Mrs. Wickett were vacationing in Chandler, Arizona. A Church fireside was arranged and Mr. Danforth was asked to speak to the young people of the Church. This was a great privilege for them, as Mr. Danforth almost singlehandedly had built up the great Ralston-Purina Company beginning with one bushel of wheat and a mule. He had also established the Danforth Foundation to assist deserving college students. At that time, this was one of the largest charitable foundations in the United States, with assets of over one hundred ten million dollars. He was also the author of an inspiring little book for young people entitled "I Dare You." This meeting was attended by some four hundred people. As a part of the program, they sang the hymn *Have I Done Any Good in the World Today.* This made a great hit with Mr. Danforth, as it coincided exactly with his philosophy of life. They also sang *Put Your Shoulder to the Wheel* and *Carry On,* which were also in the Danforth tradition. Mr. Danforth said that these were the most spirited and practical songs that he had ever heard and he asked the group to sing *Carry On* three times. Then he requested my nephew, Dilworth Brinton, to send him all of the song books of the Church. Later he told Dilworth that he was so taken with the song *Dare To Do Right* found on page 108 of the Primary song book that the Ralston-Purina Company had adopted it for their theme song for the entire company.

Mr. Danforth told me that he wished all of his family would join the Mormon Church. He said all of the members of the Church with whom he was acquainted were outstanding people and were living the teachings of Christ better than any other people that he knew.

The University of Utah presented me with an honorary Doctor of Laws degree on June 9, 1953. When the possibility of this award was discussed with me a couple of months before it was made, A. Ray Olpin, President of the University, said that they wanted to make the presentation at the 1953 commencement because he felt sure that if it was allowed to go for another year that by that time I would be a General Authority of the Church. He wanted the University to lead the parade by making this presentation before any action should be taken by the Church.

I was appointed a General Authority of the Church in April of 1954, which was ten months after receiving the honorary Doctor of Laws Degree, and I feel confident that even the President of the Church did not know at the time of the presentation of the degree that I was to be a General Authority.

I have been grateful to my very good friend and stake president, Governor Henry H. Blood, who over the years has said some very complimentary things about me and had indicated that he thought I had an important future in the Church. Most of these statements were made on occasions when I was not present and came to me from those who heard them made, which again I paid very little attention to at the time. But they have assumed a new interest and importance in view of what has taken place since, and especially since I have been trying to put some of the facts and conditions of my life down on paper.

Whether these statements were inspired from some source higher than human knowledge, or whether they were the result of some natural logic or personal opinion on the part of those concerned, I do not know. But in any event, I am very grateful for the expressions beginning with the patriarch and added to by my very good friends, as they have all given me encouragement which makes me more grateful and adds to my determination not to disappoint any of those concerned, from the Lord and President of the Church who made the appointment, down to those who over the years have given me this confidence, encouragement, and support.

Chapter Nineteen

My Social Life

Man is a gregarious animal. I am sure that it was intended by creation that human beings should live and work and play together. God himself arranged that we should be divided up into races and nations and governments and communities and families. Some of the great influences and conveniences of our day responsible for our miracle of production, our high standards of living, come from our ability to work together. Some of the instruments of our cooperation are our great corporations like General Motors, American Telephone, International Business Machines, the great newspapers, the airplane industries and the giant agricultrual and manufacturing industries. These are made possible by many human beings developing specific skills, then joining together to serve the general welfare. We also have the great educational, religious, social, and political organizations which teach us to work together for our common good.

From many points of view the family is the chief unit of society. It is the program of the Creator that parents are permitted to come to the earth a few years ahead of their children so that they can provide them with a home, teach them righteousness, and help them with their education. Then the children associate with other people and form their associations, political connections, etc.

Probably the most unpleasant major part of my life, at least during the early years, might come under this heading of sociability, or the lack of it on my part.

Besides myself, there were only two other boys in my age range who lived on Easy Street: Vernon Robbins and Quincy Adams. Both of them were a couple of years older than I was, though we played together and usually spent our Sundays together. I had one social advantage in that my father had an apple orchard and he bought an old secondhand cider press. Very frequently on Sunday afternoons the three of us and some others that were attracted from more distant places would come to our place and we would make apple cider during those periods when apples were available.

But if they had given grades in sociability, recreational participation, etc., I would have received a pretty low score.

We had a large family and poor accommodations. We ate on a little fold-away table that folded up against the wall so as to give more room in the house. But we ate on tin plates or whatever we could get. Very infrequently did we have any visitors at meal time. Though the Church and my activity in it has done a great deal through the years to better my social situation, yet as a social person, I have fallen down pretty badly in a lot of ways. Although I have tried to overcome this deficit in all the years since, I still have some serious shortcomings. It is my opinion that in my early years I had about the most highly developed set of inferiority complexes that anyone has ever had. In fact, I thought that I was the only person who had them. And I am still bothered by some of them. I have blamed some of them on the poor financial circumstances in my family, our lack of housing and clothing, but that does not tell the full story. I think I was just not present when the social graces were handed out to begin with. Someone has penned in jest:

> When they passed out noses,
> I thought they said roses, so I took a big red one.
> When they passed out brains,
> I thought they said trains, and I missed mine.
> When they passed out looks,
> I thought they said books, and I didn't want any.

I have tried to lay the blame on other things. For example, we didn't have very much money to spend on clothing, athletic equipment, transportation, or other things that can promote social standing. I remember on one occasion, when I was probably in the third or fourth grade, that we were playing a kind of ring-around-the-rosy game. The girl who held my hand in the circle suddenly dropped it and said, "Let's not let Sterling play because he doesn't have any socks on." Socks seemed to be a kind of unimportant commodity in my life at that time. Inasmuch as I had a lot more serious problems to solve, I hadn't thought socks were necessary. But the fact that she thought socks were important made them a lot more important to me thereafter. If she felt toward me then as I feel about that unfortunate breed that frequently goes around without shoes or stockings, intentionally dressed in the most ludicrous cothing, I think I can more clearly understand her feelings. My lack of clothing was partly due to necessity and partly because of my insensitivity to some of the social graces that I should have been more aware of. However, I didn't argue the point with anybody, I merely dropped out of the game in obedience to her suggestion and stood with my feelings crushed and watched the others as they went on with their game.

I remember when I was in the seventh grade, it was customary among the students for someone to have a party on Friday night and invite other members of the class. I remember that I was only invited on one occasion throughout the year and that was to the home of the boy who had about the worst scholastic and social standing in the school. I eagerly accepted his invitation, but I was the only one who attended. That is, all of the other of his invited guests either ignored the invitation or failed to show up for some other reason. And the party that he and I had together was not one that you would call a howling, social success.

In that year during the baseball season, the boys used to choose up sides and play baseball at the recesses and noons. But because I didn't have a baseball or a bat or a glove and had had no experience and no great social consciousness, I was usually left out of the game. And only on very infrequent occasions was I ever invited to participate. I remember that some of the boys would choose up sides out of the common pool, and I would be the last one left as the usual thing. I was desperately anxious for someone to let me play and loan me his mitt, but that usually didn't happen.

I remember on one occasion there were eighteen of us to play. They chose up sides and I was the only one left unchosen. One team had nine players and the other had only eight. If they had chosen me, there would have been nine on each side, but the one captain said, "We are short one player, but we will beat you anyway." If they had chosen me, it would have made the teams even; but I suppose the captain felt that it would have been a bigger disadvantage to have nine players if one of them was me than to have eight if I was not on his side. Many years later, I heard my good friend, Paul Dunn, tell about being selected to play professional baseball at a very early age, and I thought what a boost that must have given to his spirit as compared with me standing on the sidelines praying that some day I would be good enough to go inas the junior substitute at the noon practice of Layton 7th grade.

My situation reminds me of the story of the boy away to school who wrote to his parents telling them about a football game in which he was a player. He explained their defeat by saying, "The opposing team found the hole in our line and it was me." I probably did better than average in the classroom, but I certainly flunked my noons and recesses.

If something like that should happen now, I think I would do something to correct the situation. I would either try to make myself more acceptable or at least protest a little harder against being dropped. But back in those days I would merely stand there with my heart breaking but would do nothing to make the correction. I do not know why I have never had heart trouble. I have had it broken enough times.

Some time ago, I found some verse that reminded me of this experience. It seems that an old professional baseball player had been told that he had developed cancer and that he would soon have to drop out of activity. He played as long as his health would permit, and finally he went to bed. Sometime later when they went into his room in the morning, they found him dead. But on the table by his bed he had written a verse which someone had entitled, "The Game Guy's Prayer." It said,

> The doctor knows what his trained eyes see,
> And he says it's the last of the ninth for me.
> One more swing as the clouds loom dark
> And I must leave this noisy park.
> 'Twas a glorious game from the opening bell,
> Good plays, bad plays, thrills pell-mell.
> The speed of it burned my tears away,
> But I thank God that he let me play.

And while I still hit quite a few foul balls and possibly struck out more frequently than I should, yet in more recent years, I have usually been able to get into the game on some kind of basis and I am grateful to be on the team even though I don't always hit a home run as I would like to do.

My freshman and sophomore years in high school seemed to belong to my grade school social years in Layton. But it seems to me now that I received some good even out of these experiences. I have a natural tendency to think in parables and I make a comparison of my social problems with the sugar beets I used to grow. There is an interesting lesson that we might learn from the culture of a sugar beet plant. When the seed of a beet is planted, the ground usually has enough moisture to help it sprout and get up to the surface. Then the beets are thinned. But as the ground dries out, the beet with its root that goes only an inch into the topsoil begins to wilt and cry for moisture. If a rain comes, that solves the problem temporarily, but sometimes I have seen these young beets so dry that their leaves have been wilted and flattened out on the ground, as though they were dead. I used to have a temptation to irrigate them so that they would not die, but this would have been disasterous. If a sugar beet is given water every time it gets thirsty, then there would be no necessity for the beet to send its roots deeper down into the earth searching for moisture, and the sugar beet would become a little nubbin on the top of the ground. But as the sugar beet is left to suffer a little bit, it sends its root deeper and deeper into the earth according to the great law of necessity with which God has equipped it. And then after the sugar beet has done all that it can for itself, and cannot stand the thirst any longer, then the water is applied, and the sugar beet fills itself out and is much greater in total size because of the added length it has acquired in its search to supply its own moisture. I am certain that many of the problems of our lives are given us for the same reason. To a certain extent we have the ability to solve our own problems, and in giving us our human nature, God so arranged it that we should do the very best we could on our own power. And then he supplies the necessary help in the form of his irrigation water.

As I grew older, things began to pick up a little for me socially. In my junior year in high school I was vice-president of the Agricultural Club, which was at least a start. In my senior year, which is the only year I ever began when school began, I made my letter in football. I was in the school play, I was president of the senior class, and played class basketball. But during my entire four years in high school I only danced three times, though I attended the school dances as the usual thing. And I think I had only one or two dates with girls during that entire four year period. However, the last year of my high school was one of tremendous experience, and I think it helped me to get started on my way.

I was still plagued with the money problem however, and because I had to work, it was not possible, in my opinion, for me to go to college, though I did borrow enough money to attend the USAC during the winter quarter of 1921 and 1922. However, my social life had a little relapse during this period among these strangers. Then I dropped out of school in favor of trying to make a living on the farm. From the point of view of any great expectations for life either social or financial, these were awful years as all of my occupational prospects already were very unpromising and I had a feeling that life had already passed me by. But from another point of view, these may have been among the most profitable years in my life. From the point of view of my own industry and handling of the situation or my attitude about it, I think these were very successful years. I felt not even the slightest rebellion or unhappiness with life itself, and I think I actually made great progress without myself being aware of this fact.

In the second year I ran my father's farm, I made enough money to get myself started on a mission in January 1924. The best way I can describe my mission is to say it was a fantastic experience. On the farm I had formed the habit of working long and hard. This was continued in the mission field when my companion's industry would permit. From my very earliest years I had been in continual Church activity and before I went on my mission I was well versed and practiced in the doctrines of the Church, every one of which I accepted wholeheartedly. My mission was also very pleasant to me. It gave me the opportunity of associating on a very pleasant basis with other missionaries as well as with many other people including members and non-members. It was in the mission field where I felt almost completely capable of taking care of myself. I felt that the quality and quantity of my work was not inferior to any of the other missionaries. This gave some uplift to my social presence. My life was really beginning to get started, and without being particularly aware of it, I was laying the foundation for a much better economic, social and educational future.

The marks of my sociability graph went down again after I was released from my mission while I was trying to figure out what I was going to do with my life occupationally. The sharpest rise on my graph came with my marriage and permanent employment, which started out at about the same time. Because of my habit of prolonged hard work, I soon began to win some distinctions and honor in my business, which gave an upsurge to my self-confidence and social standing.

My wife was much more socially advanced than I was, and she had many more intimate friends than I did. And as best she could she has been trying to lift me upward ever since.

Over the years, because of my wife's advanced sociability, we have belonged to four wonderful social groups where we have mingled together for dinner and some form of sociability once a month in each one during each year, which has been very helpful and profitable to me. My Church assignments such as my bishopric, my Sunday School General Board work, and my assignment as a General Authority have also given me some additional confidence in myself. I am very grateful for all of the many wonderful friendships that have come to me during my lifetime from many sources. And while I still frequently feel the pains from my social inferiority complexes, yet I think even they have added something to my general good and I am very grateful for them.

Someone has said that there are three things in life which one must have and do in order to make his life succesful. Number one is to love, number two is to be loved, and number three is to feel that his own life has been worthwhile. I am aware of the fact that I will receive love in about the same proportion as I give love. We need to love God. We need to love our families. We need to love our neighbors as ourselves. We need to love our work and our opportunities, and righteousness, and all righteous love is worthwhile. And I feel that my life has been a great success from the point of view of my loves. I have heard of so many people who hate their jobs, or their associates, or their family members, but in my case this is an experience that is almost completely unknown to me. The second of these, to be loved, is not so easily appraised, but in this also I feel very fortunate. As to number three, my life has certainly been very interesting. It has been extremely worthwhile to me, and I hope that God will feel that it has some of those qualities that make it worthwhile to others.

I know some of the pains involved in being excluded socially. As other people have come in to ask for counsel on their problems, I have had the experience of understanding something of what it might be like to feel excluded intellectually, physically, and morally. Someone is supposed to have described the ups and downs of her marriage by saying there were three ups and 9,422 downs. If I could draw out my social chart with its many ups and downs and know what caused the changes of direction, it would be very interesting. But in programming my life for the future, I think of continuing this graph beyond the borders of this life and I hope and plan for some new future highs.

Chapter Twenty

That Ye Might Have Joy

Since time began, people have been asking each other what is the supreme good, what is the noblest object of desire, what is the outstanding virtue to covet. In answer to this question, Henry Drummond wrote his great literary classic describing love as the greatest thing in the world. His argument is based upon St. Paul's famous thirteenth chapter of First Corinthians which is one of the masterpieces of our literature. Some translators interpret Paul's central word as charity, others call it love. Both are very strong words, and one scripture describes charity as the pure love of Christ. (Moroni 7:47.)

Paul says, "Though I speak with the tongues of men and of angels, and have not love, I am become as sounding brass, or a tinkling cymbal. And though I have the gift of prophecy, and understand all mysteries, and all knowledge; and though I have all faith, so that I could remove mountains, and have not love, I am nothing. And though I bestow all my goods to feed the poor, and though I give my body to be burned, and have not love, it profiteth me nothing. Love suffereth long, and is kind; love envieth not; love vaunteth not itself, is not puffed up, Doth not behave itself unseemly, seeketh not her own, is not easily provoked, thinketh no evil; Rejoiceth not in iniquity, but rejoiceth in the truth; beareth all things, believeth all things, hopeth all things, endureth all things. Love never faileth: but whether there be prophecies they shall fail; whether there be tongues, they shall cease; whether there be knowledge, it shall vanish away.... And now abideth faith, hope, love, these three; but the greatest of these is love." (I Cor. 13:1-8, 13.)

But there are some other great words. Jesus said, "I am come that ye might have life, and have it more abundantly." (John 10:10.) The greatest commodity in the universe is life. Without life even

271

love would have little significance. The apostle Paul says that love is the fulfilling of the law. Love is a great word and life is a great word, but law is also a great word. As a summation of all good, the prophets have said, "Keep the commandments, obey the law of the Lord." But success is also a great word. Jesus might have said, "I am come that you might have success and have it more abundantly." Success includes all other good things, and God has placed into our very natures a success instinct. Because everyone wants to make the best and the most of himself, God had given us this upward reach, this striving after better things.

But there is another great word, and that is joy. Some of the scriptures also seem to point to this word as the supreme good, the greatest word. In speaking for the Lord, an ancient pre-Columbus American prophet said, "Man is that he might have joy." (2 Nephi 2:25.) Love would mean nothing if it were not for life, but even life would have little meaning if it were not for joy. There can be no success without happiness. There can be no triumphs without joy.

We sing for joy, we shout for joy, we laugh for joy. The greatest characteristic of real love is joy. One of the finest manifestations for success is for one to have joy in his work, to exult in the happiness of his wife, to glory in the success of his children. We read for enjoyment, we think for enjoyment. The colors and the fragrance of the flowers were given for our enjoyment. We don't just eat to live, the taste and flavors of food were created that we might have joy. We don't just get married to multiply and replenish the earth. One of the main purposes of marriage is to have joy in our companion and in our posterity.

An eighty-five year old lady who has been widowed for many years recently said to her neighbor, "Did you ever know my husband?" Upon being answered in the affirmative, she said, "Wasn't he good looking?" She meant, "Wasn't he a fine person!" "Wasn't he a great husband!" From any point of view it was a magnificent joy for her in her old age to remember him. Her children may neglect her, her financial resources may be exhausted, but she will come through as long as she remembers her husband with love and life and success and joy.

Many of the greatest values in our world are represented to our minds by symbols. It may be a ring on the finger or a light in the window or a flag in the sky. Someone has made an interesting reference to the skylark as the symbol of high purpose and great happiness.

It has been said that no bird equals the skylark in heart or voice. The skylark's mission is music. In a still hour, you can hear the thrilling notes at nearly a mile's distance. Long after its form is lost to sight, it still floods a thousand acres of sky with song. The movement of the skylark is swift and sure. In almost perpendicular flight, it rises quickly toward the upper areas of the sky. It seems to be lifted up by the ecstasy of its own happy heart. On the earth the skylark seems timid, silent, and unsure of itself. It has little of color, feature, or form to recommend it. Its inspiration is that it is always soaring and always pouring out its rapturous song in a flood of shrill delight. And although the skylark flies high, it always builds its nest upon the ground.

Dr. Henry Jowett once said that the apostle Paul had a mind like a skylark. He was always soaring. He flew high enough to catch the vision of life at its best. He attained the mental heights of a searching education. The song of his heart radiated with devotion. He rose quickly from his experience on the Damascus road and thereafter believed without reservation. Never did he do things poorly or by halves. He flew high, yet he never lost the common touch. He taught a philosophy of exaltation, and yet never got his feet off the ground or lost the balance of his down-to-earth common sense. He served the God of heaven untiringly with voice and life but he kept his base of operations among humble men.

Each of us may need a little more of the spirit of the skylark to give our life the significance it needs. An increased elevation in our point of view gives us a clearer look at life. A happier song leads to a greater accomplishment. The inspiration of this little citizen of the sky can enlarge our vision and increase our pulse. Its inspiration is an antidote for boredom, a deterrent to sin, and a preventative of negative living. It teaches us that "the best education is to be perpetually thrilled by life."

A story is told of a lady who once bought the wrong typewriter. In requesting an exchange, she pointed out that none of this typewriter's keys had any exclamation points. She said, "My letters are just full of exclamations." To her, a typewriter without exclamation points would be worse than useless. But how much more serious a handicap it would be to have a mind and heart without exclamation points! How drab a skylark's life would be without exclamation points, or without her love of the upper air, or without her thrilling speed of flight. Suppose some tragedy required the skylark to lower her altitude. The perspective is less interesting when one flies at the treetop level of life, and the exhilaration is lost when our flying is slowed to a snail's pace. It is significant that the pace that kills is the crawl. Most of the darkest moods of life are born on the lower levels of living while we are using our snail's pace gear. Only when one flies high can he see the beauty of creation and feel the full joy of being alive.

A joyous spirit does good like a medicine. With a skylark's love of life, one is likely to have better health, clearer thoughts, and greater purpose in living than those of the mudlark whose sustenance comes from the slime of the low tide. We can even live on less when we have more to live for.

The spirit of the skylark in the heart of Isaiah made him say, "Sing O heavens; and be joyful, O earth; and break forth into singing, O mountains: for the Lord hath comforted his people, the Lord hath redeemed Jacob and glorified himself in Israel." (See Isa. 44:23.)

What a tremendous privilege it is to be a great human being, a child of God, an heir of salvation with the inestimable privileges of endless growth, eternal progression, and everlasting happiness.

Jesus loved the high places. He was transfigured upon a high mountain. His greatest discourse was the Sermon on the Mount. He made his atoning sacrifice upon Mount Calvary and he ascended to heaven from the top of Mount Olivet. But even more important, Jesus lived all of the years of his mortality on the heights of excellence and righteousness.

Solomon said, "Righteousness exalteth a nation." (Prov. 13:34.) But it also exalts our individual lives. The gateway to eternal life is on the earth, but its course lies upward through the skies. Eternal life and eternal joy are up. The Master did not do things by fractions. He said, "These things have I spoken unto you that your joy might be full." (John 15:11.) We must be at our best even to imagine a fullness of joy or a fullness of success, or a fullness of God's glory, and the best way to have joy tomorrow is to be worthy of joy today. Life is a rehearsal for eternity. To be a great soul in heaven one needs to be a great soul here. And one can best increase this soul quality by an enlarged appreciation of life and the high flight of greater accomplishment.

King David was called a man after God's own heart, and he had the spirit of the skylark when he said to God, "When I consider thy heavens, the work of thy fingers, the moon and the stars, which thou hast ordained: What is man that thou art mindful of him? and the son of man, that thou visitest him? For thou hast made him a little lower than the angels, and hast crowned him with glory and honour. Thou madest him to have dominion over the works of thy hands; thou hast put all things under his feet...." "O Lord, our Lord, how excellent is thy name in all the earth." (Ps. 8:3-6, 9.) And we might echo the refrain and say how excellent indeed.

It was the spirit of the skylark that made Isaiah say, "...They that wait upon the Lord shall renew their strength; they shall mount up with wings as eagles;..." (Isa. 40:31.) And the Son of God himself went beyond all others into the upper air when he projected our future by saying, "Ye are Gods and all of you are children of the most high." (Ps. 82:6.) This means that we fly high, that we make the most of these great words of love and life and law and beauty and joy.

An American diplomat in France was once asked how he was getting along with the language. He replied, "All of my French is excellent, except the verbs." But how can one get along without verbs? What wings are to the skylark, verbs are to action. And they are the most important part of accomplishment. They are also the most important part of life. They are the most important part of success. And they are the most important part of joy. Jesus used some powerful verbs which lead to glorious action. Some of them are *arise, come, follow, pray, believe, know, do, give, watch, wait, love, go, work.* These words should be underlined and powerized in our lives.

A prominent American poet, Edgar Lee Masters, once wrote a beautiful poem to his daughter. Some of the most meaningful words he put in capital letters. When the poem was published, a reader wrote to Mr. Masters and asked him why those particular words had been set apart from the others. Mr. Masters replied that the regular letters were not large enough. He said that the love he bore his daughter could only be adequately expressed in capital letters.

Similarly, we need to form our virtues in the larger mold. We need to adopt more of the spirit of the skylark in its role as the symbol of high accomplishment and great joy. Great industry is wonderful. Good judgment enriches our lives. A few good problems can strengthen our muscles and even a little suffering can enrich our souls. But we must not miss the joy.

Henry Thoreau once said, "I am afraid that at the last I may discover when it is too late that I have missed the joy." We need to know the joy of being alive, the joys of excellence. The joys of truth. We need to know the joys of labor, the joys of family, the joys of being genuine. It is wonderful to make a profit, it is great to develop prominence, it is stimulating to acquire fame; but even glory has no halo if we miss the joy.

During my many years I have loved life, I have been broadened by the law, I have been inspired by love, I have been thrilled by success, I have gloried in struggle and hardship. But I thank the great God of the universe that I have not missed the joy.

Chapter Twenty-One

My Great Expectations

It is with some sadness that I come to the last chapter in recounting the story and philosophy of my life. It has been a lot of fun for me, as I have written these pages, to go back in imagination and live my life over again. I have contemplated my antemortal existence. I have re-experienced the miracle of my birth. I have re-felt emotions of great gratitude for my parents, my brothers and sisters, my wife, my children and my grandchildren. I have also renewed my appreciation for my friends and the great army of my benefactors. I have made a detailed re-examination of my philosophies of life. I want my friends and posterity not only to know what I have done, but what I have thought about success and faith, and life and love. The years of my mortal probation that have already passed by to this point have been very pleasant and profitable to me.

I now stand facing the sunset, with my hand trying to shade my anxious eyes from the light which makes it difficult for me to see that sign which lies down the roadway—that sign which will state the simple truth, saying "The End."

I do not know how much longer my mortal life may continue, in which I may run this finishing cantor so that the step will not be too abrupt. I hope to have a little longer period than that to enable me to take care of some of that unfinished business of which I have a great deal.

I expect that these remaining years will be the most productive in my life, as I have now accumulated some of the mental, spiritual, and material resources that I have never had before. However, I am not straining my vision very hard to see what lies beyond, as I have a great faith in God, my Eternal Heavenly Father. I believe that death was ordained by him and is good. I am content that he has provided for the future happiness of his children beyond what any of us is able to realize. I have also made some preparation for the future which I hope will be acceptable to him.

I pray to him now that whatever I may have done that is amiss in his sight, that he will accept of my repentance and grant me his forgiveness. I also express this same prayer to the members of my family and to all of the people in my life with whom I have had to do, that they will pardon any thoughtlessness, unfairness, or wrong that may have been a part of me.

I have always been impressed with that philosophy in the law of Moses that if a man steal a sheep, he might make restitution by paying four sheep back as damages for the one stolen. I do not know of any stolen sheep, but I do hope that during my life I have contributed enough sheep to the general good that my eternal account may show a profit after any possible unknown damages may have been paid.

Branch Rickey, the famous baseball manager, was once asked to describe the most important day that he had ever had in baseball. He said, "I can't because I haven't had it yet." Most of our important days will come after we have crossed the borders of this life.

Many years ago, Charles Dickens wrote his enchanting book called *Great Expectations,* much of which I have appropriated to myself. This interesting word "expectations" might indicate one of our most important attitudes of success. A strong expectation gives a more powerful pitch to whatever accomplishment we contemplate.

An ancient American prophet once said that God grants unto every man according to his desires. Our desires are closely entwined with our expectations. Both of these help to make up our finest constellation of success traits and concepts. A great expectation includes an intense hope and a real anticipation that our clearly outlined future objectives may be attained. Our expectations involve a love of, and a longing for, the things expected.

There is an ancient Chinese tradition to the effect that when one went into the home of an ancient Chinese and admired some particular article, he may find that the Chinese would wrap it up and send it to him as a present. They believe that when you admired it sufficiently, that made it yours.

However, life has a program that is exactly like that. Whatever we truly love and admire we get. If we love honesty, we get honesty. If we love industry, we get industry. If we admire great faith in God, life wraps it up and sends it to us free of charge. If we sufficiently and effectively desire to forever live with God in the celestial kingdom so that we do those things that he has outlined, God will grant us our greatest desires.

Mr. Dickens has written across the pages of his book some ot those human ambitions and motivations that operate in people's lives on various levels of expectation. The story itself is centered in the experience of a little orphan boy by the name of Philip Perip. (Per-ip') As he grew up under the most humble circumstances he was called Little Pip, but his little education, his little opportunity, his little ambition, and his little abilities were enlarged by his great expectations. In fact the size and quality of anyone's expectations always exerts a powerful influence in every field of human interest, including those that lie beyond the horizon.

As we look beyond the bounds of mortality, our expectations greatly expand all of life's dimensions. The result of our expectations will determine whether or not we are traveling toward a higher or a lower floor in life. We can get some extra zest into our expectations by studying the great scripture, by following the word of the Lord, by making up our minds. We can watch the most accomplished authors draw aside the shades and make us familiar with those techniques by which a Little Pip can climb to greatness and nobility merely by increasing the effectiveness of his hopes, ambitions and expectations.

Several years ago I knew a young man who had some great expectations about becoming a medical doctor like his father. He loved learning and he had a strong desire for that skill necessary to produce health in sick people. He had a strong appetite to serve and a full confidence in his own potentiality. This was all supported by a great expectation and a complete determination to do whatever was necessary to reach the objective. He felt that he was bigger than any obstacle that could bar his way and that he was stronger than any temptation that could draw him from his course. He had an unshakable expectation that he would never get off schedule in becoming a great medical man. The power of his expectations pushed every doubt aside. It overcame every fear and eliminated every weakness. The compass of his expectations always pointed straight forward toward his star. The beckoning lights that distracted smaller people and won away the affections of those who were less resolute, had no power over him. He was constant and true to an unwavering purpose that never varied, either in sunshine or in storm. He is now one of the most competent of medical men.

The most productive area for great expectations is in the field of the spirit. God has created us in His own image, and endowed us with His attributes and potentialities. He has provided that the offspring of God may eventually become like their eternal parents. What a wonderful blessing it is to have great expectations!

I believe in God. I believe in my own designed destiny. I believe in every promise that God has made to his children. I believe in the eternity of the family unit. I believe in everlasting life, in everlasting progress, and in everlasting happiness. I believe the statement of Paul to the Corinthians when he said, "Eye hath not seen nor ear heard, neither hath it entered into the heart of man the things that God hath prepared for those that love him."

In spite of my many weaknesses, sins, and complexes, I have believed thoroughly. I have worked hard, I have loved much, and I have the greatest expectations; and as my mortality draws to its close, I thank God for my life, both here and hereafter.

Index